The Global
Environmental
Movement

Reviews of the First Edition

"A detailed, careful and thoughtful piece of contemporary history of the environmental movement . . . McCormick is to be congratulated for providing his readers with such a clear and pertinent history of ideas"
Howard Newby, in *The Geographical Journal*

"McCormick is highly readable . . . This is a fine overview faithful to the facts and spirit of very significant issues"
Forest and Conservation History

". . . scholarly and well researched"
Stephen Cotgrove, in *Nature*

"[a] solid, well-crafted and useful volume which delivers on its promise, constituting the soup to nuts of the global green activist's banquet in a digestible form"
Environmental Politics

"McCormick has provided a considerable service by examining the evolution of the international environmental movement . . . the style is easy on the eye and the mind, and . . . the book can be assimilated at any speed which the reader pleases"
Timothy O'Riordan, in *Transactions—*
Institute of British Geographers

"A reasoned and insightful analysis of the transformation of environmentalism from a private to a public issue, and from a national to a global issue"
Natural Resource and Environmental Administration

"A highly useful historical overview"
New Scientist

"A fascinating, lucid account"
International Affairs

"A valuable guide through a complicated subject"
American Historical Review

The Global Environmental Movement

SECOND EDITION

John McCormick

JOHN WILEY & SONS

Chichester · New York · Brisbane · Toronto · Singapore

British Library Cataloguing in Publication Data

A catalogue record for this book is available from the British Library

ISBN 0-471-94940-X

Typeset in 11/13pt Palatino from author's disk by
Mayhew Typesetting, Rhayader, Powys
Printed and bound in Great Britain by Biddles Ltd, Guildford and King's Lynn

This book is printed on acid-free paper responsibly manufactured from sustainable
forestation, for which at least two trees are planted for each one used for paper production.

Contents

Preface to the Second Edition

Since the first edition of *The Global Environmental Movement* was published in 1989, the world has gone through dramatic changes. The Soviet Union has collapsed, Eastern Europe has been freed from the Soviet hegemony, Germany has reunified, the European Community (now European Union) has become a single integrated market, and the newly industrialising countries (NICs) of southeast Asia and Latin America have continued their dramatic economic growth. All these events have important implications for the global environment.

- The collapse of the Soviet bloc has not only allowed the rest of the world to see (and confirm) its fears about the environmental devastation caused by Stalinism, but has also created nearly 20 new sovereign states, bringing a new degree of complexity to the political and legal response to that devastation.
- The continued integration of Western Europe has forced national governments in that region to tighten their environmental laws in response to the pressure to harmonise laws and standards. The response of the European Union to environmental problems gives us important clues regarding the prospects for improved environmental management in other parts of the world considering regional economic integration.
- Rapid economic growth in the world's NICs provides their governments with both opportunities and challenges; can they learn from (and avoid) the record of the older industrial states,

where rapid industrialisation was achieved to a large extent at the cost of environmental decay?

For the global environmental movement, the issue of the balance between economic growth and environmental protection was brought to a head in 1992 in Rio de Janeiro, Brazil. Twenty years after the landmark Stockholm conference, representatives from 178 countries met at the United Nations Conference on Environment and Development. The Earth Summit (as it came to be known) was the largest meeting of its kind ever held, and for two weeks focused the spotlight of media and public interest on the global environment.

The conference had enormous symbolism, but even before it was over, questions were being raised about just how soon its principles would or could be converted into action. Rio failed to resolve the growing differences between industrialised countries and poorer states (the North–South divide), its goals were compromised by governments placing national sovereignty above the good of the global environment, and corporations were able to avoid anything beyond a voluntary adherence to environmental management. Within months of the conference, it had become obvious that there was still a yawning chasm between the promises and the deeds of national governments.

At the same time, economic growth is improving the quality of life for growing numbers of people. As this happens, the quality of the environment will become an increasingly important issue for more people. Environmental awareness has never been stronger than it is today in both rich and poor societies, the body of national and international environmental law is growing rapidly, and the political will to address environmental problems becomes stronger by the day. The next few years will be critical for the future of the global environment.

It has been very gratifying to see how well the first edition of *The Global Environmental Movement* has been received: it has been published in five countries and three languages, and has become a standard text on the global environmental movement. The need for a new edition began to grow after the 1992 Rio conference (for which a Portuguese-language edition was published in Brazil). My goal with this second edition has been to bring the story up to date; to do that, I have edited, shortened and updated all the existing chapters (with the goal of bringing out the more important events and arguments), added two new chapters (one on green parties, and one on the Rio conference), and – in response to some of the reviews of the first edition – expanded my analysis.

The first edition began life as a master's thesis for the University of London. In that regard I want to thank Philip Lowe, who guided the development of the thesis; his comments kept it on track and stopped it becoming unmanageable. Max Nicholson took time to talk in some depth about the early years of IUCN, and commented on the first two chapters, and Martin Holdgate commented on Chapters 5 and 6. Lynton Caldwell of Indiana University, Richard Andrews of the University of North Carolina, and Tim O'Riordan of the University of East Anglia read through the whole manuscript and made many useful comments, and David Brower, Czech Conroy, Duncan Poore, Robert Prescott-Allen and Richard Sandbrook discussed specific aspects of the movement with me, and in some cases commented on sections of the manuscript.

I wrote the first edition while I was working for IIED in London; my colleagues there provided an inspiring environment in which to work, and I thank them for their support and help. The second edition was written after I joined the Department of Political Science at the Indianapolis campus of Indiana University. My thanks to my students and colleagues for providing such a congenial workplace.

Introduction

Of all the political, economic and social revolutions of the last century, none has so fundamentally changed human values and behaviour as the environmental revolution.

Tracing its roots to the late 19th century, it fed off changes in economic structures, social relations and scientific understanding before being finally pushed onto the public policy agenda by a rebellious new generation after the Second World War. Environmentalism has since spawned a mass movement with millions of followers, generated new bodies of law, hatched new political parties, encouraged a rethinking of economic and social priorities, and become a central issue in international relations. Above all, it has changed the way we look at the world and compelled many of us to change the way we live. For the first time, humanity has awakened to some of the basic truths about the interrelatedness of the biosphere, and has been alerted to the basic truth that nature is finite, and that our mismanagement of the environment ultimately threatens our own existence.

Misuse of the environment has a history almost as long as that of civilisation. Nearly 3700 years ago, Sumerian cities were being abandoned as the irrigated lands which had produced the world's first agricultural surpluses became saline and waterlogged [1]. Nearly 2400 years ago, Plato bemoaned the deforestation and soil erosion brought to the hills of Attica by overgrazing and the cutting of trees for fuelwood [2]. In 1st century Rome, Columella and Pliny the Elder warned that poor husbandry threatened crop failures and soil erosion [3]. In the 7th century, the complex 400-year-old Mesopotamian irrigation system began to break down under the strain of mismanagement [4]. Population growth brought about the 10th century collapse of the Mayan civilisation [5]. Byzantine, Venetian and Genoan shipbuilding reduced the coastal forests of the Mediterranean [6]. Air pollution from coal-burning in England was bad enough by 1661 to prompt the diarist and naturalist John Evelyn to complain about the "Hellish and dismall Cloud" which made London resemble "the Suburbs of Hell, (rather) than an Assembly of Rational Creatures" [7].

For all these early warnings, there was little sense of wider concern until well after the industrial revolution, when threats to the environment worsened and a combination of increased social mobility and improved education allowed more people to see and understand the causes and effects. The first significant public response came in the second half of the 19th century, with nature protectionist groups in Europe and a two-pronged movement of wilderness preservationists and resource conservationists in the United States. Their early converts were few, but as science revealed more about nature and the threats it faced, and as the middle class grew, became more mobile, and looked beyond its immediate surroundings, the environmental movement grew and spread.

- In 1863, Britain passed the first broad-ranging air pollution law in the world, and created the first pollution control agency. By 1971 there were still only 12 national environmental agencies; today virtually every country has one. Few have adequate powers, but that is at least in part because few policy-makers yet fully understand the breadth and depth of environmental management needs, and because political and economic priorities still militate against taking adequate action.
- The world's first national environmental interest group (the Commons, Footpaths and Open Spaces Preservation Society) was founded in Britain in 1865; today the world has more than 20 000 such groups, which have become the foundation of national movements.
- The first international agreement on the environment was signed in 1886; today there are more than 300, most of which

have been signed since 1960. Many remain unenforced, but most have encouraged changes in national policy.

- In 1972, representatives from most of the countries of the world met in Stockholm under the auspices of the United Nations to discuss the problems of the human environment. They met again in Rio de Janeiro in 1992 in an Earth Summit designed to consider policies into the 21st century. Stockholm and Rio symbolised the ongoing process of reordering global priorities.
- In the wake of Stockholm, the United Nations created a new environmental programme; by 1980, almost all the major international organisations – from the World Bank to the European Union and the Organisation for Economic Co-operation and Development – had developed their own environmental policies.
- Dissatisfied with the response of conventional ideologies, new green parties emerged to challenge the old order. The first were founded in Tasmania and New Zealand in 1972; by 1991, more than 35 countries had national green parties, of which 22 had returned members to their national legislatures. In response, many of the older established parties rewrote their environmental policies and began to take notice of the green vote.

There is no denying the size and scope of the movement, and yet – with the notable exceptions of the work of Max Nicholson and Lynton Caldwell [8] – there have been very few studies of environmentalism as a global phenomenon. This has left many of the questions about environmentalism unanswered. How, where and why did it begin? What forms does it take, and what are its underlying goals and values? Is it a way of life, a state of mind, an attitude to society, or a political philosophy? Why is it also (confusingly) called "ecology" or "conservation"? How does "protection" differ from "preservation"? How does "conservation" differ from "sustainable development"? What *is* "sustainable development"?

The Global Environmental Movement sets out to answer some of these questions, to address some of the misconceptions, and to provide a study of environmentalism as a global political, social and economic phenomenon. It is primarily a history of the movement, and sets out both to describe the key events in the evolution of that movement, and to provide analysis that helps explain that evolution and place it in its broader context. Its central argument is that environmentalism must be seen not simply as a series of separate national movements, but as part of a cumulative, broad-ranging, long-term change in human attitudes arising as a reaction to industrialism and leaving almost no society untouched. It also argues that few environmental problems can be addressed by individual states acting alone, but that we must develop regional and global policies that recognise the regional and global links between cause and effect.

It is also a study of how and why the environment has been transformed from a private issue into a public political issue. It argues that most of the credit must go to private individuals and a popular mass movement, and that most governments and policy-makers have done little more than react to public pressure. It focuses on the internal dynamics of that movement, and the effects on society and on public policy. It is less a study of environmental problems than of the evolution of a mass movement.

The movement has been far from homogeneous. At the local and national level, debates rage about the causes of the environmental crisis and about the appropriate responses; should policies change to deal with problems as they arise, or is the key a fundamental reordering of human attitudes towards the biosphere and even towards each other? The US environmental movement was once described as "the biggest assortment of ill-matched allies since the Crusades – young and old, radicals of left and right, liberals and conservatives, humanists and scientists, atheists and deists" [9]. One study of American environmentalism identifies three main traditions: the biocentric (nature for and in itself), the ecologic (based on scientific understanding of interrelationships and interdependence among the parts of natural communities), and the economic (the optimal use of natural resources) [10].

Taken to the global level, the diversity of philosophies, tactics and aims is even greater.

- The issues range from the protection of orchids to the protection of whales, from the diposal of toxic wastes to the theoretical dangers of global warming, from the effects of affluence to the effects of poverty.

- Environmental groups range from multi-million member organisations operating out of designer offices in Washington DC, London or Geneva, to Himalayan village associations fighting to preserve their livelihood.
- Tactics range from public education, to careful and sustained lobbying in national and local legislatures, to occasionally violent confrontation between activists and corporations.
- Philosophies range from accommodation between the needs of development and economic growth to uncompromising anti-growthism.

For present purposes, environmentalism is defined as the promotion of values, attitudes and policies aimed at reaching an accommodation between human needs and the limits of the natural environment. The focus of most of this book is on Europe and North America, not because I want to belittle or overlook other societies, but because the world's most serious environmental problems have emerged as a result of economic and social changes coming out of the European industrial revolution, and because the citizens of industrial states were the first to respond, and because those states still make most of the key decisions affecting the global environment. However, as I argue towards the end of the book, environmental problems in Asia, Africa and Latin America are worsening, and attention is increasingly shifting to the problems of less developed countries.

Chapter 1 provides a prelude to the rest of the book by looking at the roots of environmentalism in the 19th and early 20th centuries, mainly in Britain and the United States, but also in Australia, South Africa and India. These developments are then related to one of the first truly regional environmental issues – the African wildlife question – and finally to the first signs of an international nature protection movement.

Chapter 2 follows these threads through to the post-Second World War era: the first major international conservation conferences, the creation of the first international conservation bodies, early neo-Malthusian worries, and the beginnings of an understanding of the conservation/development debate in post-colonial Africa.

Chapters 3 and 4 focus on New Environmentalism in industrialised countries between 1962 and 1972. Chapter 3 assesses some of the reasons why the new movement emerged when it did: the reaction to affluence, the fear of nuclear fallout, the influence of Rachel Carson, the impact of environmental disasters, and the influence of other social movements. Chapter 4 then looks at the debate generated by the prophets of doom.

Chapter 5 focuses on a single event: the 1972 Stockholm conference on the human environment. This was such a watershed that global environmentalism can be divided into two phases – before and after Stockholm. The performance of the most tangible institutional outcome of Stockholm – the United Nations Environment Programme – is assessed in *Chapter 6*.

Chapter 7 describes the politicisation of the environment in liberal democracies. Slightly before – but mainly after – Stockholm, New Environmentalism began to be translated into political action by governments: new laws, new government agencies, and new international conventions.

Chapter 8 deals with the very different problems faced by poorer countries trying to resolve the conflict between development goals and sustainable environmental management. Without coherent policies, accurate data, broad-based economic development, a reduction in population growth, and a more equitable distribution of resources (natural and financial), the future for the human environment in many of these countries looks bleak.

Chapter 9 describes the rise of green parties, explaining how and why they emerged, and why they developed when and where they did. It also describes and assesses the main ideas behind green philosophy, and the criticisms levelled by greens at conventional economic and political ideas.

Chapter 10 takes the broad view by examining international cooperation in addressing global and regional environmental problems. It looks at the development of international environmental law and at the work of international organisations, and illustrates the underlying motives of international cooperation with case studies of acid pollution and threats to the ozone layer.

Chapter 11 looks at the second of the big global environmental conferences, the 1992 Rio conference on the environment. It looks at the motives behind Rio, and at the consequences of the conference, and concludes by summing up the significance of environmentalism, and looking at prospects into the 21st century.

Acronyms and Abbreviations

ASP	African Special Project
CCOL	Co-ordinating Committee on the Ozone Layer
CDSN	European Committee for Conservation of Nature and Natural Resources
CEQ	Council on Environmental Quality (United States)
CFCs	chlorofluorocarbons
CIDA	Canadian International Development Agency
CITES	Convention on International Trade in Endangered Species of Wild Fauna and Flora
CND	Campaign for Nuclear Disarmament
CO_2	carbon dioxide
CPRE	Council for the Protection of Rural England
CSE	Centre for Science and Environment (India)
DAC	Direct Action Against Nuclear War
DESCON	Consultative Group for Desertification Control
DGSM	Dasohli Gram Swarajya Mandal (India)
DoE/DOE	Department of the Environment
ECB	Environment Co-ordination Board
ECE	Economic Commission for Europe (United Nations)
ECOSOC	United Nations Economic and Social Council
ECY	European Conservation Year
EEB	European Environmental Bureau
EIS	environmental impact statement
ELC	Environment Liaison Centre

EPA	Environmental Protection Agency (United States)
EU	European Union
FAO	Food and Agriculture Organisation of the UN
FoE	Friends of the Earth
GEMS	Global Environment Monitoring System
GNP	gross national product
GRID	Global Resource Information Database
IAEA	International Atomic Energy Agency
IAWGD	Inter-Agency Working Group on Desertification
IBP	International Biological Programme
IBPGR	International Board for Plant Genetic Resources
ICBP	International Council for Bird Preservation
ICSU	International Council of Scientific Unions
IGO	inter-governmental organisation
IGY	International Geophysical Year
IIEA	International Institute for Environmental Affairs
IIED	International Institute for Environment and Development
ILO	International Labour Organisation
IMCO	International Maritime Consultative Organisation
INFOTERRA	International Referral System
INGO	international non-governmental organisation
IOPN	International Office for the Protection of Nature
IRPTC	International Register of Potentially Toxic Chemicals
ITC	International Technical Conference on the Protection of Nature
IUBS	International Union of Biological Sciences
IUCN	International Union for Conservation of Nature and Natural Resources
IUPN	International Union for the Protection of Nature
IWC	Inland Waterways Commission
LDC	less developed country
LRTAP	long-range transboundary air pollution
MAB	Man and the Biosphere
MAP	Mediterranean Action Plan
MDC	more developed country
MEP	Member of the European Parliament/ Mouvement D'Écologie Politique

MIC	methyl-isocyanate
MIT	Massachusetts Institute of Technology
NASA	National Aeronautics and Space Administration
NATO	North Atlantic Treaty Organisation
NCEP	National Committee on Environmental Planning (India)
NCS	national conservation strategy
NEPA	National Environmental Policy Act
NES	National Environment Secretariat (Kenya)
NGO	non-governmental organisation
NIC	newly industrialising country
NO_x	nitrogen oxides
OAS	Organization of American States
OAU	Organisation of African Unity
OECD	Organisation for Economic Cooperation and Development
OPEC	Organisation of Petroleum-Exporting Countries
PACD	Plan of Action to Combat Desertification
PPM	Project on the Predicament of Mankind
RSP	Regional Seas Programme
RSPCA	Royal Society for the Prevention of Cruelty to Animals
SCEP	Study of Critical Environmental Problems
SO_2	sulphur dioxide
SPNR	Society for the Promotion of Nature Reserves
SPWFE	Society for the Preservation of the Wild Fauna of the Empire
SWMTEP	System-Wide Medium-Term Environmental Programme
UN	United Nations
UNCED	United Nations Conference on Environment and Development
UNCOD	United Nations Conference on Desertification
UNCTAD	United Nations Conference on Trade and Development
UNDP	United Nations Development Programme
UNEP	United Nations Environment Programme
UNESCO	United Nations Educational, Scientific and Cultural Organisation
UNFPA	United Nations Fund for Population Activities

UNICEF	United Nations Children's Fund
UNSCCUR	United Nations Scientific Conference on the Conservation and Utilisation of Resources
UNSO	United Nations Sudano-Sahelian Office
USAID	United States Agency for International Development
VPE	Les Verts-Parti Écologiste
WCS	World Conservation Strategy
WHO	World Health Organisation
WISE	World Information Service on Energy
WLCSC	Wild Life Conservation Special Committee
WMO	World Meteorological Organisation
WWF	World Wildlife Fund/World Wide Fund for Nature

A note on terminology

This book uses the terms "more developed countries" (MDCs) or "the North" to describe wealthier industrial or post-industrial states (Europe, Russia, North America, Japan and Australasia) and "less developed countries" (LDCs) or "the South" to describe the rest of the world.

1

The Roots of Environmentalism

The global environmental movement had no clear beginning. There were no landmark events which sparked mass outrage, no specific leaders who inspired a mass movement, and no sudden changes in human thinking. The global movement grew out of a series of independent responses to local issues, in different places at different times. Individuals came together to form local groups in the mid- to late 19th century, responding to different issues for often different reasons. Local groups slowly became national movements, combined after the Second World War to become a multi-national movement, and have today become a large, complex and disparate global movement.

The roots of the movement lay in the technological, economic and social changes brought by the industrial revolution in Europe and North America: these included improved scientific understanding, increased personal mobility, and the spread of human settlement. For Europeans, the movement arose partly out of a response to the threats posed to nature, and partly as a reaction to the horrors of life in industrial cities. In those parts of the world settled by Europeans – notably North America, Australia, South Africa and some African colonies – conservation and protection emerged as a reaction to the exploitation of natural resources. As settlers moved west in North America in the 19th century, some began arguing that the west should be protected from the kind of changes made by human settlement in the east. Others disagreed, and argued that the resources should be exploited, but in a more rational and sustainable manner. Similar arguments were made in some of Europe's African and Asian colonies.

Ideas were exchanged among professional foresters and planners, while the growth of the natural sciences alerted naturalists to the dangers posed to nature by unthinking economic development. By the early 20th century, the first tentative moves were beginning to be made to share knowledge across national boundaries, and to see threats to nature and natural resources as being international, and as demanding international responses.

Victorian Britain: in search of Arcadia

The British environmental movement was born when scientific discovery shed new light on the ways in which human activity was threatening nature, and when social and economic change led to the rediscovery of the human relationship with nature. This led first to a movement to protect wildlife, and then to demands that rural amenity be provided as relief for the inhabitants of cities that were growing bigger and dirtier.

The first major influence was the birth of popular interest in natural history. During the 16th, 17th and 18th centuries, the foundations of modern botany, zoology and other life sciences were laid by the work of a succession of amateur field naturalists [1]. Among these was Gilbert White, whose seminal *The Natural History of Selborne*, published in 1788, became the fourth most published book in the English language, and influenced several generations of naturalists, including Charles Darwin. White epitomised the Arcadian view of nature, based around the idea that simplicity and humility were needed in order to restore humans to peaceful coexistence with nature.

The Romantics and the primitivists found emotional solace in nature, and became offended by its subjugation. The writer William Gilpin complained that "wherever man appears with his tools, deformity follows his steps. His spade and his plough, his hedge and his furrow, make shocking encroachments on the simplicity and elegance of landscape" [2]. William Wordsworth wrote of the "violated rights" of nature, and in 1820, more than 50 years before the creation of the world's first national park, suggested that the English Lake District should be regarded as "a sort of national property, in which every man has a right and interest who has an eye to perceive and a heart to enjoy" [3].

The beauty of nature was brought to a wider public by the work of botanical illustrators, and by the invention of lithography in 1796–98. The work of artists such as Thomas Bewick combined with the discoveries of the naturalist John Ray, the Swedish botanist Carl von Linne (Linnaeus), and the findings of scientists such as Wallace and Darwin to promote a rediscovery of the relationship between humans and their natural environment.

Victorian confidence and self-assurance led many to think that mastery over the environment was essential for progress and for the survival of the human race. In reaction, what Worster calls a "biocentric conscience" [4] gradually emerged, encouraging people to rediscover their lost sense of kinship with nature, and to accept the moral responsibility to protect the earth from abuse. Darwin provided a major stimulus to this view; evolution suggested that humans were one with all other species, and distanced themselves from nature at their peril.

By the end of the 19th century, more was understood and appreciated about the balance of nature, and its sensitivity to human interference. Changes which in the past had been seen as positive now aroused passionate opposition, at least among an influential minority of intellectual Victorians [5], who increasingly criticised as vandalism the idea of "improving" the environment (by demolishing buildings, controlling vermin, or draining marshes). There was a growing realisation among naturalists that individual concerns had to be combined to generate group action to protect nature.

Changes in transport in the 19th century made the countryside accessible to the increasing number of Victorians looking for education, leisure and self-improvement. So many took up the study of nature that, by the 1880s, several hundred natural history societies and field clubs had been founded, attracting a combined membership of about 100 000 [6]. They initially emphasised contemplation and study rather than preservation, but this changed as specimen collecting posed a growing threat to wild plants and animals. Most collectors were interested in research, but the more thoughtless naturalists began competing to build bigger and better collections of birds, eggs and plants. For their critics, the desire to preserve nature now became implicit in the study of nature.

The damage inflicted by collectors was compounded by the growing popularity of field sports. Hunting was one thing, but wanton slaughter and cruelty quite another. Among the worst examples of this in England were the annual shoots of seabirds off Flamborough Head in Yorkshire. Opposition to slaughter of this kind gave rise to the second major influence on early British environmentalism: the wildlife protection movement. This traced its roots to growing revulsion at cruelty to animals, which led to the creation in 1824 of the Society for the Protection of Animals. The Society initially campaigned against cruelty to domesticated animals, but soon turned its attention to wild animals, was given a royal charter in 1840, and became the Royal Society for the Prevention of Cruelty to Animals (RSPCA). By the 1870s it was investigating vivisection, pigeon-shooting, stag-hunting and rabbit-coursing. Because cruelty to animals was seen as an indication of the most savage and primitive elements in human nature, protectionists believed that in saving wildlife, they were helping preserve the fabric of society [7]. Most of the support for the RSPCA came from the middle and upper classes.

Social reform movements often borrow techniques from one another, and attract support from the same quarters. Just as the environmental movement of the 1950s and 1960s overlapped for a time with protests against nuclear testing, civil rights and the Vietnam War (see Chapter 3), so naturalists and the critics of cruelty to animals began to influence each other, and the idea of protecting wildlife won growing support. The turning point probably came in the 1860s, when protectionists mustered forces around the issue of the killing of birds to provide plumage for women's fashions [8].

The East Riding Association for the Protection of Sea Birds, probably the first wildlife protection body in the world, was founded in 1867 to campaign against the shoots off Flamborough Head [9]. Although new legislation in the 1860s and 1870s gave some protection to wild birds and helped stem the flow of feathers from local sources, new supplies began arriving from the tropics in the 1880s. In the six months to April 1885, for example, the plumage of nearly 775 000 West Indian, Brazilian, East Indian and other birds was sold on the London market [10]. The opposition to the killing of birds for plumage was led by women, who deliberately excluded men from their organisations, such as the Plumage League (1885), the Selborne League (1885), the Fur, Fin and Feather Folk (1889), and the Society for the Protection of Birds (SPB) (1889), which was given a royal charter in 1904 and went on to become one of Britain's biggest and most influential environmental interest groups. The SPB pledged its members to boycott plumage, and set up a network of national and overseas branches; the Indian branch was behind one of the earliest laws against international traffic in wildlife: the 1902 Indian government order banning the export of bird skins and feathers [11].

The third major influence on British environmentalism was the growing reaction to the environmental costs of urban development. The industrial revolution had seen a dramatic increase in the number of town-dwellers, making Britain the most urbanised country in Europe. The new industrial centres also became the most polluted in Europe, leading to growing pressure to act. The first demands for action came from an unlikely source: a clergyman named J E N Molesworth, leader of the Manchester Association for the Prevention of Smoke, one of the first anti-pollution pressure groups in the world. Molesworth's brother-in-law, W A Mackinnon, was a member of parliament, who between 1843 and 1850 (prodded by Molesworth) kept up a parliamentary campaign to introduce anti-smoke laws [12]. He failed, but he had struck a note with a public becoming increasingly alarmed at the quality of Britain's urban air. Lord Palmerston, home secretary in 1852–53, took up the cause, and Britain's first significant anti-pollution law – the Smoke Nuisance Abatement (Metropolis) Act – was passed in 1853.

The focus then shifted to the problems created by the alkali industry, which made sodium carbonate for use in the manufacture of soap, glass and textiles, but also produced damaging emissions of hydrochloric acid. The emissions could be reduced by washing them with water, but without legal controls producers were unwilling to take action unless their competitors did likewise. *The Times* reported on 12 May 1862 that "Whole tracts of country, once as fertile as the fields of Devonshire, have been swept by deadly blights till they are as barren as the shores of the Dead Sea". Farmers and landowners complained, but little was done until Lord Derby, whose estate near St Helens was affected, took up the matter in the House of Lords, and helped bring about the passage of the world's first broad-ranging pollution control law, the Alkali Act of 1863.

Enforcement of the law was made the responsibility of the new Alkali Inspectorate, the first government department set up specifically to deal with pollution. The Inspectorate was to be run for its first 21 years by Robert Angus Smith (1817–84), a Scottish chemist who – among his other achievements – published a report in 1872 that coined the term "acid rain" and outlined for the first time the link between air pollution and acidification [13]. Against a background of growing public pressure, Smith lobbied the government to strengthen the laws against pollution and to broaden its definition of the kinds of problems it should be addressing. Parliament took further action in the 1880s, but the strength of public opinion was still too limited to generate an effective response. It would be 1956 before Britain passed a Clean Air Act, and Smith's findings on acid pollution were to be largely ignored until the Scandinavians made acid rain a major public issue in the 1960s (see Chapter 10).

Revulsion at the squalor of life in the industrial towns had meanwhile combined with the desire for open space and nature to produce the fourth major thrust of early British environmentalism: the amenity movement. The countryside came to be associated increasingly with rest and relaxation, and threats to the countryside now took on a new significance. One possible answer was to set aside pieces of land as nature reserves, an idea that had already taken hold in the United States. The world's first private environmental group – the Commons, Open Spaces and Footpaths Preservation Society – was founded in 1865 to campaign for the provision of land for amenity, particularly the urban commons that were often the nearest "countryside" available to urban workers. The Society's pressure tactics were successful, but it did not have the corporate status needed to allow it to buy land. That job was left to the National Trust, founded in 1895 with the goal of saving

Britain's cultural and natural heritage from industrial development. By 1910, the Trust had bought 13 sites, but it was as much interested in sites of cultural and historic value as those of natural value, and naturalists criticised the almost random way in which potential nature reserves were acquired, apparently with little regard for the national significance of their plants and animals [14].

In 1912 the Society for the Promotion of Nature Reserves (SPNR) was created to encourage the National Trust to pay more attention to creating reserves. This it did by making a national inventory of sites worth protecting, and mobilising public support for the acquisition of those sites. Even so, the need for protected areas was still seen as less urgent than the need to control specimen collectors and to curb cruelty to animals. Nature reserves were regarded by most people as an expensive way of supplementing legislation [15]. Although the first had been created on the Norfolk Broads in 1888, it was not until after the Second World War that the idea of habitat protection won wider support in Britain.

Ironically, the National Trust was condemned, by its own success in acquiring land and property, to spend more and more of its time and money on managing that land and property. This opened the way for the creation in 1926 of the Council for the Protection of Rural England (CPRE), founded to coordinate the voluntary movement, lobby for new laws, give advice to landowners, and promote countryside preservation. In 1929, thanks in part to CPRE pressure, the Addison Committee was set up to look into the question of national parks. Its 1931 report supported the creation of parks to protect flora, fauna and areas of exceptional natural interest, and to improve public access. But British national parks did not come until after the Second World War, and even then took on a very different role from parks elsewhere. Instead of protecting wilderness, they preserved land of natural value on which people already lived and made a living [16].

Conserving the empire: India, Australia and South Africa

Imperialism promoted the spread of European ideas about development – and then about protection and conservation – to other parts of the world, with varying results. For India, colonialism meant the testing – at the invitation of British administrators – of German principles of forest management. When German foresters were invited to India, they not only spread forest science ideas more widely, but also helped lay the foundations of global conservation. For Australia and South Africa, by contrast, colonialism meant the spread of uncontrolled exploitation, with devastating results.

Forestry had been taught in German universities since the early 18th century and sustained yield methods used in German forests since the late 18th century. Britain appointed the first conservator of forests in Bombay in 1847, and the second in Madras in 1856 [17], charging both with managing forests as a source of revenue for the state. When Britain acquired Lower Burma in 1856, the German forester Dietrich Brandis (a relative by marriage of the Governor-General of India, Lord Dalhousie) was appointed forest superintendent and charged with preventing deforestation. In 1864, Brandis was appointed inspector-general of forests for India, and the first Indian Forest Act was passed the following year. Brandis now began the organised recruitment of forestry officers from Britain, all of whom spent time in Germany, France and Switzerland as part of their education. After their work with the Indian Forest Service, many moved on to other parts of the Empire, notably Australia and East Africa, where their services were often badly needed.

The earliest settlers in Australia saw forests as obstacles that had to be removed. The uncontrolled cutting of timber and the cultivation of riverbanks in New South Wales brought serious soil erosion and flooding as early as 1803 [18]. During the early 19th century, the clearing of forest for sheep grazing led to overgrazing across vast areas of inland Victoria, New South Wales and Queensland, but little was done to curb the damage, or to protect wildlife. By the 1830s there were too few seals left to make sealing economically viable, and by the 1850s, whaling too had dwindled, thanks largely to the practice of killing females at the time of calving.

The idea of game laws was anathema to many Australians, because the right to hunt game had been a privilege of landowners in Britain, and many convicts had been shipped for breaking game laws. With the apparent abundance of animal life in Australia, the new settlers saw hunting as a basic right, and rejected conservation as a hated relic of the Old Country [19]. Bustards, emus, wallabies and smaller marsupials became increasingly rare, and one British visitor to Western Australia noted in 1849 that although vast herds of kangaroo existed in the interior, the trade in kangaroo skins had taken such a toll that "no increase can bear up against this wholesale animal slaughter" [20]. Matters were made worse by the introduction of new plant species (which often replaced native species), and of animal pests, notably the domestic dog and cat, and the rabbit.

The first signs of a response came in the late 19th century. From the 1860s, state governments began reserving coastal foreshore and lake and river banks for public amenity [21]. In 1866 a reserve was established at Jenolan Caves in New South Wales. In 1879 the New South Wales government declared the Royal National Park south of Sydney, but – like the parks later created in other Australian states – the Royal was created more for public recreation than wilderness preservation. The Tasmanian parliament passed laws to protect selected bird species in 1860, and natural history societies on the British model were formed in Victoria and New South Wales in the 1880s. New South Wales introduced laws protecting selected marsupials in 1903, and in 1909 a Wildlife Preservation Society was formed in Sydney.

Commissions of enquiry in Tasmania and Victoria (1898) and Western Australia (1903) meanwhile argued that forests could not continue to be regarded as a limitless resource, but needed sustainable management. A new law in Queensland in 1906 gave the government the power to create national parks in areas with little marketable timber, and in 1915 Tasmania passed a Scenery Preservation Act. But these were exceptions to the rule; although forestry commissions based on the Indian model and staffed largely by ex-officers of the Indian Forest Service were set up in every state between 1907 and 1920, the result was not always improved forestry management.

In southern Africa, environmental destruction and protection had followed in short order within years of the first permanent

European settlement in 1652. By 1658, proclamations were being issued to control the clearance of forests for firewood, and to protect penguins shot for food, seals for skins, and elephants for ivory (although the controls on elephants were imposed because the Dutch East India Company wanted to monopolise the ivory trade). The laws had little effect, though, because enforcement was almost impossible in a colony whose white settlers were becoming increasingly dispersed and isolated, and who saw wood, skins, hides and ivory as accessible forms of barter and valuable sources of income. Hunting spread during the 18th century, with some elephant hunters setting out on journeys of up to nine months. By the 1830s, the Eastern Cape had lost most of its elephants.

The uncontrolled clearance of forests, and subsequent soil erosion and sand blow, finally prompted the passage of an 1846 ordinance aimed at the "better preservation" of the Cape Flats area near Cape Town. A forest commission was set up in the Cape in 1854, and conservancies set up in the Eastern Cape in 1856. A drought in 1862 emphasised the need for new legislation on land management, and proved a turning point in settler and farmer attitudes [22]. An 1864 Select Committee on soil erosion, drought and associated problems noted the links between soil erosion and veldt-burning, and the clearance of vegetation.

J C Brown, Cape Botanist from 1862 to 1866, launched a one-man crusade to draw attention to the links between human activity and environmental degradation. His warnings were undermined, however, by the apparent abundance of land for settlement, and the influence of the timber trade [23]. Of more immediate concern was the question of wildlife preservation. New laws aimed at protecting wildlife were passed in Natal, the South African Republic and the Orange Free State in the second half of the 18th century, the first state game reserves in Africa were set up in 1857 in the Knysna and Tsitsikama forests, and private game reserves were created elsewhere by large landowners from 1875. These did little to curb the killing, however, and by 1858 ivory had become Natal's most valuable export. In 1866 one Orange Free State company alone exported 152 000 blesbok and wildebeest skins. In 1873, 62 000 zebra and wildebeest skins were exported [24]. But the costs were already being felt: in the peak year of 1877, more than 19 tonnes left Natal (roughly the produce of 950 elephant); by 1895 the annual export had fallen to just 30 kg (66 lb).

Professional hunting became a popular occupation in the mid-19th century further north (particularly in present-day Botswana and Zimbabwe), where demand was strongest for ivory, ostrich feathers, rhino horns, hippo teeth, hides and meat [25]. In 1872–74 alone, an estimated 50 tonnes of ivory – the spoils of about 2500 elephant – were collected by Ndebele and European hunters. As the herds shrank, hunters had to travel further north, and by 1880 elephant were so rare south of the Zambezi that it was no longer possible to make a living out of elephant hunting in the area [26]. In August 1883 the last quagga died in Amsterdam Zoo, emphasising the threat faced by southern African wildlife. In the same month the first wildlife conservation body in South Africa – the Natal Game Protection Association – was founded. A game reserve created in 1894 at Pongola in the eastern Transvaal later became part of the Kruger National Park.

The roots of American environmentalism

Although there were parallel motives behind the growth of environmentalism in Western Europe and North America (there was a similar flowering of interest in natural history, and the influence of Romanticism was comparable), there was one major obvious difference: where Europe had long been settled and exploited, vast new areas of western North America were being opened to settlement, just as they had been in Australia and South Africa.

Attempts had been made to preserve nature along the eastern seaboard during the early years of European settlement, such as William Penn's ruling in the late 17th century that settlers in Pennsylvania leave an acre of trees for every five acres cleared [27]. But most settlers saw wilderness as a barrier to settlement, and saw nature as a ready source of food, fuelwood and shelter. The hope that the New World was a second Eden was shattered when it was found that the land was often hostile and desolate, a discovery that allowed abundant opportunity for the expression of Judaeo-Christian biases against wilderness [28]. Already by

1700, over 200 000 hectares (500 000 acres) of woodland had been cleared for farming in New England [29]. From about 1620 to 1870, wood was the major source of energy in the United States and the primary building material, but there was little under-standing of woodland management techniques.

At the same time, the growing popularity of natural history alerted scientists – as it had in Britain – to the extent of environ-mental change. The beauty of North American wilderness inspired the writings of Romantics, philosophers and travellers throughout the 18th and early 19th centuries. The scientist, writer and poet Alexander Wilson expounded on the beauties of nature, and in 1808–14 published a nine-volume study of American birds which raised interest in ornithology. John James Audubon's research for *Birds of America* (1827–38) alerted him to the rapid deforestation of the Ohio Valley [30].

Later in the 19th century, Henry David Thoreau studied wood-land management, and warned that clearing forest and planting rye for short-term profits was "a greediness that defeats its own ends" [31]. While the westward advance of settlement during the 19th century pitted settlers and mining and lumber companies against the wilderness, it also helped the nature-lovers, drawn by the spectacular beauty of the Rocky Mountains and the Far West.

Two seminal events occurred in 1864. The first was the publi-cation of *Man and Nature* by George Perkins Marsh (1801–1882), a co-founder of the Smithsonian and then US Minister to Italy. *Man and Nature* was remarkable for outlining ideas that would not be more widely discussed for another century. Marsh argued that waste and destruction were making the earth unfit for human habitation, and ultimately threatened the human race with extinction. Society, he warned, was "breaking up the floor and wainscoting and doors and window frames of our dwelling, for fuel to warm our bodies and seethe our pottage, and the world cannot afford to wait till the slow and sure progress of exact science has taught it better economy . . . the teachings of simple experience . . . are not to be despised" [32]. Marsh's ideas influenced French writers and Italian and Indian foresters, and Stewart Udall described *Man and Nature* as representing the beginning of "land wisdom" in the United States [33].

The second event was the 1864 Act of Congress transferring the Yosemite Valley and the Mariposa Grove of Big Trees to the State of California on the condition that they be held inalienably for "public use, resort and recreation" [34]. The idea of setting aside land for recreation has been traced back to the early 19th century. During his travels in the west in 1829–32, the artist George Catlin concluded that buffalo and native Americans alike were threatened with extinction, argued that the "primitive" was worth preserving, and suggested that native Americans, buffalo and wilderness could be protected if the government were to establish "a nation's Park, containing man and beast, in all the wild[ness] and freshness of their nature's beauty!" [35]. Americans travelling to Europe came home with a new appreciation of the value of wilderness and of the urgent need to preserve it before it was gone.

In 1858, Thoreau wrote of the desirability of "national preserves" [36] and suggested that preserving wilderness was ultimately important for preserving civilisation [37]. The man credited with developing the idea of national parks as a practical policy, however, was Frederick Law Olmsted, the landscape architect who designed Central Park in New York City, and helped campaign for the creation of a park around Niagara Falls. Olmsted argued that it was the duty of government to "democratise" nature in the sense of making natural beauty available to more than a privileged few, as was the norm in most of Europe [38].

A second Act of Congress, signed in 1872, designated an area of 800 000 hectares (two million acres) in Wyoming as Yellowstone National Park, the world's first national park. Nash argues that the invention of national parks was made possible in the United States by the existence of land in the public domain, by the fact that wilderness still existed at a time when the demand for its preservation developed (which was not the case in most of Europe), and by the coexistence of developed and undeveloped land [39]. At the same time, he notes that Yellowstone was created less to preserve wilderness than to prevent private acquisition of its "natural curiosities" [40]. Similarly, the creation of the Adirondack Forest Preserve in New York State in 1885 was less to protect wilderness than to protect the watershed and the local water supply [41]. Rather than being focused on the protection of nature, Runte suggests that American national parks originated in the search for a national identity and the glorification of the natural beauty revealed by westward expansion [42]. Whatever the short-term motives, the long-term effects of the establishment of Yosemite, Yellowstone and the Adirondack park were to preserve wilderness, and to give substance to the philosophies of Catlin, Thoreau, Marsh and others. They also provided models that were imitated in other countries, such as Australia (Royal National Park, 1879), Canada (Banff National Park, 1885) and New Zealand (Tongarivo National Park, 1894).

At the turn of the century, American environmentalism divided into two camps: the preservationists (who wanted to preserve wilderness from all but recreational and educational use) and the conservationists (who wanted to exploit the continent's natural resources, but to do so rationally and sustainably). The champion of wilderness preservation was the Scottish-born naturalist John Muir (1838–1914). His earliest campaigning helped bring about the creation in 1890 of Yosemite National Park, the first park specifically designed to protect wilderness [43]. Buoyed by this success, Muir in 1892 helped found the Sierra Club, which worked to make the mountain regions of the Pacific Coast accessible for recreation, and became a rallying point for the preservationists.

Although he often used practical justifications when arguing his case, Muir spoke and wrote of wilderness in religious terms, remarking that while God's glory was written all over his works, in the wilderness the letters were capitalised. When Ralph Waldo Emerson visited Yosemite in 1871, Muir hoped he could persuade Emerson to join him "in a month's worship with Nature in the high temples of the great Sierra Crown beyond our holy Yosemite" [44]. He felt that civilisation had distorted man's sense of his relationship to other living things, and spoke of "protecting" or "preserving" the environment, often implying that wilderness be used for nothing but recreation and contemplation.

The conservationists disagreed, arguing that resources such as land, forests and water could be exploited as long as this was done sustainably. Tree-planting had begun in the prairie states in the 1860s [45], and a Forestry Division had been created within the Agriculture Department in 1876, but it had neither money nor power. The real work was undertaken by amateurs, such as the wealthy botanist Charles Sprague Sargent. Inspired by Marsh's book, Sargent surveyed American forests for the federal government in 1880 and recommended that federally owned timber be protected until a comprehensive study could be made by experts.

The first suggestion for a forest service of scientifically trained specialists came from Gifford Pinchot (1865–1946), a wealthy Pennsylvanian who – with the help of Dietrich Brandis – had studied forestry in Europe, where he had learned that forests could be both protected and managed for sustained yields. (The European influence continued in 1886, when the German forester Bernhard Fernow became the first trained forester to be appointed to direct government forest work in the United States [46].) Pinchot, Sargent and others pursued the idea of a government-sponsored commission, which was established in 1896. The commission confirmed that American forests were in a parlous condition, but argued that they should not be withdrawn completely from use.

Pinchot believed that conservation should be based on three principles: development (using existing resources for the present generation), the prevention of waste, and the development of natural resources for the many, not the few [47]. He claimed that his conservation policy was "breaking new ground", but – as Worster argues – he was ignoring a tradition of progressive, scientific agriculture that stretched back to the 18th century. Pinchot's contribution was to bring the tradition of progressive agriculture to the management of public lands, particularly forests [48].

Early American conservation is often described as a battle between the people and private interests set on exploiting the nation's natural resources for selfish ends. But there was very little in the way of a popular movement. American conservationists were professionals in fields such as forestry, hydrology and geology. They were influenced less by public opinion than by loyalty to their professional ideals in ensuring rational planning and efficient exploitation of natural resources. They opposed those who wanted to withdraw resources from commercial development, arguing that grassroots democracy would have defeated what Hays calls the "gospel of efficiency" [49]. Jones suggests that Progressive leaders were not the product of popular discontent but the self-appointed guardians of the public interest [50].

Pinchot's utilitarian philosophy was supported by Vice-President Theodore Roosevelt, who became President in September 1901. Pinchot in effect became Roosevelt's "Secretary of State for Conservation", and resource management became a matter of public policy at the federal level for the first time. Roosevelt also sought Muir's opinions, and the demands of the preservationists were met during the Roosevelt era by the addition of Yosemite Valley to the surrounding national park, and the creation of 53 wildlife reserves, 16 national monuments and five new national parks [51]. On the whole though, Roosevelt leaned towards the promotion of professional conservation based on the rational management of natural resources.

If forestry was one inspiration of American conservation, water was another. Conservationists emphasised the importance of rivers in inland transport, domestic and commercial water supply, flood and erosion control, and hydroelectric power, and noted that water was the only major resource still in public possession. Multi-purpose river development was seen as a prime example of the planned and efficient use of resources. In March 1907, Roosevelt, at the suggestion of Pinchot [52], created the Inland Waterways Commission (IWC), ostensibly to prepare and report a comprehensive plan for the improvement and control of American rivers. In fact it went far beyond this. Roosevelt insisted that any plan for the utilisation of inland waterways should consider flood control, the prevention of erosion and siltation, and the construction of dams. The Commission concluded that any plans for the use of inland waterways should regard rivers as a national asset and take full account of the conservation of all resources connected with them. Its findings were published in February 1908, and immediately opposed by the US Army Corps of Engineers (which had a narrow view of water use and development [53]), and by Congress, which was against the idea of an all-encompassing planning agency.

In 1908–09, as his term drew to a close and his conservation programme appeared to be ebbing, Roosevelt began working to give conservation a national audience [54]. At an IWC meeting in May 1907, Frederick H Newell (an engineer in the US Geological Survey, a colleague of Pinchot's and a member of the IWC) suggested that the Commission stage a national conference to help draw attention to conservation. The plan was agreed, and the White House Conference of Governors on Conservation was held on 13–15 May 1908, and attended by 44 state governors and delegates from 70 national organisations. Muir, Sargent and other preservationists were not invited.

Although initially limited to a discussion of water resources, the agenda was widened to take in all natural resources. State's rights was a key issue, with most governors declaring their opposition to more than the most marginal federal government involvement in the control of resources. They recommended that each state create a conservation commission to work with other state commissions and the federal government.

Thanks to the publicity surrounding the conference, the conservation debate was brought to the attention of the wider American public for the first time. Within three weeks, Roosevelt had announced the creation of a National Conservation Commission, entrusted with making the first survey of natural resources in the United States. Pinchot headed the executive committee, which completed the inventory in six months. When it was laid before Congress on 22 January 1909, Roosevelt described it as "one of the most fundamentally important documents ever laid before the American people" [55]. Congress, however, refused to approve continued funding because of a prevailing resentment at Roosevelt's expansion of executive power [56].

Seeds of a global movement

By the close of the 19th century, the first attempts were being made to promote greater international cooperation, particularly in the field of wildlife protection. It had occurred to several European protectionists that the spread of human settlement was increasing the pressure on wildlife. Given that European countries

Table 1.1   Foundation of selected private environmental organisations, 1865–1914

Year	Organisation	Country
1843	Manchester Association for the Prevention of Smoke	Britain
1865	Commons, Open Spaces and Footpaths Preservation Society	Britain
1867	East Riding Association for the Protection of Sea Birds	Britain
1870	Association for the Protection of British Birds	Britain
1880	Fog and Smoke Committee (National Smoke Abatement Institution from 1882)	Britain
1883	American Ornithologists Union	US
	Natal Game Protection Association	S. Africa
1885	Selborne League (later Society)	Britain
1886	Audubon Society (lapsed 1889, revived 1905)	US
1889	Society for the Protection of Birds	Britain
1892	Sierra Club	US
1895	National Trust	Britain
1898	Coal Smoke Abatement Society (later National Society for Clean Air)	Britain
1903	Society for the Preservation of the Wild Fauna of the Empire	Britain
1909	Swiss League for the Protection of Nature	Switzerland
	Swedish Society for the Protection of Nature	Sweden
	Wildlife Preservation Society	Australia
	National Conservation Association	US
1912	Society for the Promotion of Nature Reserves	Britain
1913	British Ecological Society	Britain

were so small and so closely situated to each other, cooperation had its own logic, especially as each country faced the common experiences of growing populations, widening human settlement, urbanisation, industrialisation, and an increasingly urgent need for natural resource planning. National nature protection groups were founded in several countries in the closing decades of the century, many taking their inspiration from the national parks movement in the United States [57]. By the first decade of the 20th century, enough national groups existed to make the need for international collaboration more obvious and its achievement more practicable.

The protection of birds provided the first focus of attention. The spread of human settlement, combined with the trade in birds and feathers, led to suggestions that the role of birds in agriculture should be studied more closely, and lists made of which birds were pests and which were useful to agriculture. An international agreement to protect animals useful to forestry and agriculture was suggested at a meeting of German foresters and agriculturalists in Vienna in 1868, and in 1872 the Swiss Federal Council proposed a commission to look at the possibility of an international agreement on bird protection. A convention to protect birds useful to agriculture was finally signed by 12 European countries in March 1902, and came into force in 1905. Opposition to its utilitarian character, combined with its restriction to birds, formed a rallying point for groups seeking a more ambitious document and a permanent international nature protection body [58].

The hunting and plumage debates had meanwhile helped draw the attention of naturalists to the problems of the wildlife of Europe's African colonies. They were particularly concerned about East Africa, which had begun to attract hunters to the game made accessible by the declaration of German and British protectorates in 1885 and 1896. The building of the Uganda railway in 1895–1902 and of the Tanga–Moshi railway in 1896–1912 made the interior even more accessible to white settlers and hunters, who sent home reports of abundant game. As the number of visiting hunters grew, the number of game animals fell. Although game reserves were created in East Africa at the end of the 19th century, they were planned as hunting grounds for the sport of soldiers and administrators [59].

In 1897, responding to pressure from preservationists and hunters equally concerned about the future of game, the British Prime Minister, Lord Salisbury, suggested to the German government the need to control ivory exports from East Africa. A note was circulated to other governments in 1899, and in 1900 the world's first international environmental agreement – the Convention for the Preservation of Wild Animals, Birds and Fish in Africa – was signed at a conference in London by Britain, France, Germany, Italy, Portugal and the Belgian Congo. Game preservation was at the root of the convention, and there was little interest in non-game animals, which it was assumed were in no danger because they were not being hunted [60]. The Convention was designed to control the trade in ivory, fish, skins and trophies, and suggested protective measures such as closed seasons. Although signed, it was never put into effect; its real importance lay in the precedent it created for later legislation.

The protection of colonial wildlife was also the motivation behind the creation in 1903 of the world's first international environmental organisation, the Society for the Preservation of the Wild Fauna of the Empire (SPWFE) (now the Fauna and Flora Preservation Society). Sponsored by hunters and naturalists, the Society aimed to encourage the protection of fauna (in effect, birds and the larger mammals) in the colonies. Within a year, its hunter sponsors were being nicknamed "the penitent butchers" [61].

Among those most actively warning of the decline of African wildlife were Sir Harry Johnston, Special Commissioner in Uganda (1899–1901) and a founder member of SPWFE, and the German naturalist C G Schillings, who collected specimens for German museums and pioneered wildlife photography in the region. In 1906 Johnston wrote that funding was desperately needed to pay for nature protection in East Africa, that public opinion should be encouraged to strengthen government action, and that Britain could learn something from the lessons being learned in Africa. He had little time for European hunters: "It seems to be still the accepted panacea in Britain or Continental society that a young or middle-aged man, who has been crossed in love, or who has figured in the Divorce Court . . . must go out to Africa and kill big game" [62].

Schillings – who had attended the 1900 London conference and was concerned that the destruction of South African wildlife should not be repeated in East Africa – wrote of the "tragedy of civilisation" in man bringing more and more of nature under control and killing animals at an unprecedented rate. He found it regrettable that Germans knew so little of the animal life in their colonies, and, in his books *With Flashlight and Rifle* and *In Wildest Africa*, made impassioned pleas for greater protection and more research. He felt the most urgent task was to collect accurate data on wildlife and then design practicable measures for protection. Like Marsh before him, Schillings argued that no epoch had seen such progress in industry and knowledge, yet was so blinded to the effects: water and air pollution, deforestation, the extinction of animal species, and the reckless exploitation of coal reserves [63].

By 1910, about 150–200 shooting parties were visiting British East Africa annually, killing about 10 000 animals [64].

The vogue for hunting began to recede almost as suddenly as it had begun, due largely to the influx of permanent white settlers, which reduced the area of public hunting territory. By 1919 there were two game reserves in British East Africa: the Northern (between Lake Rudolf (now Turkana) and Mount Kenya), and the Southern (between Nairobi and the Tanganyika border, running down as far as Mt Kilimanjaro). The Northern Reserve covered semi-desert unsuitable for settlement, while the Southern had been created almost arbitrarily, and it was only during First World War military operations that it was found to contain land suitable for settlement. One observer noted at the time that there was little chance that the reserve would be kept inviolate unless settlers were convinced that it did not retard development of the colony: "wherever you pick the area to be reserved for game, it is sure to be a Naboth's vineyard to someone, and . . . game is likely to get a worse name through this supposed usurpation than if such land were actually thrown open for settlement" [65]. (This prescient observation was to apply equally well to the problems that were to arise much later when newly independent African governments tried to balance the exploitation of natural resources with demands that wildlife be protected.)

Hunting was to remain fashionable for several decades yet, but the spread of European settlement brought two more problems in its wake. First, there was the suspicion that animals such as the eland and the buffalo carried parasites that posed a direct threat to domestic livestock. Second, speculators were beginning to see the commercial possibilities in exploiting East Africa's forests. The colonial government – which was in favour of conserving forests – felt it would be premature to sell off concessions until it had a workable re-afforestation scheme. Nevertheless, about 100 000 hectares (250 000 acres) of forest (or a quarter of the proclaimed forest area) were destroyed in 1894–1919 [66]. The direct cause was clearance and conversion to crops by peasant farmers; the indirect cause was government policies that forced peasant farmers to move off their traditional farmland. By the Forest Ordinance of 1911, just over 800 000 hectares (two million acres) of forest were protected from cutting except under licence.

The extermination by colonial authorities of wild animals regarded as pests or carriers of disease to domestic stocks began taking a heavy toll following the First World War; a total of 321 518 animals were killed, for example, in anti-tsetse fly operations between 1924 and 1945 in Southern Rhodesia alone [67]. Concern for the implications was one of the main motives behind the convening in London, on British initiative, of the 1933 International Conference for the Protection of Fauna and Flora. This resulted in the signing of a convention on the Preservation of Fauna and Flora in Their Natural State, which was later ratified by most of the colonial powers.

Superseding the long-defunct 1900 Convention, the new agreement was designed to curb threats to African wildlife by creating protected areas, such as national parks and reserves. It brought preservationists, scientists and governments together in common cause, made its signatories aware of the problems of each other's African colonies, and established the precedent of non-governmental organisations playing a technical advisory role in such initiatives [68]. It even included appendices of endangered and rare animal species. But the signatories were not bound by its rules, there was no provision for regular follow-up meetings, and there was no monitoring committee. It may also have begun making local populations hostile to wildlife protection, because animals were being protected for no practical reason and with no regard to traditional hunting rights. This would later become a critical factor in post-independence attempts to promote conservation (see Chapters 5 and 10).

Conservation and the New Deal

With attention in the United States focused more closely on domestic issues, there was little support for, or interest in, the international dimension of protecting or conserving nature. Pinchot was one of the few who saw the need for cooperation. Aware that a new president was unlikely to be as sympathetic to conservation as Roosevelt, he followed his work on the Governors' Conference by promoting two more conservation conferences, this time international in scope. The first was the North American

Conservation Congress, held in Washington DC on 18 February 1909 with Pinchot in the chair. Ten delegates from Canada, Newfoundland, Mexico and the United States discussed the principles of conservation espoused by Roosevelt, Pinchot and the Governors' meeting. The most notable outcome was an agreement that conservation was a problem broader than the boundaries of one nation, and a proposal that Roosevelt call a world conservation conference.

The North American Congress was still in session when Roosevelt issued invitations to 58 countries to attend a world congress in The Hague. Roosevelt left office in March, and nearly half the countries had accepted, when the conference was called off by President Taft. Pinchot was bitterly disappointed. Further national conservation congresses were held in September 1910, September 1911, October 1912 and November 1913, but Taft had not repeated his request to Congress, made as President-elect, to maintain the National Conservation Commission, and appeared undecided over his attitude to conservation policy. Pinchot was removed from the leadership of the Commission in 1910 and became president of the National Conservation Association (founded in 1909).

Conservation was not to become a central part of federal government policy again until 1933, when Franklin D Roosevelt took office to preside over a nation in deep financial crisis. Roosevelt harkened back to Pinchotism, and his New Deal administration applied professional management and efficiency as a cornerstone of economic recovery, notably in the Tennessee Valley Authority, the apogee of the multi-purpose development philosophy. Similarly, the Civilian Conservation Corps deployed unemployed men in forestry, soil erosion prevention, flood control and similar projects.

Elsewhere, attitudes to "rational management" were changing, as exemplified in the extermination (begun with federal funding by Theodore Roosevelt) of animals regarded as pests. The wolf, the prairie dog and the coyote were particular targets. Pinchot had little interest in wildlife, and paid little heed to the ecological complications of eradicating a species that interfered with the productivity of resources in which people had an interest [69].

Opposition to the extermination of predators was led in the postwar years by the American Society of Mammalogists, and by 1936 the killing of all predators in national parks had stopped.

The changing view is encapsulated in the career of Aldo Leopold (1887–1948). Leopold, a graduate of the Yale Forestry School founded with Pinchot family money, published in 1933 his book *Game Management*, which became a key text for the wildlife profession. In it he declared that "effective conservation requires in addition to public sentiment and laws, a deliberate and purposeful manipulation of the environment" [70]. But he had already become concerned at the US Forest Service obsession with forestry to the exclusion of wildlife management. In 1924 he was instrumental in the creation of the Gila National Forest in New Mexico as a wilderness, and in 1935 he helped found the Wilderness Society.

Leopold's conversion from progressive conservation was confirmed in his enormously influential *Sand County Almanac*, published posthumously in 1949. "Have we learned", he asked, "the first principle of conservation: to preserve all the parts of the land mechanism? No, because even the scientist does not yet recognize all of them" [71]. He warned of the inadequacy of land conservation as a purely economic question: "We abuse land because we regard it as a commodity belonging to us. When we see land as a commodity to which we belong, we may begin to use it with love and respect" [72].

Meanwhile, the wilderness preservation movement underwent a revival during the New Deal. As the United States emerged from the Depression, visits to national parks soared from 6.3 million in 1934 to 16.2 million in 1938. Despite his deep care for land, trees and water for human use [73], Roosevelt was personally unimpressed by many parks, but he saw them as essential to the process of national spiritual rejuvenation. He hoped they could be made more accessible, particularly for residents of the over-populated eastern states. He was opposed in this by the wilderness preservationists, who argued that the roads being built into parks to make them more accessible threatened to destroy wilderness. The continuing rift between conservationists and preservationists came to a head in 1935–39 with the debate over

Kings Canyon in the Sierra Nevada. Muir had long before campaigned without success to have it declared a national park; in 1935 the planned construction of an access road and the commercial development it would bring helped pull the Sierra Club out of the rut into which it had by then settled. Concentrated campaigning resulted in the declaration of Kings Canyon National Park in 1939.

The mid-1930s saw one of the greatest man-made environmental disasters in history: the Dust Bowl. Between 1934 and 1937, more than 200 regional dust storms hit the Great Plains [74]. Some were dense enough to blot out the sun and create drifts up to six metres (20 feet) high; others blew dust as far as Chicago, Washington DC and the Atlantic. By 1938, more than half the Great Plains – about 1.29 million km^2 (500 000 square miles) – had been eroded, 16 states had been affected, and the United States had been obliged to make up for lost farm production by importing wheat. Immediate blame for the Dust Bowl was placed on the wind and on the drought of 1931–34, but the real blame lay with more than half a century of ill-advised agricultural practices: ploughing long straight furrows, leaving fields bare of vegetation, reliance on a single cash crop, and the destruction of the native sod that was a vital buffer against wind and drought [75].

Reporting in 1936, the Great Plains Committee emphasised the role of disturbances to the balance of nature, the pursuit of self-interest and unregulated competition, and the belief that nature could be shaped at will to suit human convenience [76]. Before the Dust Bowl, resource management in the United States had been uncoordinated, and founded in immediate economic needs; as a direct consequence of the Dust Bowl, Worster believes, conservation began to move towards a more inclusive, coordinated, ecological perspective.

The effects of the Dust Bowl were felt far beyond the borders of the United States. Anderson argues that the alarm created by images of the Dust Bowl was one of several factors which combined to encourage a reassessment of agrarian policies in Britain's African colonies [77]; the others included the effects of the Depression on export markets for colonial produce, recognition that rapid increases in the human and stock populations of African reserves were exerting serious pressure on the land, and concern for the consequences of an increasing incidence of drought in much of East Africa. By 1938, soil conservation had become a major public policy issue in East Africa, a development which Anderson sees as part of a wider transition in British colonial thinking. The transition now fed into accelerated attempts to develop a multi-national response to environmental problems, especially in Europe.

2

Conservation and Reconstruction (1945–1961)

In 1909, European nature protectionists met in Paris at the International Congress for the Protection of Nature. Reviewing the record of nature protection in Europe, they argued the need for a multi-national response, and proposed the creation of an international nature protection body [1]. The idea was taken up by Paul Sarasin (the founder in 1914 of the Swiss National Park). With the support of the Swiss Federal Council, he approached the governments of Austria, Argentina, Belgium, Britain, Denmark, France, Germany, Hungary, Italy, Japan, The Netherlands, Norway, Portugal, Romania, Russia, Spain, Sweden and the United States. All except Japan and Romania agreed in principle.

In November 1913, an Act of Foundation of a Consultative Commission for the International Protection of Nature was signed in Berne by 17 European countries. The Commission was to collect, classify, and publish information on the international protection of nature, and propagandise on behalf of the cause. The first step was to have been a conference to talk about such issues as whaling, international trade in skins and feathers, and migratory bird protection, but the outbreak of war led to the cancellation of the conference and effectively laid the 1913 Commission to rest. The only progress made during the war years was the signing in 1916 of a migratory bird agreement between the United States and Britain (on behalf of Canada).

Post-war attempts to revive the Commission met with little success. It was clear that the idea of an international body was little more than the pipe-dream of a few committed disciples, among them the Dutch protectionist P G van Tienhoven. In 1925, van Tienhoven founded The Netherlands Committee for International Nature Protection as a base from which he could promote his plans for an international body to take over the mantle of the 1913 Commission. The creation of national nature protection bodies in Belgium and France in 1925–26 seemed to augur well, but there was no support from Britain.

In 1928, working through the International Union of Biological Sciences, van Tienhoven created a Dutch-subsidised international coordinating office, which was reconstituted in 1934 as the International Office for the Protection of Nature (IOPN). Like the 1913 Commission, IOPN was ahead of its time, and was doomed to fail; without an international authority it could lobby, or a quorum of mature national groups, it had nowhere to go.

The only progress made during the inter-war years belonged once again to the ornithologists. The International Committee for Bird Protection (ICBP) (later International Council for Bird Preservation) was founded at a meeting in London in June 1922. The moving light was Gilbert Pearson, president of the Audubon Society from 1910 to 1934, who hoped that the ICBP would strengthen links between American and European bird protection groups. The ICBP was less ambitious than the 1913 Commission, seeking "transnational co-ordination rather than international integration" [2]. The key to ICBP's success lay in the autonomy it gave to its national committees, which between them helped draw public attention to the depletion of species, the threats faced by migratory birds, and the dangers of the international trade in feathers [3]. The need for international action and legislation was on the agenda of other gatherings of ornithologists during the 1920s and 1930s, notably of the International Conference on the Protection of Migratory Waterfowl, held in London in 1927.

While Europe was diverted during the late 1930s by the escalating threat of war, the Americans reached two international wildlife protection agreements: the 1937 Migratory Birds Treaty (signed with Mexico and Canada), and the Convention on Nature

Protection and Wild Life Preservation in the Western Hemisphere (or Western Hemisphere Convention). Administered by the Organization of American States (OAS), the Western Hemisphere Convention was opened for signature in 1940 to all American countries. It was the most broad-ranging agreement of its time, covering wildlife, scenery, geological formations, wilderness, and regions and objects of aesthetic, historic or scientific value. Contracting governments undertook to set up new national parks, consolidate existing parks, maintain wilderness preserves, draw up legislation, encourage research exchange with one another, protect migratory birds, control trade in wildlife, and give special protection to species listed in an annex. This was all very impressive, but by the end of the war only eight states had signed, and the Convention – lacking adequate administration – was to lie almost forgotten until 1976 when the OAS launched a campaign to revive it. By then, though, it had little practical value [4].

The work of SPWFE, IOPN and ICBP, and the signing of the 1900 and 1933 African conventions and the Western Hemisphere Convention represented the seeds of an interest in international cooperation, and an acceptance (if only as yet by a minority) that national conservation and protection movements ultimately had interests that transcended national frontiers. But it was to take another world war before the climate was right for the hopes of a few to be converted into the actions of many.

Protection, conservation and the United Nations

The Second World War transformed attitudes towards internationalism. The determination of the allied powers to avoid a repeat of the problems that had led to two devastating conflicts in 30 years encouraged them to work more closely with each other than ever before. The new United Nations and its specialised agencies were to lead the way, and although the UN would not turn its attention to the environment for another 20 years, its creation was enough to inspire a new interest in international cooperation, and to revive Pinchot's idea for an international conference on the conservation of natural resources, and van

Tienhoven's idea for the creation of an international organisation for the protection of nature.

Since the cancellation of Theodore Roosevelt's proposed international conference in 1909, Gifford Pinchot had periodically tried to revive the idea. After fruitlessly approaching Wilson, Harding, Coolidge and Hoover, his friendship with Franklin D Roosevelt gave him influence once again in the White House, but it was to be June 1944 before he felt the time was right to raise the matter with Roosevelt. The president responded favourably, noting in a letter to Cordell Hull, his Secretary of State, that he was surprised "that the world [knew] so little about itself", and describing conservation as "a basis for permanent peace" [5]. In a draft conference invitation to the allied governments, Pinchot argued that peace could only be achieved by removing the incentives to war, one of which was the demand for land and natural resources.

The State Department was less than enthusiastic about the idea, arguing that two new UN agencies – the UN Economic and Social Council (ECOSOC) and the Food and Agriculture Organisation (FAO) – would make conservation part of post-war economic planning, and doubting whether much agreement could be reached on conservation without considering the development and marketing of natural resources. Conservation, it argued, was only one (albeit important) part of the total problem of collaboration on resource planning and exploitation. FAO would be looking at conservation as it related to agriculture, fisheries and forestry; the Anglo-American Petroleum Agreement then before Congress included the goal of an "orderly" development of world petroleum resources, and conservation had already been raised in international commodity discussions [6].

Roosevelt dismissed these arguments, saying that they failed to grasp the real need for looking at the bigger picture and finding out more about the world's resources. In January 1945 he told Pinchot that he would take up the idea of the conference with Stalin and Churchill at Yalta later that month [7]. There is no evidence that he kept his promise, however, and although Pinchot's plans for the conference were awaiting Roosevelt upon his return, the president appears to have had second thoughts. He drafted a memo to Pinchot in March suggesting that, given the attention FAO, ECOSOC and the World Bank planned to devote to conservation, the conference should be postponed. "We would not want to have a separate international organization to recommend plans and projects with respect to conservation except subordinate to, and related to, [ECOSOC]", he wrote [8]. But the memo was never sent, and Pinchot went ahead with a detailed draft plan for the conference.

He thought the conference should consider the creation of an international organisation to promote resource conservation, fair access to raw materials by all countries, information exchange, and the writing of an inventory of natural resources and a set of principles on their conservation. Pinchot established with the chairman of the UN Interim Commission on Food and Agriculture that there would be no conflict between the conference and FAO's plans, and claimed that everyone he had spoken to in government was supportive, with the exception of the State Department.

Roosevelt's death in April 1945 brought an end to direct White House interest in the matter. In a letter to the State Department soon after Roosevelt's death, William Clayton, the Assistant Secretary of State for Economic Affairs, pointed out that Pinchot's draft plan of March "confirms our early misgivings. The suggested agenda (and recommendations and conclusions) . . . all indicate a coverage of discussion that would overlap at almost every turn" with the functions of FAO, ECOSOC and a proposed World Trade Conference. Clayton felt the information could be better collected by experts working with each other through "normal channels", and that it was unlikely that countries could agree on working together on conservation action until they had resolved the larger problems of trade and commodity arrangements [9]. In May, Pinchot spoke to President Truman, and in December gave him another set of plans for the conference [10], but the initiative was now out of his hands, and he was left to devote his last months to his autobiography. He died in October 1946, aged 81.

Ironically, the UN had in fact begun thinking about an international conference on the conservation and use of resources, to be based on the "need for continuous development and widespread application of the techniques of resource conservation and utilization" [11]. In September 1946 the US representative at the United Nations wrote to ECOSOC proposing that a conference be held in the United States to "consider the conservation and effective utilization of natural resources" [12] in the light of the wartime drain on natural resources and their importance to reconstruction. ECOSOC was agreeable, and called a conference to allow "the exchange of ideas and experience on these matters among engineers, resource technicians, economists and other experts in related fields" [13]. The conference – the United Nations Scientific Conference on the Conservation and Utilisation of Resources (UNSCCUR) – was scheduled for the summer of 1949. In form and content, it was nearly identical to Pinchot's stillborn conference.

FAO, food security and the neo-Malthusians

Food production and the elimination of hunger was one of the main items on the UN agenda. In October 1942, Frank McDougall, adviser to the Australian representative to the League of Nations, and someone long involved in League activities on nutrition, had sent a memorandum to governments proposing a UN campaign for freedom from hunger. Roosevelt had responded by hosting a conference in May 1943 at Hot Springs, Virginia, to explore long-term global food problems and talk about food supply and demand, increased production, and better distribution. Conservation was mentioned only in passing [14].

The UN Food and Agriculture Organisation (FAO) was founded at a conference in Quebec in October 1945, with Sir John Boyd Orr as first director-general. Boyd Orr (1880–1971) was a Scottish physician who had begun specialising in nutrition after seeing the suffering of Glasgow slum-dwellers. FAO was "born out of the idea of freedom from want" [15], and Boyd Orr's first priority was to cope with a world food crisis then predicted to last well into 1947, and to deal with long-term food supply. He proposed a World Food Council that would buy, hold and sell important tradeable agricultural commodities, thereby controlling prices and supplies. The Council would work with ECOSOC and the World

Bank (created in 1944), and would build food reserves large enough to cope with famine emergencies. The proposal was rejected in late 1947, a defeat that was to be instrumental in Boyd Orr's decision to resign his post the following year. (In 1949, in recognition of his work at FAO, he was awarded the Nobel Peace Prize.)

Given its interests, FAO could not avoid making resource conservation a central item on its agenda. Article 1 of its constitution listed "the conservation of natural resources and the adoption of improved methods of agricultural production" [16] as one means of achieving its goals. It also set out to rebuild the world timber industry, and to promote the protection and extension of forest cover to check soil erosion, protect watersheds, control floods, act as windbreaks, and shelter wildlife. It ran training courses and workshops in forestry, gave technical help to less developed countries, studied timber trends, and held conferences in 1947, 1948, 1949 and 1952 to discuss timber production in Europe, Latin America, Asia and the Pacific, and the Near East, and long-term plans for forest rehabilitation.

In 1951, FAO held a conference in Ceylon on land use in Asia and the Far East. Population was at the core of the debate, and shifting cultivation was blamed for falling soil fertility, the clearance of vegetation, flooding, soil erosion, river siltation, and reduced water supplies. Two critical points were made at the conference:

1) Research into tropical soils was urgently needed; the tendency in the past had been to apply the results of research and experience in temperate zones to the tropics, with often disastrous results. Tropical soils clearly had to be understood on their own terms.
2) More attention needed to be paid to the needs of peasant farmers.

The new thinking among professionals was exemplified by comments made by Sir John Russell in his presidential address to the annual meeting of the British Association for the Advancement of Science in September 1949. Warning of the social and political roots of soil erosion, and alluding to anti-soil erosion programmes in different parts of the world, he noted the importance of ecology in promoting crop production: "The old idea that science would enable the farmer to go anywhere and produce anything has given place to the more realistic principle that every acre of land should, as far as possible, be used in the way to which it is best adapted. Extensions of the cultivated area, treatment of eroded land and improvement of wild pasture are already seen as ecological problems but the range is much wider and the possibilities great" [17].

It was now becoming clear to economists and conservationists that resource mismanagement and population growth were standing in the way of a solution to the food crisis. Boyd Orr wrote in 1953 of the "wasting asset" of fertile land, caused by the soil erosion brought on by the clearance of trees (especially on sloping land), and by overgrazing and overcultivation. "The present world food shortage", he noted, "has raised again the spectre of Malthus" [18].

Boyd Orr's warnings were only the latest in a new round of neo-Malthusianism. In 1936, the economist Stuart Chase had warned of the depletion of natural resources [19]. In 1937, at the height of the Dust Bowl, Paul Sears had written of the dangers of spreading deserts in his book *Deserts on the March* [20]. In 1939, Hugh Bennett of the US Soil Conservation Service, and R O Whyte and G V Jacks had warned of the dangers of soil erosion and the need for conservation [21]. In 1945, Frank Pearson and Floyd Harper had described the relationship between hunger, population and land in their book *The World's Hunger* [22]. Concerns about the relationship between population growth and resource depletion were now revived in two influential books published in the United States in 1948: *Our Plundered Planet* by Fairfield Osborn, and *Road to Survival* by William Vogt.

Osborn (1887–1969) had been President of the New York Zoological Society since 1940. Prompted partly by the memory of the Dust Bowl and partly by wartime shortages of food and wood, and quoting numerous examples from history of human misuse of the land, he argued that the story of forests, grasslands, wildlife and water resources in the United States in the previous century had been "the most violent and most destructive of any written in the long history of civilization". He complained that few people were aware of the destruction being inflicted on natural resources: "The fact that more than 55 per cent of the population of the USA lives in cities and towns results inevitably in detachment from the land and apathy as to how living resources are treated". He argued that international discord could be traced to diminishing productive lands and increasing population pressures, and warned that the tide of the earth's population was rising while "the reservoir of the earth's living resources is falling. There is only one solution: [humans] must recognize the necessity of co-operating with nature" [23].

In *The Limits of the Earth* (published in 1954), Osborn argued that when societies had had enough resources to meet basic human needs, economies, nations and cultures had flourished. "The so-called 'great periods' of history are intimately identified with this favorable relationship. Lacking it, apparently indestructible empires have dissolved" [24]. Like Marsh before him, Osborn traced the links between environmental destruction and social decay in Greece and Rome. He now asked how the earth could continue meeting the needs of a rapidly growing population.

William Vogt (1902–1968) was even more alarmed [25]. In the best-selling *Road to Survival*, he argued that the United States was overpopulated, self-indulgent, wasteful and doomed to extinction. Competition and the profit motive had been disastrous to the land, he argued, because land had been managed without regard for "the physical and biological laws to which it is subject. Man assumes that what has been good for industry must necessarily be good for the land. This may prove to be one of the most expensive mistakes in history" [26].

Surveying the effects of the imbalance between human demands and the carrying capacity of land in five continents, Vogt concluded that humans had "moved into an untenable position by protracted and wholesale violation of certain natural laws". Vogt argued that governments were unlikely to take remedial action without people leading the way, and that people had to understand their dependence on resources and be made aware of the dilemma [27]. (Among those influenced by Vogt's assessment was Paul Ehrlich, then a student of biology at Stanford University; see Chapter 4.)

Osborn and Vogt were widely read, but their warnings were undermined by the fact that the United States was just reaching the end of two decades of enforced austerity, and beginning a decade of unparalleled prosperity and consumption. Good weather produced repeated bumper harvests, incomes rose, and consumer spending and energy consumption grew. Half a century before, American conservation had been allied to Progressivism, which in turn was a product of an era of prosperity. But prosperity now produced a very different reaction; American consumers had a field day, and Western Europe entered a post-war economic boom. After the misery of the Great Depression and the Second World War, no-one wanted to hear talk of gloom and doom. That would have to wait until later.

UNESCO and nature protection

FAO was not the only UN agency looking into global cooperation on resource management. Also active was the UN Educational, Scientific and Cultural Organisation (UNESCO), although less as a result of the logic of its own agenda than of the coincidental interest of one man: its first director-general, Julian Huxley (1887–1975).

As part of a feasibility study into setting up national parks in Britain, a National Parks Committee was created in 1945, along with a Wild Life Conservation Special Committee (WLCSC) with Huxley as chair. Huxley began his work by sending a team of six scientists and administrators to Basle in June 1946 to meet with the managers of the Swiss National Park (founded 32 years before) and to learn something from their experience with national parks. One of the six was Max Nicholson, an ornithologist and former civil servant who not only played a key role in the creation of IUCN and the World Wildlife Fund, but was also co-founder of the Council for Nature in Britain, served for 14 years as director-general of the British Nature Conservancy, and became one of the most influential actors in the development of both the British and the global environmental movement.

Nicholson and the other members of the team were surprised and dismayed to find on their arrival that the Swiss had taken the opportunity to invite their counterparts from Belgium, France, Norway, The Netherlands and Czechoslovakia. IOPN, which had moved from Brussels to Amsterdam in 1940, had been trying to revive interest in creating a network of protectionists, and had produced a report on international wildlife protection during the war. P G van Tienhoven of IOPN and Dr Charles Bernard, president of the Swiss League for the Protection of Nature, now decided to broaden the discussions. The purpose of bringing everyone together now, they said, was to discuss the future of international nature protection [28].

Bernard assured the meeting that no decisions could be taken: "our aim is to enable each of us to state his ideas on the subject. Our conversations will be informal, as none of us have come in our official capacity. Also there are not enough nations represented here" [29]. The result was an informal agreement on the "desirability" of setting up a new international nature protection organisation ("adequately financed, and with adequate terms of reference") to facilitate cooperation between national bodies [30]. The British were doubtful, arguing that it was too early to be talking about international initiatives; Switzerland had remained neutral, they argued, while the rest of the world had been fighting a devastating war. Not only was reconstruction an overriding priority, but few countries had either the resources or the national agencies needed to make up a viable international network [31].

While his colleagues in Britain now worked on the situation at home (the Nature Conservancy was founded in 1949, and an Act of Parliament passed that cleared the way for the creation of Britain's first national parks), Julian Huxley in 1946 became the first director-general of UNESCO, and used his influence to give nature protection a new audience. UNESCO had been founded in November 1946 to promote cooperation in education, science and culture. Its Department of Natural Sciences was one of the smallest of its seven departments, attracting only 12 percent of UNESCO's budget for 1948 and employing less than 6 percent of its staff [32]. The word "conservation" appeared in UNESCO's constitution, but in relation to books and works of art, not natural resources.

But UNESCO needed technical advice, and had to go to some of the existing non-governmental bodies, such as the International

Council of Scientific Unions (ICSU). At the suggestion of the Cambridge biochemist Joseph Needham, ICSU became attached to UNESCO in Paris. UNESCO had also given itself powers to help create new non-governmental organisations if needed. Huxley submitted a proposal to the UNESCO General Conference in 1947 that the organisation include nature protection in its brief. He managed to persuade the conference that "the enjoyment of nature was part of culture, and that preservation of rare and interesting animals and plants was a scientific duty" [33]. Single-handedly, Huxley had made one of the UN's most influential agencies agree to put nature protection on its agenda, even if no specific action was yet proposed.

Meanwhile, the new international nature protection body pro-posed by the Europeans was discussed in more depth at a second meeting sponsored by the Swiss and held between 28 June and 3 July 1947 at Brunnen. Better organised than the informal Basle meeting the year before, it was attended by 70 delegates from 24 countries (all European except Argentina, Australia, Guatemala, the Dutch East Indies, New Zealand and the United States); 14 governments had given their representatives powers to speak on their behalf, leaving Britain, Belgium and Switzerland as the only Western European countries without government representation. Again, it was made clear that no final decisions would be taken; the task was to "establish the basis of an organisation that would be definitively created in the near future" [34].

Some of the delegates were obviously worried that the initiative was going to be lost to the United Nations, and argued that they should move ahead because UNESCO lacked "the special knowledge required to put such an organisation on its feet" [35]. The British delegates disagreed, saw the UNESCO link as a boon, and suggested that UNESCO be asked to manage the creation of the new organisation, using the model of the 1913 Commission. They had to be reminded that both Huxley and Needham had told the Swiss League that UNESCO had no wish to commit itself to specific action on nature protection.

A French delegate, Professor Bresson, who had been closely involved with the foundation of IOPN in 1926, warned that nothing could be achieved without official government help [36].

The Americans supported the British view that the help of a UN agency was needed if governments were going to take the new organisation seriously; besides, the Americans asked, how could the new body be truly international when so many countries (notably the USSR, China, India, Canada and South Africa) were missing from Brunnen?

Despite the doubts and disagreements, the conference adopted a draft constitution for a Provisional International Union for the Protection of Nature (IUPN). A draft constitution was sent to UNESCO with the request that they pass it on to governments for comment, the idea being to build IUPN's credibility by its public identification with UNESCO. Its goals were to promote co-operation between governments and non-governmental organisations on nature protection, promote public education, scientific research and legislation, and collect, analyse and disseminate data and information. It also agreed to begin work on a global convention for the protection of nature.

IUPN was formally created at a conference held in early October 1948 at Fontainebleau, attended by representatives from 18 governments, seven international organisations, and 107 national organisations. At the request of Max Nicholson, the British Foreign Office had drawn up a new draft constitution, which provided the basis for most of the discussion at Fontaineblue [37]. The most controversial issue was the relative power of governments and interest groups, with the former not wanting to be in a position where they could be outvoted by the latter. In its final form, IUPN was a hybrid of governmental and non-governmental bodies that, even today, is almost unique.

The constitution emphasised that the destruction of nature could be reversed if people were "awakened in time to a full realisation of their dependence upon exhaustible natural resources and [recognised] the need for their protection and restoration as well as for their wise and informed administration in order that the future peace, progress, and prosperity of mankind may be assured" [38]. This was clearly a mix of protectionist and conservationist principles; aesthetic considerations were minimised, and the ethics of conservation mentioned not at all. IUPN saw humans standing at the heart of the natural system with conservation directly serving their interests and needs.

In his memoirs [39], Huxley was to describe IUPN as "the organisation for Nature Conservation I had founded and built up while at UNESCO". The claim was exaggerated, but should not detract from his role, and certainly IUPN benefited from its public association with UNESCO. At Huxley's urging, and despite US opposition, UNESCO now agreed to convene a technical conference on nature protection at the same time as UNSCCUR. This was to be arranged in cooperation with IUPN; a contract was signed in November, with UNESCO pledging financial support. Although IUPN now existed on paper, and physically existed in new offices in Brussels, it faced two enormous problems: turning its principles into action, and establishing some credibility. Its biggest handicap was a lack of money, a problem that was to grow increasingly serious over the next decade. Much now depended on the results of UNSCCUR, where experts in resource conservation and management would be meeting for the first time under UN auspices.

The UN Scientific Conference on the Conservation and Utilisation of Resources (UNSCCUR)

UNSCCUR was held at Lake Success, New York, between 17 August and 6 September 1949. Organised by FAO, UNESCO, the World Health Organisation, and the International Labour Organisation, it was then the biggest international conservation conference ever held, attended by more than 530 delegates from 49 countries (excluding the USSR). At 54 separate meetings, the delegates discussed the increasing pressure on global resources; the interdependence of resources; the development of new resources; shortages of food, forests, animals and fuels; education in less developed countries; and the integrated development of river basins.

The conference was intended solely as a forum for the exchange of ideas and experience on resource conservation techniques [40]. Delegates focused on science, not policy, and they made no binding decisions, nor even recommendations to governments.

They knew that little of what they discussed would result in real action until the necessary funding was available, but at least they were beginning to compare notes and make plans. The central theme of the conference was the balance between resource supply and human demand; it was argued that science could help the world to find or create new resources, and to better understand those already in use.

Many of UNSCCUR's themes and conclusions were ahead of their time, so much so that it was to be another two decades before they were more widely reflected in international conservation policy. Most environmental historians unfairly ignore UNSCCUR; in Nicholson's view it was successful only so far as "it marked a breakthrough for conservation onto the agenda of intergovernmental business" [41]. But this underrates the remarkable breadth and foresight of its agenda, which would not be repeated until the 1968 Biosphere Conference and the 1972 Stockholm Conference (see Chapter 5). Without question, it was a major step in the rise of the global environmental movement.

The concurrent IUPN/UNESCO conference – the International Technical Conference on the Protection of Nature (ITC) (Lake Success, 22–29 August) – was attended by representatives from 32 countries and 11 international organisations, and focused on education and human ecology. Many of its resolutions went beyond nature protection and were remarkably conservationist, calling for a careful study of human ecology, the promotion of conservation education, ecological impact assessments of large-scale development projects, the controlled use of pesticides ("more attention should be drawn to the control of [pesticides] and biological methods from the point of view of protecting the equilibrium of nature" [42]), detailed research into threatened fauna and flora, and cooperation between UNESCO and FAO on the conservation of food resources. Perhaps the most far-sighted resolution was No. 7, which suggested that IUPN should look into promoting ecological impact assessments of development projects in less developed countries. It would be another 20 years before environmental groups or aid agencies began taking this idea seriously.

The resolutions that came out of ITC could have formed the foundation of an organisation that based its activities on the relationship between development and the environment. In the event, the promise of ITC was to stand in stark contrast to the reality of the far more limited interest in nature protection that characterised IUPN policy in its early years.

IUPN: The first 21 years

IUPN was not the product of a popular movement, but the creation of a few enthusiasts. Nicholson recalls that, until 1954, when the administration was taken over by "scientists", the Union was run by "emotionally inspired" missionaries [43]. It began life with a healthy supply of enthusiasm and dedication, but little else. It was a small and exclusive body concerned with a narrow range of interests. It had little organisational ability and financial support, few national bodies or committees with which it could work, and very little hard scientific evidence on which to base an agenda and design policies. By distancing itself from UNSCCUR and huddling at the separate ITC, it had distanced itself from the UN system, and perhaps missed an opportunity not only to push the environment up the UN agenda but to benefit from the political influence and financial resources that closer involvement with the UN might have brought.

At its second General Assembly in Brussels in 1950, a note of frustration was evident in the words of the Secretary-General Jean-Paul Harroy: "It is not unreasonable to claim that the UN should place the Union on a level with its principal specialized agencies and endow it with numerous collaborators disposing of very substantial credits" [44]. Without money it could not sponsor research or fund conservation, and it could barely afford the kind of professional staff needed to establish it as an international scientific organisation. Nicholson believes the Union was an imaginative body that foresaw problems such as the effect of toxic chemicals and the problems likely to arise from attempts to find and develop new stocks of energy [45]. Yet it fell short of the promise contained in the preamble to its constitution, which defined nature protection as "the preservation of the entire world biotic community, or man's natural environment, which includes the earth's renewable natural resources of which it is composed"

[46]; it chose instead to devote itself almost exclusively to nature protection.

During his term as secretary-general (1948–1955), Harroy "continually heard the Union criticised as being behind the times" because of its limited view [47]. Few governments had more than a passing interest in nature protection; in Britain, Nicholson recalls, it was regarded as "the amiable eccentricity of a number of people who had to be humoured" [48]. At the 1952 General Assembly in Caracas, a group including Vogt, Osborn, Harold Coolidge and Harroy tabled a resolution suggesting that IUPN ask the UN secretary-general to assign one of the specialised agencies to look at population issues. This led to a debate so bitter that Charles Bernard (the President of IUPN) feared for the stability of the Union and requested the withdrawal of the resolution [49]. (The resolution was, in the event, adopted at the 1954 General Assembly.)

Of all IUPN's handicaps, few were greater than the sheer lack of hard data. Individual scientists had long known that some species were threatened with extinction, but often the only clue lay in depleted numbers; why they were threatened, and what could be done to help, was conjecture. A tentative list of threatened species was compiled after ITC, and state members of IUPN were encouraged to draw up national lists of threatened species, but none did so until the late 1960s. The IUPN Survival Service was created as an advisory network linking specialists in different countries, and the launch of the *IUPN Bulletin* in 1952 provided a forum for news and information. But the Survival Service faced the problem of finding individuals and organisations qualified, capable or even willing to provide current and dependable information. IUPN made such little progress with mammal conservation that the American Society of Mammalogists resigned from the Union in 1954.

A private donation from the United States in 1955 finally allowed IUPN to undertake its own field research. It commissioned an American ecologist, Lee Talbot, to undertake a survey to determine the status of threatened mammals, notably those on the IUPN list. Talbot (who went on to become director-general of IUCN in 1980–83) travelled widely through Africa, south Asia, and the Near and Middle East during 1956–57, not only adding weight to IUPN's information, but providing data that could be used for education and publicity. Talbot's work, together with other surveys carried out during the late 1950s in cooperation with the Fauna Preservation Society, resulted in a much clearer picture of the situation, and the first hesitant corrective action. In 1958 the Survival Service published a list of 34 endangered species. This led to the publication in 1960 of the Red Data Book, a loose-leaf file of 135 endangered mammal species. ICBP and IUCN together drew up an additional list of threatened birds. Both lists grew during the 1960s and ultimately formed the basis of the current series of Red Data Books, the major reference source on the status of the world's threatened and endangered species.

ITC had concluded that the number of threatened species of fauna *and flora* [50] was growing, but plants were all but ignored in the early work of IUPN, as were smaller mammals, reptiles, amphibians, insects and molluscs. "Fauna" in effect meant only the larger (and more visible and popular) mammals. The Survival Service Commission Threatened Plants Committee was established only in 1974, and a plants Red Data Book was finally published in 1978. Boardman believes that this reflected not so much a lack of appreciation of the ecological importance of plants, as the difficulties involved in listing and assessing threats to the thousands of species involved [51]. Mammals and birds were more visible, the threats they faced more easily identified, and corrective action more readily suggested. Nicholson believes that much can also be explained by historical accident; ornithology had entered a dynamic growth phase in the 1920s, and so tended to eclipse the other sciences for some time. Botany was simply in a recession of interest following the war [52].

The second of IUPN's major networks, in addition to the Survival Service, was the Commission on Ecology. This was set up in 1954, under the chairmanship of the American ecologist Edward Graham, to coordinate ecological research and promote contact between ecologists. By 1956 the Commission had decided that its priority was research into the biotic conditions governing certain types of "landscapes", the study of human influences, and the best long-term use of these landscapes. There were early suggestions that plants could only be protected if habitats were protected; by 1980 the Red Data Books confirmed that two-thirds of all threatened species were threatened by the loss or contamination of their habitats [53]. Inaction by IUPN over the problem of habitat destruction had earlier caused some discontent, notably in the United States. At the International Zoological Congress in London in 1958, Coolidge noted the "greater realization of the importance of preserving habitats instead of individual species" [54]. The importance of conserving representative ecosystems now attracted greater attention.

Between 1948 and 1956, influenced by the Commission on Ecology's warnings that people should be aware of the ecological consequences of their activities, IUPN's interests gradually broadened to include conservation. The change of focus was confirmed in 1956 by the Union's decision to change its name (largely on US insistence [55]) to the International Union for *Conservation* of Nature and Natural Resources (IUCN). The new emphasis on conservation began in 1961 when IUCN launched Project MAR (a name derived from the common three letters of the word for "marsh" in different languages) to underline the threats to wetlands, and convened a conference on wetlands in the French Camargue in November 1962. The second focus was on national parks. For nearly 90 years, parks had developed in national isolation, with individual states responding to domestic needs and all but ignoring what other states were doing. Arguing that more coordination was needed, and concerned that some countries had not yet even established national parks, IUCN sponsored the First World Conference on National Parks in Seattle, Washington, in July 1962.

Of all the problems that plagued IUCN during the 1950s, lack of money was the most serious; the Union could barely support itself, let alone finance outside projects. Some funding had come initially from UNESCO, but this had proved irregular, and it became increasingly clear that an organised fund-raising system was needed. The idea for a separate fund-raising body cannot be credited entirely to any one individual; against the background of IUCN's financial problems, it must have weighed heavily on more than one mind during the 1950s. However, it was Julian Huxley and Max Nicholson who started the ball rolling.

The World Wildlife Fund

Max Nicholson was director-general of Britain's Nature Conservancy from 1952 to 1966. While the Conservancy had adequate statutory powers and a small but growing income, he noted the concern in Britain at the "lack of a strong support movement to share the burdens and provide political muscle". Since the threats to nature were global, he felt it would be "morally obligatory and also a source of added strength to use our British base to build up an effective world network" [56]. In May 1961, IUCN issued the Morges Manifesto, which outlined IUCN's belief that the ability and skill needed to tackle threats to wildlife existed, but not the "support and resources", and that money was the most essential of all needs [57].

Following a visit to East Africa in 1960, Julian Huxley wrote three articles for the London weekly *The Observer* on the growing threats to African wildlife, particularly from the spread of cultivation, increasing numbers of cattle, poaching, deforestation, overgrazing, and the spread of semi-desert conditions. Huxley broached the fund-raising idea with Max Nicholson, whose involvement with IUCN during the 1950s had convinced him that the Union was incapable of running its own affairs (especially financial affairs) efficiently, and had given him the idea of a twin body to IUCN which would be responsible for fund-raising; its job, as Nicholson bluntly observed, would be to salvage IUCN [58]. He suggested a new body consisting of a trust registered in Switzerland, an operations group responsible for establishing priorities and allocating funds, a supporters' club of wealthy members, and several national appeals. The concept was discussed at the Arusha conference (see below) in September 1961, and the World Wildlife Fund (WWF) was launched in London later that month. In December, national appeals were launched in the United States and Switzerland, to be followed by appeals in The Netherlands in 1962 and West Germany and Austria in 1963. Altogether, 20 national appeals were launched during the first ten years of operation.

According to Harold Coolidge, WWF "was founded without question for the purpose of raising funds to finance the budget of IUCN" [59], but it rapidly set off on a parallel course to IUCN.

"Instead of taking care of us first," Coolidge recalled, "[WWF] stated we were the highest priority, but they had to take care of their own administrative expenses and then they also had certain projects they wanted to fund" [60]. This caused problems, with IUCN constantly in deficit and WWF consistently performing well financially, and eventually outgrowing IUCN [61]. (By the mid-1980s, the artificiality of the divisions between the two organisations led to an attempt to mould their shared Swiss headquarters into a new World Conservation Centre.)

WWF funded projects in five categories: individual species, wilderness areas, support for existing organisations, conservation education, and "miscellaneous" conservation matters. WWF also directly lobbied governments. In 1965, for example, it persuaded the Ugandan government not to build a hydro-electric power station in the Murchison Falls National Park. In 1968, it persuaded the Tanzanian government not to build a new hotel in the Ngorongoro crater. Representations were also made to several countries to set up national parks or to launch national conservation plans.

By 1967, WWF was spending more than $370 000 per year on conservation, and had funded 183 projects, but there were imbalances in the way the money was spent. While the majority of projects (56 percent) were in Africa and Asia, they attracted only 26 percent of the funds. Inversely, Europe and North America, with 27 percent of the projects, attracted 52 percent of the funds. This could be explained by the fact that most of the European and North American projects involved buying or renting land for new protected areas, always an expensive proposition. That Africa had more projects and attracted more money than all the other less developed regions combined was explained by the fact that it had simply submitted the most applications [62].

By 1969, the proportion of money spent on North American and European projects had risen even further, to nearly two-thirds of total expenditure, with Africa, Asia and Latin America combined receiving just 15 percent. WWF admitted that these were not the percentages "the founders of WWF had in mind at the time of its inception, [but] it is clear that if WWF wishes to raise considerable funds in future it has to show tangible results in the countries in which money is available *now*" [63]. The figures were to change significantly over the next eight years: the proportion of funds spent in Europe fell from 50 percent in 1971 to 10 percent in 1977; in 1969, North America received 40 percent of the funds, and in 1975 just 0.5 percent; funds for Africa fluctuated wildly, while the proportion spent in Asia rose from 6.5 percent in 1968 to nearly 20 percent in 1975. As for WWF's primary purpose of funding IUCN, only 12.8 percent of WWF expenditure between 1962 and 1967 went directly to IUCN, and by 1969 the proportion had dropped to 9 percent [64]. This figure did not, however, include funds given to IUCN-approved projects.

Conservation and the African Special Project

As IUPN/IUCN struggled through its first decade, it realised that nature protection was not the best response to the growing post-war pressure on natural resources; the focus should instead be on promoting conservation as an integral part of development. This kind of thinking had been reflected in some of the resolutions agreed at Lake Success: Resolution No. 1 noted the importance of understanding the ecological implications of UN technical assistance to less developed countries; No. 3 resolved that "organizations concerned with nature protection and conservation, and those concerned with the utilization of resources, should collaborate to the greatest possible extent"; No. 7 noted that large development projects could have serious unforeseen effects on nature, and that IUPN should promote ecological impact surveys.

The 1900 and 1933 African conventions had both set nature aside in protected areas. While European governments had been free to impose their own concepts of wildlife protection on their colonies without much reference to the wishes or needs of local people, this would obviously no longer be possible in the post-colonial era. As Africa emerged from colonialism, European conservationists felt it was essential to encourage African governments to make conservation a part of their national development plans.

On Belgian initiative, the Third International Conference for the Protection of the Fauna and Flora of Africa was held in Bukavu in the Belgian Congo in 1953. It set out to discuss African resource issues and a possible revision of the 1933 convention to bring it "up to date and in line with modern conservation concepts" [65]. In what amounted to a tangential departure from previous thinking, delegates agreed that nature protection in Africa involved far more than simply protecting fauna and flora. The problems of the African environment, they noted, could not be solved "solely by the creation of nature reserves and the protection of certain species". Instead, governments needed to consider a new, broader-based convention designed to conserve natural vegetation, soil, water and natural resources in the interests of Africans themselves [66].

At its 1956 General Assembly, IUCN noted that "landscape-planning based on ecological research" should be the starting point for development in less developed countries (LDCs) [67]. At its 1960 General Assembly, IUCN concluded that conservation was a particularly urgent priority in Africa and that foreign aid was "prone to overlook conservation and the value of wildlife and habitat as a continuing economic, scientific, and cultural asset" [68]. IUCN's response was to launch the African Special Project (ASP) in an attempt to encourage new African leaders to publicly identify themselves with conservation, and to convince them of "the virtue of living off the income of their natural resources, not the capital" [69].

The ASP had three stages. In the first, the FAO Forestry Officer for Africa, Gerald Watterson, on secondment to IUCN as its secretary-general, toured 16 African countries and reported on conservation policies in each. Stage II was the Pan-African Symposium on the Conservation of Nature and Natural Resources in Modern African States, held in Arusha, Tanganyika, in September 1961, three months before Tanganyikan independence. Attended by representatives from 27 countries (21 in Africa), and co-sponsored by FAO and UNESCO, it was notable for being the first occasion on which Africans themselves had been represented at a forum for the discussion of their own natural resources. (The 1900 and 1933 conventions had been restricted to the representatives of European colonial powers.) The Arusha conference, by attempting to draw newly independent and near-independent states into the debate, opened discussion on the needs of local people and their attitudes to nature. Opening the conference, Sir Richard Turnbull, the Governor of Tanganyika, outlined three issues for consideration: that wildlife and nature were valuable resources of revenue and so should be rationally exploited where this was the best form of land use, that the support of public opinion was essential, and that international aid was needed if African wildlife was to be preserved [70].

Arusha brought a significant change in the direction of IUCN policy, and of attitudes towards environmental protection in less developed countries more generally. One of the participants was the journalist John Hillaby; reflecting on IUCN's "chequered history", he noted the week before the conference that the Union appeared to have been "entirely revitalised" [71]. There was an emphasis during the conference on *using* wildlife. The point was made that "only by the planned utilisation of wildlife as a renewable natural resource . . . can its conservation and development be economically justified in competition with agriculture, stock ranching and other forms of land use" [72]. It was argued that the value of wildlife as a resource was in no way incompatible with the demands of agriculture and forestry, nor with the overall economic and social development of a country.

A Sudanese forester, Sayed Kamil Shawki, argued that natural resources were "more fundamental to the economic development of underdeveloped countries than they are to more highly developed states" [73]. Wildlife management outside and adjacent to national parks depended on the needs, way of life and cooperation of local communities. Traditional African bonds with nature – which had been undermined by European economic development models of the sort that had caused the destruction of nature in Europe – needed to be revitalised. The point was raised that preservation alone was not the answer, and that rational management based on clear objectives was needed. The following were among the major recommendations of the conference: the intensive use of unsuitable land by farmers and pastoralists should be avoided; greater attention should be paid to the economics of resource development programmes; and African governments should formulate wildlife policies. IUCN offered to help them integrate wildlife management with overall land-use development plans.

Stage III of the ASP was originally to have involved the creation of a specialised unit within IUCN to provide consultancy services to African governments; in the event, it came down to a tour of African states during 1962–63 by two land-use specialists – Thane Riney and Peter Hill – to advise governments on integrating resource use and economic development. Their visits to Sahelian and West African countries in early 1962 revealed an urgent need for an international service to emphasise the importance of land-use planning based on ecological principles [74]. There was also clearly a need for a convention binding African states to the conservation of nature, as had been suggested at Bukavu. FAO had in fact set up a working party in 1960 to draft just such a convention. Two resolutions drawn up at the Seattle national parks conference referred to the importance of conservation in development programmes and the need for development agencies to incorporate environmental considerations into their planning.

The African Special Project was the first and most effective of IUCN's regional programmes. A South-East Asia Project along the same lines was launched in 1964, with Lee Talbot once again sent out to undertake field research, and a conference held in Bangkok in late 1965 to discuss resource conservation in southeast Asia. (In 1968 IUCN organised a conference at San Carlos de Bariloche, Argentina, to do the same for Latin America.)

In December 1962 the UN adopted a resolution supporting the argument that natural resources were vital to economic development, and that economic development in less developed countries could jeopardise natural resources if it took place "without due attention to their conservation and restoration" [75]. IUCN deliberately chose Nairobi as the site of its 1963 General Assembly, and focused on the problems of tropical environments. Much of the discussion concentrated on the balance between population and environment, and the effects of population pressure on land.

IUCN concluded that "if the purely political considerations which have dominated the African scene during the last few years can now be subordinated to the more precise consideration of primary human and animal needs – which are usually complementary – plans can be prepared which, if realistically implemented, will lead to a reasonable and improving standard of living for the African peoples" [76]. Speaking at the assembly, the US Secretary of State for the Interior, Stewart Udall, said the world was in need of a conservation ethic: population growth jeopardised conservation, he argued, and furthered the obsession with over-exploitation: "This is simply a 'plunder now, pay later' policy. [Population growth] makes all the more necessary a wise policy of conservation. Conservation is not a luxury; it is a necessity" [77].

Speaking at the 1967 WWF Congress in Amsterdam, Russell Train, then president of the US Conservation Foundation, warned against the tendency among conservationists to think of people and nature as mutually exclusive concepts; this approach was self-defeating. He was encouraged to note that conservationists were increasingly understanding of the fact that long-term conservation objectives "cannot be pursued successfully in isolation from other national objectives but can best be achieved as integral elements of overall national development programs" [78].

Between 1963 and 1967, FAO and IUCN worked on rival drafts of the proposed African convention, FAO having gone ahead independently in the belief that the IUCN draft paid too little attention to wildlife as a resource to be exploited, and that FAO was more experienced than IUCN in the drafting of conventions [79]. But it was the IUCN draft which was eventually accepted by the Organisation of African Unity (OAU) in 1967, and formed the basis of the African Convention for Conservation of Nature and Natural Resources. Adopted by 33 OAU member states in Algiers in September 1968, it entered into force in 1969. The philosophy of the convention was founded on the "conservation, utilisation and development of soil, water, flora, and faunal resources in accordance with scientific principles and with due regard to the best interests of the people" [80].

The changed emphasis in IUCN's thinking was confirmed at its tenth General Assembly in New Delhi in 1969 when it was agreed that, after 21 years of a "fire brigade" approach to curing individual conservation problems as they arose, the time had come for an approach based on prevention *and* cure [81]. The Assembly defined conservation as the "management (which includes survey, research, administration, preservation, utilisation . . .) of air, water, soil, minerals, and living species including man, so as to achieve the highest sustainable quality of life" [82].

Even as IUCN and WWF developed a broader and more universally useful definition of the concept of conservation, however, environmentalism was already entering a new, more activist phase. At some time in the late 1950s and early 1960s, circumstances gave rise to a new protest movement based on concerns about the state of the human environment and about human attitudes to the earth. Nature and natural resources were now no longer the sole concern; the new movement addressed everything from overpopulation and pollution to the costs of technology and economic growth. New Environmentalism went beyond the plight of nature, and challenged the basic assumptions about human attitudes to the entire human environment.

3

The Environmental Revolution (1962–1970)

In the late summer of 1962, a new book by Rachel Carson went on sale in American bookstores. Despite its seemingly impenetrable topic – synthetic pesticides and insecticides – *Silent Spring* struck a chord with its readers, sold half a million copies in hard cover, stayed on the best-seller list of the *New York Times* for 31 weeks [1], and prompted the creation of a presidential advisory panel on pesticides.

In April 1970, 300 000 Americans – perhaps more – took part in Earth Day, then the largest environmental demonstration in history. Cover stories and newspaper headlines proclaimed the arrival of the environment as a major public issue. For *Time* magazine, the environment was *the* issue of 1970 [2]; for *Life*, it was a movement that promised to dominate the new decade [3]. British Prime Minister Edward Heath decided to start the new decade by creating the Department of the Environment; Richard Nixon and the US Congress, for their part, passed the National Environmental Policy Act and created the Environmental Protection Agency. Elsewhere, work began on preparing one of the biggest United Nations conferences ever held, which would take the representatives of 113 countries to Stockholm to discuss the problems of the global environment.

The eight years between *Silent Spring* and Earth Day saw environmentalism transformed. If in 1962 there was growing unease about the state of the environment, by 1970 there was a new insistence on change in a global society seemingly bent on self-destruction. The concerns of a few scientists, administrators and interest groups blossomed into a mass movement that swept North America, Western Europe and Japan. The old conservation and protection movements were bypassed and left to catch up as best they could. New Environmentalism was more dynamic, more broad-based, and won much wider public support. Some of the older organisations flowed with the tide, but a wave of new organisations emerged, differing from their precursors in at least two major respects.

First, if nature protection had been a moral crusade centred on the non-human environment, and conservation a utilitarian movement centred on the rational management of natural resources, New Environmentalism addressed the entire human environment. For protectionists, the issue was wildlife and habitat; for conservationists, the issue was natural resources; for the New Environmentalists, human survival itself was at stake. There was a broader conception of the place of humanity in the biosphere, a more sophisticated understanding of that relationship, and a note of crisis that was greater and broader than it had been in the conservation movement [4]. Americans were not just limiting themselves to "the great outdoors", but were applying their moral and aesthetic appreciation of nature to the total environment [5]. The new movement was underpinned by a new fear for the future of life and the vulnerability of the human race; after two centuries of industrialism and urbanisation, people now began to rediscover the idea that they were part of nature [6].

Second, New Environmentalism was much more overtly activist and political. Many of the older protectionist groups had essentially charitable aims, while the conservationists based their arguments on economics; the New Environmentalists by contrast wanted a more direct political impact. Their message was that environmental catastrophe could be avoided only by fundamental and radical changes in the values and institutions of industrial societies [7]. New Environmentalism can be seen as part of a wider social transformation then taking place in Western society, generated by a reaction to the values that had led to world wars, the Berlin and Suez crises, the cold war, the threat of nuclear annihilation, institutionalised racism, and pollution. The new movement took positions that were both reactive and anti-establishment. Its leaders relied less on hard scientific evidence than on instinct. It was a social and political movement, and the issues it addressed were ultimately universal.

Like its precursors, New Environmentalism was not an organised and homogeneous phenomenon, but an accumulation of organisations and individuals with varied motives and ideals, with roughly similar goals but often different methods. Sandbach makes the distinction between the older ecological/scientific form of environmentalism, and the newer anti-establishment form [8]. The first – exemplified by people like Marsh, Theodore Roosevelt and Pinchot – saw the priority as the sustenance of a viable physical and biological environment, and attempted to influence policy by presenting a valid, scientifically argued case. The second was more instinctive, less concerned with systems analysis than with humanism.

New Environmentalism contained elements of anarchism, evangelism, social reform, political reform, and hard science. It politicised science to the point that it was often called the ecology movement. In 1970, a professional ecologist told a US Congressional committee that "ecology is no longer a scientific discipline – it's an attitude of mind" [9]. For Michael McCloskey, executive director of the Sierra Club, the components of the new movement in the United States reached beyond the old alliances to include "the consumer movement, including the corporate reformers; the movement for scientific responsibility; a revitalised public health movement; birth control and population stabilisation groups; pacifists and those who stress participatory democracy . . .; young people who emphasize direct action; and a diffuse movement in search of a new focus for politics" [10].

New Environmentalism grew out of industrial society, and was a product of forces both internal and external to its immediate objectives. The change began with the reaction to post-war affluence and social conservatism, but accelerated as more evidence emerged of the extent to which human activity threatened not only the environment, but human existence itself.

New Environmentalism and the affluent society

The growth of new environmental groups in Britain in the early 1970s has been characterised as part of a pattern tied to phases in the world economic cycle; similar growth had occurred before (in the 1890s, late 1920s and late 1950s) towards the end of periods of sustained economic expansion [11]. The environment is often seen as a "quality of life" issue, meaning that it attracts the most attention and concern when people have enough disposable income and job security to turn their attention to apparently less immediate problems that threaten their security. Environmental concern grew simultaneously in all industrialised capitalist countries as more and more people turned to count the mounting external costs of unbridled economic growth and sought to reassert non-material values [12]. As O'Riordan puts it, environmentalism does not aim to slow down economic growth but "to ensure continued progress in economic well-being and reasonable spread of the benefits of growth across the population at large . . . maybe the threat of scarcity is necessary to remind a greedy population enjoying the hedonism of affluence of the need for efficiency and frugality" [13].

The emergence of New Environmentalism was part of a broad, cumulative process of social and political change growing out of the prolonged and steady growth witnessed by all the major industrialised economies. Affluence gave more people more time to think about – and develop a resentment of – social injustice and threats to peace. The juxtaposition of affluence and insecurity ultimately gave rise to frustration with government and a belief that only direct action could bring unconventional issues to the attention of the political establishment [14]. This was to be extended in the 1960s to the view that environmental degradation posed as great a threat to material security as war; hence the many parallels between environmentalism and the anti-war movement. Both were social reform movements and both derived much of their support from young, well-educated and dissatisfied activists.

In the United States, and to a lesser extent in Britain, the 1950s were a time of apparent calm, equanimity, consensus and affluence. Big business re-established the reputation it had lost in the Depression. To the American middle class, it was a time of material comfort, increased leisure time, and the promotion of "traditional" values. Commenting on the weakened state of American conservation in 1952, Steven Raushenbush complained that the ultimate function of all the raw materials in the world was apparently to support the high American standard of living, and that conservation was in danger of becoming a lost cause [15]. By the middle of the decade, the United States, with 6 percent of the world's population, was producing and consuming over one-third of the world's goods and services. Large families were common, and the death rate was declining, so population grew rapidly [16]. Intellectuals avoided social criticism; the middle class had faith in the ability of government – in the context of a booming economy – to address pollution, urban problems and unemployment.

Britain too enjoyed some of the hedonism of affluence. Even if the boom of the Macmillan years was only brief and superficial, it did appear for a time that the British really had never had it so good. Keynesian economics appeared to have brought permanent full employment and steady economic growth, and the young had more disposable income than ever before, giving them increasing independence. (Japan and the continental European countries were too busy at this time rebuilding their political and economic systems; environmentalism came to each of them relatively late.)

Yet the contentment and conformity of the late 1950s was apparently superficial, for there was in fact a deep and latent discontent, particularly among the young. Although the United States in the 1950s appeared calm, the problems that led to the activism and conflict of the 1960s were already emerging. Post-war prosperity obscured the more significant reality of economic and social inequality; the wealthiest 5 percent of Americans were earning 21 percent of national income, while the poorest 20 percent received a constant 5 percent. For industrial workers, life became dull and mechanical, there was little room for personal pride in mass-produced goods, and the prospect of growing automation brought a feeling of insecurity.

In the affluence of the 1950s, the middle-class young of America enjoyed home comforts and extended education, and were generally conservative and conformist, raised as they were on a diet of "Leave It To Beaver" and cold war anti-communism. But they became increasingly critical of the complacency and indifference of the older generations. Increased leisure time and greater prosperity helped shift attention from the accumulation of material security, and the very comfort of middle-class existence served to draw attention to social inequality. The young were alarmed by the prospect of nuclear conflict and the accumulation of power by the military–industrial complex.

In 1958, John Kenneth Galbraith, then professor of economics at Harvard, published *The Affluent Society*. Motivated partly by the post-war market revival and the belief that all social ills could be cured by more production, and also by concern at the remarkable degree of poverty and deprivation that remained in a country which enjoyed apparent prosperity and wealth, he criticised materialistic consumption. Increased production was not the final test of social achievement, he warned [17]. Affluence brought with it higher aspirations and more demanding standards; public dissatisfaction stemmed not from the poorer performance of the system, but from the growth in people's expectations of the system [18].

Nuclear testing and the threat of global destruction

Out of the cold war came the first of the truly global environmental issues: atmospheric nuclear testing. The first explosion of an atomic bomb by the Soviet Union in 1949 signalled the beginning of an increasingly competitive race to build bigger and better nuclear arsenals. The United States launched its test programme in 1951, followed by Britain in 1952, the USSR in 1953, and France in 1960. France began testing in Algeria, but miscalculated meteorological conditions, with the result that a radioactive cloud crossed into the Iberian peninsula [19]. The French test site was subsequently moved to French Polynesia.

The earliest British tests were carried out in Australia and the Pacific; the first British device was detonated on a British frigate off the Australian coast in October 1952 [20]. Eleven more major tests were carried out there and in the interior of South Australia until 1957, and more between 1956 and 1958 around Christmas Island. The official secrecy which surrounded the tests encouraged the circulation of rumours, generating strong local opposition. (A Royal Commission reported in 1985 that the tests had been carried out without adequate attention being paid to meteorological conditions, or the dangers posed to aborigines, and that British attempts to clean up had been wholly inadequate.)

Between 1945 and 1962, a total of 423 nuclear detonations were announced by the United States (271), the USSR (124), Britain (23) and France (5) [21]. Attempts to reach agreement on nuclear disarmament began within weeks of the Hiroshima bomb, but the first tangible result did not come until the signing in 1963 of the Partial Nuclear Test Ban Treaty, which ended atmospheric testing by the US, the USSR and the UK. Ward, Dubos and Commoner claim the treaty as the first victory in the campaign to save the global environment [22]. Maddox takes a different view, suggesting that although the issue of radioactivity in the environment was an element in the equation, the powers signing the treaty were moved more by the fact that they had completed the development of long-range missile warheads, calculated that the treaty would help postpone the time when other nations could become nuclear powers, and so felt they could afford to accept the environmental argument [23].

Was the treaty a victory for environmentalism? An early indication of the environmental costs of nuclear testing came in October 1952, when abnormally radioactive hailstones fell 2800 km (1750 miles) from the first British test off Australia [24]. In April 1953, radioactive rain fell in New York state, apparently contaminated by tests in Nevada. The debate about this new phenomenon soon spread within the scientific community [25]. In *The Closing Circle*, Barry Commoner recalled that he "learned about the environment from the United States Atomic Energy Commission in 1953. Until then, like most people, I had taken the air, water, soil, and our natural surroundings more or less for granted". He now became concerned by the new and destructive force of nuclear energy [26].

The tests became a matter of wider public concern in March 1954 when an American hydrogen bomb test, codenamed BRAVO, was held on Bikini Atoll in the western Pacific. The explosive yield was twice that anticipated, and an unexpected shift in the wind caused radioactive ash to drift over the inhabited Marshall Islands, instead of falling into the ocean as planned. About 18 000 km² (7000 square miles) of ocean was contaminated by a radioactive cloud which extended 410 km (220 nautical miles), and was as wide as 75 km (46.5 miles).

Two weeks after the test, a Japanese tuna trawler – the *Fukuryu Maru No 5* (*Lucky Dragon*) – returned to port with all 23 of its crew members suffering radiation sickness. The boat had been downwind of the BRAVO test; whether it was inside or outside the "off-limits" sector set by the United States was unclear. Fish subsequently arriving at Japanese ports from other vessels in the region were found to be contaminated. All of Asia, notes Voss, was "galvanised" into action to stop further testing. Albert Schweitzer, Albert Einstein and Pope Pius XII joined the outcry. The death of one of the *Lucky Dragon* crew members six months later touched off a wave of anti-Americanism in Japan, and strained US–Japanese relations [27]. Matters were perhaps made worse – then and later – by the secrecy with which the US Atomic Energy Commission approached the question of fallout, raising public suspicions that something frightening was being withheld.

Despite the outcry, media and public opinion in the United States on the cessation of testing was divided. Opinion polls showed a steady (albeit inconsistent) majority in support of testing, with the figures fluctuating according to the level of cold war tensions (e.g. a 71 percent majority in support in 1954 changed to a 77 percent majority against in 1959, but was back to 55 percent in support in 1962, following the U-2 incident and the Cuban missile crisis [28]). Although the 1955 Geneva disarmament conference (and continuing UN discussions) failed to reach agreement, the US, USSR and UK all announced in 1958 a moratorium on nuclear testing pending further discussions. Testing became an issue during the 1956 presidential campaign when Democratic candidate Adlai Stevenson, moved by the BRAVO incident, called for a ban on hydrogen bomb tests. During his 1960 election campaign, John F Kennedy committed himself to seeking an accord on nuclear testing.

In the wake of all the tests, fears had grown about the presence in the atmosphere of strontium 90 and other toxic ingredients of fallout. In hearings before a US Senate sub-committee on disarmament in the late 1950s, scientists, church leaders, and members of Congress voiced concern about the dangers of fallout, particularly to human health [29]. But opinion was divided, and there were those – notably Edward Teller, a senior scientific advisor to the Eisenhower administration – who argued that radiation was a minor worry. In the view of Barry Commoner, the tests showed how little was known about the environment, because it was mistakenly assumed that much of the fallout would remain in the stratosphere for years, out of harm's way; in fact it returned to earth within months [30]. In 1958, Commoner and others at Washington University in St Louis formed the St Louis Committee for Nuclear Information with the object of drawing attention to the implications of fallout.

Despite such fears, fallout was at first only a minor public concern. In 1961, only 21 percent of Americans felt there was enough fallout in the atmosphere to constitute a danger [31], but they had learned much more about fallout. In 1955 only 17 percent of Americans could correctly define fallout; by 1961 the figure had risen to 57 percent [32]. As media support grew for a test ban treaty, and President Kennedy expressed himself in favour, not only did public support for the treaty grow, but so did the importance of fallout as an issue. In July 1963, 52 percent gave unqualified support to the treaty, and 12 percent quoted fallout as the major consideration. By September, the figures were respectively 81 percent and 21 percent, with fallout replacing a general need to end tests as the most oft-quoted justification for the treaty [33].

The view in US government circles was similarly divided. Kennedy was deeply concerned about fallout [34], as were his scientific advisors and the Arms Control and Disarmament Agency created in 1961. Among other government agencies and in the US Senate, however, the issue was much less important than military considerations; some senators even saw contamination as an acceptable cost for continued testing [35]. Opinions varied from that of Senator Wayne Morse, who felt that fallout control was the central purpose of the treaty, to conservative

Republican Senator Strom Thurmond, who dismissed the fallout issue as "propaganda", to Senator Bourke Hickenlooper who argued that radiation – in moderation – could actually be beneficial to health [36].

In 1961 – with negotiations on a test ban apparently stalled [37] – the USSR and the US resumed their tests, followed in 1962 by Britain. The Geneva disarmament conference was adjourned, then resumed in July 1963 after bilateral contacts between the US and the USSR. By then, it was clear that there was growing international opposition to atmospheric tests, motivated partly by significant increases in fallout levels following the 1962 test series. Furthermore, US stockpiles of nuclear weapons had by 1962 reached such a high level that there were fears about command problems leading to an accidental war [38]. In August 1963, the Partial Test Ban Treaty was finally signed in Moscow by the United States, the Soviet Union and Britain, banning tests in the air, above the atmosphere or at sea (but not underground).

Because the US and the USSR were unable to agree on methods of verifying compliance with underground tests, the final treaty – much to Kennedy's dismay – was only partial. In a radio and television address to the nation in July 1963, Kennedy listed the abolition of fallout as a key advantage of the treaty, second only to the reduction of world tension. Commoner argues that one of the benefits of the Treaty was that it established that nuclear weapons were a *scientific* failure inasmuch as regardless of the outcome of nuclear war, neither major power would survive the holocaust – the failure of nuclear "defence" lay in the ecological disasters it would set off [39]. (This was an issue that was to be revived in the 1980s with the nuclear winter debate.)

The claim that the Partial Test Ban Treaty was the first global environmental agreement is credible. The question of global security would have been enough reason in itself, but the environmental element was a key supporting factor, even though it apparently played only a minor role until just before the actual signing of the treaty. The preamble to the treaty lists the principal aim as "the speediest possible achievement of an agreement on general and complete disarmament . . . which would put an end to the armaments race", but puts the desire to "put an end to the contamination of man's environment by radioactive substances" next on the list [40]. In the text of the treaty tabled at the 17-nation Geneva disarmament conference in August 1962, the preamble made no mention at all of fallout; the change was made only in the final few months of negotiations [41]. Whatever the real motives behind the Treaty, the debate over fallout unquestionably alerted public opinion for the first time to the idea that modern technology could cause unlimited environmental contamination, and that *everyone* could be affected; the global environment was seen as a whole for the first time. The idea of universal threats to the environment was now further reinforced with the publication of *Silent Spring*.

Rachel Carson and Silent Spring

The single event most frequently credited as marking the beginning of the environmental revolution was the publication in 1962 of *Silent Spring* by Rachel Carson. The book detailed the effects of the misuse of synthetic chemical pesticides and insecticides, generated much controversy, and heightened public awareness of the implications of human activity on the environment, and of the cost in turn to human society. Shea argues that the book showed for the first time "that a meticulously researched and lucidly written account of a faulty technology could arouse the public to demand a more rational approach to problems of the environment" [42]. For Schnaiberg, the book showed how the forces undermining the ecosystem operated much less dramatically but with greater impact than any lay observer could appreciate [43]. It exposed some of the social, economic and scientific infrastructure that had *knowingly* permitted ecological degradation to occur.

Rachel Carson (1907–1964) had trained as a marine biologist and worked with the US Bureau of Fisheries and the US Fish and Wildlife Service. She had established her reputation as a writer with *The Sea Around Us* (1951) (a best-seller in the United States for 96 weeks, and translated into 33 languages) and *On the Edge of the Sea* (1955). Both were unpolemical studies in natural history, and reflected her primary interest: the sea. *Silent Spring* – for which she is now best remembered – differed from these because it grew out of her observations of the *threats* posed to nature. What she saw shook her belief that "life could never assume the power to change drastically – or even destroy – the physical world" [44].

Besides the threat of nuclear war, Carson wrote, the central problem of the age was the contamination of the environment with "substances of incredible potential for harm . . .; what we have to face is not an occasional dose of poison which has accidentally got into some article of food, but a persistent and continuous poisoning of the whole human environment" [45]. The use of chemical pesticides was, she warned, interfering with the natural defences of the environment itself. "By their very nature chemical controls are self-defeating, for they have been devised and applied without taking into account the complex biological systems against which they have been blindly hurled" [46].

The focus of Carson's concern was DDT, whose insecticidal properties had been discovered in 1939. Cheap and easy to make, it was hailed as the universal pesticide, and became the most widely used of new chemical pesticides, before its environmental effects had been intensively studied. *Silent Spring* was by no means the first public warning of the environmental impact of persistent pesticides; in 1945, *Harper's*, *The Atlantic Monthly*, and *The New Yorker* had all run articles on the dangers posed to nature by DDT. Some of Carson's colleagues at the Fish and Wildlife Service had published scientific papers on the possible long-term consequences of DDT, and Carson herself had submitted an article on DDT to *Reader's Digest*, but it had been rejected [47]. The difference with *Silent Spring* was that its message was clear and direct, and that it struck a chord with a public newly receptive to concerns about the environment. Boosted by pre-publication serialisation in *The New Yorker*, it became an immediate best-seller, and during 1963 was published in 15 countries.

Carson came under attack from the US Department of Agriculture and several chemical companies, one of which had apparently attempted to suppress publication of *Silent Spring* [48]. The book also fell foul of the scepticism with which scientists often greet works which popularise science. Carson was criticised for misusing the word "mutagen", misciting or misrepresenting the writings of medical authorities, and giving credence to cancer theories which were speculative or had already been discarded [49]. Despite the detractors, President Kennedy was sufficiently impressed to refer to Carson's work in an August 1962 press conference, and to request his scientific advisor to study the pesticide issue. A Special Panel of the President's Scientific Advisory Committee was set up, and released a report in May 1963 that was critical of the pesticide industry and the federal government. The report, noted *Science*, was "a fairly thorough-going vindication" of *Silent Spring*. By corroborating Carson's thesis, the report of the President's Committee had changed the nature of the debate; no-one could any longer deny that the problem existed [50].

Why was *Silent Spring* so influential? Its impact stemmed from a combination of its moralism, the controversy it caused, and from the effect it had of taking the pesticide issue out of academic circles and technical journals and into the public arena. While almost all previous writing on the subject had been phrased in economic terms, *Silent Spring* was an ecological study designed to shock people into action against the misuse of chemical pesticides [51]. Fox notes the relative failure of a book published only six months earlier (*Our Synthetic Environment* by Murray Bookchin, written under the pen-name of Lewis Herber) which examined a broad range of the incidental effects of modern technology, from air pollution to contaminated milk [52]; Carson, by contrast, concentrated on a single issue.

Despite her alarmism and occasional errors, her approach worked. Pesticides became a public issue, and *Silent Spring* can be credited with helping instigate changes in state and federal government policy in the United States (some states banned the aerial spraying of DDT, and procedures for registering chemical pesticides were improved) and several European countries (such as Britain, Sweden, Denmark and Hungary). The public debate over pesticides continued throughout the 1960s, and all 12 of the most toxic substances listed in *Silent Spring* were eventually banned or restricted [53].

Environmental disasters and public opinion

The disquiet spawned by the nuclear fallout debate and the warnings of *Silent Spring* was compounded in the period 1966–72 by a series of environmental disasters which made headlines and dramatically drew attention to the threats faced by the environment. There had been comparable disasters before, some of them in the very recent past. For example, 20 people had died and 43 percent of the population of Donora, Pennsylvania, had fallen ill in 1948 following a sulphurous fog. A winter smog in London between 5 and 10 December 1952 was implicated by the London County Council in the immediate deaths of 445 people; altogether, more than 4000 people died, most from long-term circulatory or respiratory disorders brought on by the smog [54]. The event was directly related to the passage in Britain of the 1956 Clean Air Act.

In October 1957, a fire had broken out at the Windscale nuclear plant in northern England when one of the reactors had overheated. The fire burned for more than 85 hours, but although radioactivity was released, contamination was limited [55]. The event caused deep concern within the nuclear power industry, but the public and the media – still unfamiliar with nuclear power and therefore with the implications of such accidents – barely responded. Besides, nuclear power was still in its infancy, and was being hailed as the fuel of the future.

The accidents which occurred from the mid-1960s had much greater impact because of the heightened public sensitivity to environmental problems. One of the first in the new round of disasters was the collapse in October 1966 of a pit-heap above the village of Aberfan in south Wales, resulting in the deaths of 144 people, 116 of them children in the local school. Stanley Johnson suggests that Aberfan was important not because it had a clear place in the genealogy of pollution but because it prepared the way for a greater understanding of the implications of pollution [56]. Even more influential than the hazards of derelict land, however, was the problem of oil pollution, which had immediate, visible and often catastrophic side-effects.

The size and number of operating oil tankers had grown dramatically since the Second World War. In 1950 there was only one tanker bigger than 50 000 dead weight tons; by the late 1960s there were 602 tankers above that weight [57]. The first major disaster was the wreck of the tanker *Torrey Canyon* in March 1967. About 875 000 barrels (117 000 tons) of crude oil were spilled after the tanker struck a reef off the southwest tip of England, between Land's End and the Isles of Scilly. Hundreds of kilometres of Cornish coastline were polluted. "It was a national event of international dimensions" notes Stanley Johnson [58]. The use of untested detergents to break down the oil only added to the biological damage, helping illustrate the threat posed to marine ecosystems by tanker traffic through coastal waters.

With the cost of Royal Air Force bombing sorties intended to set fire to the spilt oil, and the £6 million bill for cleaning up the polluted coastline, it also impressed upon British taxpayers – on their own doorstep – the financial costs of pollution. The disaster revealed a lack of government preparedness, and gaps in the organisation of scientific research and of scientific advice to the British government [59]. The government response led ultimately to the creation of the Royal Commission on Environmental Pollution in 1969, and the incident was also foremost in the minds of signatories to the 1969 Convention Relating to Intervention on the High Seas in Cases of Oil Pollution Casualties, and the Convention on Civil Liability for Oil Pollution Damage.

Two years after *Torrey Canyon*, a blowout at a Union Oil Company platform off the coast of Santa Barbara, California, brought pollution to long stretches of Californian coastline. Because the spill came from a drill hole in an unstable area of the continental shelf, it took several weeks to bring the flow fully under control. It was also impossible to be sure of the precise quantity of oil spilled; estimates varied widely [60]. The blowout occurred on 28 January 1969, and took two days to bring under control, but there was a second eruption on 12 February. Seepage continued for weeks, and beaches were still being polluted in July. Although there have since been much bigger disasters (two million barrels of oil were spilled after a 1979 tanker collision in the Caribbean, and 3.1 million barrels in the 1979–80 blowout of the Ixtoc I well in the Gulf of Mexico), the *Torrey Canyon* and Santa Barbara spills were the first such incidents, and so had far greater public impact.

"Santa Barbara was neither the worst nor the most frightening environmental disaster the nation has experienced", reflected the Council on Environmental Quality in 1979; "no one was killed . . . no one suffered permanent health damage . . . no large numbers of people were threatened . . . Yet the event dramatized what many people saw as thoughtless insensitivity and lack of concern on the part of government and business to an issue that had become deeply important to them. It brought home to a great many Americans a feeling that protection of their environment would not simply happen, but required their active support and involvement" [61]. The effect of the spill was reinforced by the indignation of the disproportionately upper- and upper-middle-class nature of Santa Barbara's population [62]. Interior Secretary Walter Hickel took immediate action by closing down wells in the Santa Barbara Channel area, but within 24 hours he had ordered a resumption of drilling and production, confirming the worst fears of local residents about government priorities [63].

Torrey Canyon and the Santa Barbara spill were the most publicised oil spills of the time, but by no means the only spills; in 1968, 714 oil spills greater than 100 barrels were reported in US waters alone, and in 1969 more than a thousand [64]. Altogether, an estimated 10 000 spills of oil and other hazardous materials annually polluted the navigable waters of the United States [65]. Pollution of other kinds now began to capture wider public attention. The condition of Lake Erie – one of the Great Lakes – was often singled out as an example of the extreme effects of pollution. The lake had long been used as a sink for organic effluent from industrial centres such as Detroit and Toledo. Yields from the Lake Erie fishery had begun to fall at the turn of the century, and became progressively smaller. Annual yields of cisco, for example, which once constituted 50 percent of the fish crop of the lake, fell from about 6200 tonnes in the early 20th century to 3.6 tonnes in 1960–64. Pollution was suspected, but it took biological surveys conducted over several years before it could be confirmed, in the early 1950s, that the lake was suffering from eutrophication (consumption of the oxygen in the lake water).

The human costs of environmental pollution were illustrated in the late 1960s and early 1970s by events at Minamata in Japan. Chemical production had begun on the shores of Minamata Bay (opposite Nagasaki) in 1939, and spent catalysts containing mercury were discharged into the bay. In 1953 it was noticed that cats and birds in the area were acting strangely, and by 1956 neurological disorders were noticed among fishing families. Concentrations of mercury were discovered in fish from the bay and in local people who had died from what became known as "Minamata disease". The chemical company involved denied any relationship between mercury and the disease, but between 1961 and 1964 paid out small compensations to disease victims. A second outbreak of the disease occurred at the city of Niigata, where another factory was discharging mercury into a river. Niigata victims won a civil action against the factory in 1971, and in 1973 the Minamata factory was found similarly culpable and ordered to pay reasonable compensation [66].

There were lesser known but equally significant incidents elsewhere in Japan. In 1972 the Mitsui Mining and Smelting Company was ordered to compensate victims of *itai itai*, a disease which had appeared as early as 1920 and afflicted people drinking water from the Jinzu River (on the north coast of central Japan), into which the factory had poured untreated cadmium, zinc and lead wastes over several decades. At Yokkaichi in central Japan, site of the country's first oil-refining and petrochemical complex, air pollution – already a problem by 1959 – led to a growing incidence of respiratory diseases. An action brought by nine victims in 1967 resulted in a 1972 decision in their favour.

Inspired by the outcome of the incidents at Minamata, Niigata, Mitsui and Yokkaichi, more than 450 anti-pollution campaigns had been launched in Japan by 1971. Most took issue with the kind of single-minded economic growth pursued by Japan since the war, which had led economic planners to give low priority to pollution control and waste treatment [67]. By the late 1960s, pollution had become a critical problem in Japan. Photochemical smog afflicted urban centres and had spread to the countryside, Tokyo Bay was seriously polluted, and mass production and consumption had created a throwaway society – about 10 percent of Tokyo's garbage was plastic.

The effect of these and other environmental disasters was to draw much more public attention in industrialised countries to the threats facing the environment. People were sensitised to the potential costs of careless economic development, and now gave their support to a series of local and national environmental campaigns which generated wide media attention. In the United States, for example, there was debate over a proposed jetport near the Everglades National Park, the proposed Alaskan pipeline, polluted beaches off New York, lead in fuel, and phosphates in detergents. In Britain, in 1969, there was debate over the siting of the third London airport, with the inhabitants of short-listed localities organising vocal – and ultimately successful – opposition.

One of the results of New Environmentalism was to replace traditional concerns with new concerns. As people began to understand more fully the sources and breadth of threats to the environment, worries about wildlife and nature had to take their place alongside a growing list of broader environmental concerns. For example, a National Wildlife Federation survey in the United States in 1969 showed that water pollution (an established issue) and road vehicle emissions (an issue of more recent interest) had joined the new concern over pesticides, to leave open spaces and wildlife well behind in the issues regarded as most important by the American public [68].

Advances in scientific knowledge

Making and implementing environmental policy has always been fundamentally handicapped by the gaps in scientific under-standing of the links between cause and effect. Scientific uncertainty was a stick that the opponents and critics of environ-mentalism used against Rachel Carson, and continue to wield today (see the acid pollution debate, Chapter 10). There was no question that greater scientific certainty was needed, and that environmentalism could not feed indefinitely on instinct or supposition alone. Scientists realised this just as much as environ-mentalists, and the rise of New Environmentalism paralleled major new initiatives in international scientific research.

One impetus came in 1957–58 with International Geophysical Year (IGY), which showed how research could benefit from international cooperation. Inspired by IGY, senior members of the International Council of Scientific Unions (ICSU) and of the International Union of Biological Sciences (IUBS) talked of applying the IGY model to biological research. Professor C H Waddington, president of IUBS, noted that ecology was at that time (the early 1960s) "emerging from a descriptive to an experimental stage . . . Prominent ecologists were communicating with each other and this made the time ripe for a co-ordinated international effort" [69]. There was concern that the study of environmental biology was lagging behind other fields, such as cell biology and molecular biology.

After discussions between ICSU, IUBS, IUCN and biologists in a number of countries, the International Biological Programme (IBP) was launched in July 1964. Its theme was "the biological basis of productivity and human welfare"; its aims were to promote international study of organic production, the potential and uses of new and existing natural resources, and human adaptability to changing conditions. It was a direct response to the threats to natural ecosystems that were now the subject of so much public attention. A year was regarded as too short a time in which to collect a significant body of biological information, so three phases were planned, taking the IBP through to 1974.

Enthusiasm for IBP was guarded. On the one hand, few questioned the need for better understanding of environmental biology, and biologists saw that the sum of national efforts was nowhere near enough to meet the world's future needs for national parks, nature reserves and field laboratories [70]. Britain was probably the most enthusiastic proponent of IBP, supported by most of the countries of East and West Europe. On the other hand, there were biologists who felt that national scientific programmes were adequate, and feared the diversion of funds from those programmes to IBP. The United States, where the structure and priorities of biological research were very different, initially opposed the IBP (although it later provided active support).

Lack of funding proved a major handicap. Total income for IBP over 1964–74 was $1.88 million, of which 43 percent came from national dues and special contributions, 15 percent each from

ICSU grants and loans and UNESCO contracts, and 12 percent from publications [71]. Even so, IBP was generally regarded as a success. The Programme's *modus operandi* was to define a problem, bring together a small team of competent specialists, set up an action plan, put the plan into operation, and finally assess the results. This put specialists in different countries in touch with one another, encouraged ecological research in many countries, produced reliable research methods, had a catalytic effect on new environmental research programmes [72], and produced 40 volumes of findings. IBP is credited with helping publicise threats to the global biosphere, and with having an important input to the Stockholm conference [73] (see Chapter 5). UNESCO was particularly interested in the programme, and IBP for a time overlapped with, and transferred interests to, UNESCO's subsequent Man and the Biosphere programme (see Chapter 10). If IBP had a defect, it was that it was too broad and ambitious [74].

The influence of other social movements

Social movements often borrow methods, principles and inspiration from one another, especially if they come out of the same basic root concerns. During the late 1950s and 1960s, several social and political issues galvanised people – especially the young – into mass action, creating a new climate of public activism from which environmentalism benefited.

In Britain, the first significant movement to alert a generation to social problems and new methods of protest was the Campaign for Nuclear Disarmament (CND). The Suez crisis and the Hungarian uprising of 1956 had created a new mood of idealistic purpose on the British Left, giving rise to a mistrust of old ideologies and institutions [75]. The nuclear arms race was seen as symptomatic of the problems of the Old Order. Demonstrations during the early 1950s revealed a groundswell of public concern over nuclear weapons, and in 1957 the Emergency Committee for Direct Action Against Nuclear War (DAC) was set up to protest against a British nuclear test at Christmas Island.

CND was created in 1958, and between 1958 and 1965 was involved in several mass demonstrations, notably the marches between London and the nuclear weapons establishment at Aldermaston. Although the majority of disarmament campaigners became involved for moral, political or religious reasons, there were significant links between the disarmament movement and the later environmental movement, if only because both groups sought rational control over the technology created by advanced industrial society [76]. By the early 1970s, it was difficult to disassociate the campaigns against nuclear weapons and nuclear energy.

In the United States, the first issues to catch public attention were poverty and racism. These produced the civil rights movement of the late 1950s and early 1960s, which Schnaiberg suggests was the first social movement to capture the energies of substantial numbers of college students (shifting their concerns from private to public goals), and to extend and develop new techniques of participation in resistance to existing social forces [77].

There were no formal links between the civil rights and environmental movements, which had very different values and very different constituencies. Many studies (in the late 1960s and since) have argued that environmentalism was elitist, and that it drew most of its support from the white middle class [78]. (A 1973 survey found that 98 percent of the members of US environmental groups were white, 61 percent were college graduates, 35 percent were professionals, and 53 percent had family incomes greater than $15 000 [79].) For black Americans, the most immediate and urgent issues were social and economic justice. While the poor were fighting for jobs, education and political and social equality, environmental groups were lobbying for such apparently non-essential demands as the protection of wilderness. For many black activists, the environmental movement even threatened to divert dollars and the conscience of the middle class.

During the 1960s, the more radical segments of the civil rights movement began to exclude white liberals. The radical journalist James Ridgeway went so far as to suggest that the environmental movement was "cut off from the revolutionary surge sweeping through American society. It had no bearing on the war, political repression, blacks, the poor, or any other factor which created the currents of stress in the society" [80]. Yet the civil rights movement showed what could be achieved through mass protest, and the techniques used by Martin Luther King and other civil rights leaders to bring about peaceful confrontation with authority undoubtedly educated a new generation in the methods of effective protest.

The second protest movement of note – with which New Environmentalism had much closer links – was the anti-Vietnam War movement. In 1965, the first acknowledged American combat troops were landed in South Vietnam, and "non-retaliatory" air strikes began at the same time; the first student protests against the war followed in short order. The protests escalated in the late 1960s as Americans learned more about the real nature of the war and about the gap between official predictions and actual events. The main sources of support for the anti-war movement were white professionals, students and clergy [81]. Students were exempt from the draft, so college campuses became the head-quarters of the movement, whose moral underpinnings over-lapped for a while with wider and deeper student discontent with society. Demonstrations became almost an everyday event; in the 1967–68 academic year alone, there were 221 demonstrations on 101 campuses [82].

The anti-war movement revealed a campus population which was – according to the Cox Commission report on disturbances at Columbia – "the best informed, the most intelligent, and the most idealistic this country has ever known . . . It is also the most sensitive to public issues and the most sophisticated in political tactics" [83]. At the root of the phenomenon was a society apparently unable to live up to the ideals taught in schools and churches. "For many student activists", noted the 1968 National Commission on the Causes and Prevention of Violence, "the university represented a qualitatively different kind of social institution, one in which radical social criticism could be generated and constructive social change promoted" [84].

Student disaffection came to many industrialised nations in the late 1960s, reaching a watershed in 1968 (especially in France, West Germany and Spain). Lipset notes that a sharp increase in student activism could be expected in any society where "accepted political and social values are being questioned, in times particularly where events are testing the viability of a regime and where policy failures seem to question the legitimacy of social and economic arrangements and institutions" [85]. Searle notes three features of the student unrest of the time: the search for sacred goals and values, the creation of an adversarial relationship with authority, and the rejection of authority [86].

Heightened student concern and sensitivity created a constituency receptive to taking on issues where the prevailing social and economic system was seen to be working against an ideal. In the same way as racial discrimination and the Vietnam War seemed to be symptomatic of the sickness of the system, so environmental degradation seemed an equally acceptable focus for protest. Nash suggests that some among the American college population were attributing social problems – from imperialism to racism – to "unecological attitudes" [87]. Student disaffection also grew out of the obsession with success and security of the older generations; materialism, technology, power, profit and growth were seen as symbols of all that was worst about Western society, and as posing a threat to the environment.

Environmentalism also provided expression for the counter-culture, which was anti-industrial, rejected the work ethic, condemned consumerism and material values, and questioned the rationality of a society which "harnessed science to what were seen as the inhuman atrocities of the Vietnam war, and the ecological damage wrought by insecticides and industrial waste" [88]. The hippie movement of the late 1960s embodied the moral and anti-establishment school of environmentalism in the United States, when a return to wilderness and nature was seen as the only way of retaining earthly values in a materialist world. Nash believes it no accident that Charles Reich chose *The Greening of America* as the title for his influential 1970 book [89], because "the green world, the wild world, held essential truths" [90].

Environmentalism in the United States finally matured when it intersected with the other social movements of the day. Reaching its crest at the end of a decade of social activism, the environmental revolution borrowed from all the major movements [91], the primary link being chronological, in that activists turned to the environment at the end of the 1960s as the civil rights and anti-war movements lost momentum. In both Britain and the United States, many of the young supporters of the environmental movement had been introduced to activism through the experiences of other protest campaigns.

No longer a quiet crisis

Social revolutions have complex roots. The roots of New Environmentalism were many and varied, and it is difficult to dissociate one from the other. It was neither a single issue nor a sudden crisis that led to the formation of the movement, argues Bowman [92]. It is more than coincidental that the rise of environmental awareness coincided with the maturation of the first generation to grow up in post-war affluence; the outcry over environmental quality was more a function of changes in attitude than changes in the actual state of the environment [93], but the former would not have happened without the latter. New Environmentalism was mainly concerned with the quality of life, and how it was compromised by the pollutive by-products of economic growth. Affluence, youthful discontent, headline disasters and broader social and economic trends all played their part in bringing the change.

Other explanations have been offered. Means suggests that the goals of the traditional conservation movements may have been too narrow and – ironically enough – were being questioned because they had been surprisingly successful [94]. Schnaiberg points to the growing interest in wilderness recreation and camping, in part a reflection of metropolitan decay and the expansion of urban areas [95]. Looking at the United States, Downs suggests that so many Americans were able to participate in activities that were formerly only available to a small, wealthy minority (such as car ownership and access to national parks, suburban housing and resort areas), that the environment of the elite was deteriorating [96].

Enzensberger suggests that the environmental impact of new technological developments had become more universal, which meant that – for the middle and upper middle classes – geographical mobility was no longer an answer to avoiding problems such as nuclear fallout and oil pollution [97]. Hardin suggests that environmental concern may have been a displacement from other, more intractable problems [98]. Golub and Townsend even argue that the myth of an ecological crisis was developed by business interests as a means of encouraging greater international cooperation, thus enabling planned industrial growth by an increasing number of multi-national corporations [99].

Whatever the cause, by 1970 there had been a revolution in environmental attitudes in most industrialised countries. In the United States, for example, annual membership in the five major US conservation groups was growing at 16–18 percent in 1969–70; membership of the Sierra Club alone had tripled since 1966 [100]. Environmental spokesmen such as Paul Ehrlich and Barry Commoner (see Chapter 4) were travelling the country, occasionally speaking before audiences of up to 10 000. In a cover story in February 1970, *Time* noted that the environment "may well be the gut issue that can unify a polarized nation" [101].

New Environmentalism peaked on 22 April 1970 when Earth Day – the largest environmental demonstration in history – was held in the United States. The idea came from Senator Gaylord Nelson of Wisconsin; with federal funding, an organising committee chaired by Denis Hayes orchestrated a nationwide show of concern for the environment. Rallies and teach-ins were held at an estimated 1500 colleges and 10 000 schools; both houses of Congress recessed; Nelson himself spoke at nine college campuses, from Harvard to Berkeley; cars were banned from New York's Fifth Avenue for two hours, allowing 100 000 pedestrians to fill the thoroughfare; and in Washington DC, 10 000 people surrounded the Washington Monument for 12 hours of revelry. Shortly before Earth Day, *New Republic* dismissed "the ecology craze" as an irrelevant sideshow; six months later, it devoted an entire issue to the environment and admitted that Earth Day had been "not just a channel for frustrated antiwar energies, as we thought. It signalled an awakening to the dangers in a dictatorship of technology" [102].

In 1963 Stewart Udall, Secretary of the Interior in the Kennedy and Johnson administrations, had written *The Quiet Crisis*, a personal review of the history of American environmental philosophy, from the land wisdom of native Americans to the urban planning of Frederick Law Olmsted. The "quiet crisis" lay – he argued – in the fact that "America today stands poised on a pinnacle of wealth and power, yet we live in a land of vanishing beauty, of increasing ugliness, of shrinking open space, and of an overall environment that is diminished daily by pollution and noise and blight" [103]. Udall argued that the post-war obsession with "hot and cold wars" had diverted attention from the environment, and that progress in science had encouraged a false sense of well-being that had resulted in urgent conservation and management needs being ignored.

In July 1965, five days before his death, Adlai Stevenson (then US ambassador to the United Nations) gave a speech before the UN Economic and Social Council in Geneva on the problems of urbanisation throughout the world. In the speech (originally drafted by Barbara Ward [104]), he used the metaphor of the earth as a spaceship on which humanity travelled dependent on its vulnerable supplies of air and soil. The theme was developed further by Kenneth Boulding, an economist at the University of Michigan, in his 1966 essay "The Economics of Coming Spaceship Earth", in which he compared the open "cowboy economy" (reckless, exploitative, romantic, where consumption and production were good things) with a future "spaceman" economy concerned mainly with stock maintenance, where the essential measure of the success of an economy was not production and consumption, "but the nature, quality, and complexity of the total capital stock" [105]. The notion of Spaceship Earth was graphically underlined by the publication in 1966 of the first photographs of earth taken by Lunar Orbiter satellites, which showed the planet as a lone, finite and seemingly vulnerable oasis in space. For millions on earth, suggests Arthur C Clarke, these photographs "must have been the moment when the Earth really became a planet" [106].

By 1970, the environmental crisis was no longer a quiet crisis. A new mass movement had emerged, and an urgent new policy issue was beginning to find its way onto the political agenda. Scientific evidence confirmed the fears of activists and amateur ecologists: the human race was rapidly using up its stock of natural resources, and fouling its nest in the process. Concern mounted, and a controversial debate on the limits to growth was born, centred on the Malthusian argument that crisis and collapse were inevitable unless population growth and resource exploitation were brought under control. The prophets of doom had arrived.

4

The Prophets of Doom
(1968–1972)

Mass movements often rally around charismatic leaders. While independence and civil rights movements had such leaders, the same was less true of the environmental movement, which instead saw the emergence – in the United States at least – of theorists and philosophers who seemed to act for a while as voices for the movement. Most were academics, such as Paul Ehrlich of Stanford, Barry Commoner of Washington (St Louis), LaMont Cole of Cornell, Eugene Odum of Georgia, Kenneth Watt of the University of California at Davis, and Garrett Hardin of the University of California at Santa Barbara.

These theorists offered neither a unifying creed for the movement nor a particular sense of direction, and the more pessimistic among them were quickly described as "the prophets of doom" or "the New Jeremiahs". What they *did* provide was an intellectual focus, on three issues in particular: pollution, population growth and technology. They helped promote a more wide-ranging debate about the causes and nature of the environmental crisis. However, the contention that none of these problems *alone* fully explained that crisis eventually led to the view that it stemmed from exponential economic growth, and that there were clear limits to that growth.

The Ehrlich–Commoner debate

Early controversy was aroused by the differences of opinion between two biologists, Paul Ehrlich and Barry Commoner. Ehrlich took a well-worn theme – population growth – and made it his own; Commoner for his part focused on the quality of economic growth.

The population question had a long history, dating back to the British physician William Petty (1623–1687), who had written in 1650 of the multiplication of human population [1], speculating that it would take 2000 years for the earth's carrying capacity to be reached. Not surprisingly, his views drew little notice. Nearly 150 years later, much greater public impact was achieved by the British classical economist Thomas Malthus (1766–1834). In his *Essay on Population*, written in 1798–1803, Malthus argued that the natural rate of population growth was exponential, while that of food production was arithmetical. Unless population growth was checked, the population would outstrip the available food supply and there would be widespread famine [2]. The fact that he was a clergyman earned him the epithet "that dismal parson".

Vogt, Osborn, the Wilderness Society, the Sierra Club and others raised the question of overpopulation again after the Second World War. In 1966, David Brower, then executive director of the Sierra Club, argued that there could be no conservation policy without a population policy; population was "the root of our troubles" [3]. In 1967, Brower heard Ehrlich, then professor of biology at Stanford University, talk at the Commonwealth Club in San Francisco and commissioned him to write a short book on population for the Sierra Club. The book, *The Population Bomb*, was published in 1968, and became one of the best-selling environmental books of all time, with three million copies in paperback by the mid-1970s. (Curiously, a remarkably similar book published three years before – *The Silent Explosion* by Philip Appleman [4], a professor of English at Indiana University – sold well, but achieved nothing like the impact. Ehrlich made no reference to Appleman's work.)

Ehrlich was an unashamed neo-Malthusian. Criticisms that he was an alarmist did not upset him: "I *am* an alarmist", he said in

1970, "because I'm very goddamned alarmed. I believe we're facing the *brink* because of population pressures" [5]. It was the battle to provide for an ever-increasing human population that caused most of the problems, he argued, and the most effective environmental safeguard was birth control; "no changes in behavior or technology can save us unless we can achieve control over the size of the human population" [6]. Ehrlich warned that (1) hundreds of millions of people faced starvation in the 1970s and 1980s, (2) the limits of human capability to produce food by conventional means had nearly been reached, (3) attempts to increase food production would cause environmental deterioration and reduce the earth's capacity to produce food, (4) population growth could lead to plague and nuclear war, and (5) the only solution lay in a change in human attitudes.

Barry Commoner, then professor of biology at Washington University, St Louis, offered a different view. Commoner's environmental activism had begun in 1953 with his concern for the effects of nuclear fallout. The publicity generated by his Committee for Nuclear Information is often credited as a telling factor in public support for the 1963 Partial Test Ban Treaty. The fallout issue for him was symptomatic of the destructive impact of technology on the environment. He took his message to college campuses in the late 1960s, and by early 1970 had earned a *Time* cover story hailing him as the Paul Revere of ecology. He outlined his fears in *The Closing Circle*, published in 1971.

While population growth and affluence had intensified since the Second World War, he noted, the increases were too small to account for the dramatic growth of pollution. An additional factor must therefore be "flawed technology", particularly the massive growth in the use of synthetics, disposable products, pesticides and detergents. The issue was not so much the growth in economic activity, but *how* that growth had been achieved. It was not so much that *more* goods were being consumed, but that their production and disposal were more costly in environmental terms. The increased output of pollutants resulting from the introduction of new technologies since 1946 had, he argued, come to account for 95 percent of the total output of pollutants [7]. He emphasised that some of the most dangerous environmental perils were those that could not be seen, such as polluted air, food and water.

Their positions stated, Ehrlich and Commoner entered into an often vitriolic debate of questionable merit. Popular opinion among physical and social scientists at the time was that both parties were carrying their views to the extreme, Ehrlich being an "alarmist" and Commoner strangely obstinate in exonerating population growth [8]. Ehrlich spoke from a scientific perspective, whereas Commoner considered politics to be very much part of the equation [9]. Commoner opposed coercion in limiting population growth, arguing that action to eliminate poverty would result in a demographic transition – as societies became wealthier and more industrialised, population growth would slow. He suggested that most of the serious pollution problems of the United States either dated from the post-war years or had worsened since the war [10] (although *The Closing Circle* relates many examples of pollution that pre-dated the war, often by decades). Commoner correctly pointed out that pollution and the exhaustion of mineral resources would continue without population growth. Indeed, in *Science and Survival*, he had fleetingly described population growth as a major source of pollution; following the opening of the debate with Ehrlich, he tended to dismiss the population issue.

Ehrlich felt *The Closing Circle* to be "inexplicably inconsistent and dangerously misleading". He saw three principal defects in the book: it assumed that environmental deterioration consisted only of pollution (leading Commoner to discuss the environmental crisis "as if it had begun in the 1940s"); the argument that the cause of pollution lay in faulty technology was based on faulty research and interpretation of data; and Commoner's misconceptions about certain aspects of demography led him to draw erroneous conclusions about human "self-regulation" and viable strategies for population limitations [11].

Ehrlich occasionally appeared more open-minded than Commoner, admitting, for example, that his views changed with time and with his understanding of the issues. Commoner recalled how, in early conversations with Ehrlich and his followers, the latter "conceded [in contrast with the position expressed in *The Population Bomb*] . . . that population growth is not *alone* responsible for environmental impact, and that technological factors are also significant. I was gratified by this indication that they were prepared to modify their position on the basis of the new data" [12]. In 1973 [13] and again in 1974 [14], Ehrlich appeared to soften his disagreement with Commoner by suggesting that the components of the environmental crisis caused by population growth, affluence or technological errors were difficult to differentiate; it was preposterous, he argued, "to try to sort out which of three multiplicative factors is responsible for the whole thing, when quite obviously we have to attack all three" [15]. In 1970, he argued that he had written *The Population Bomb* because he thought too many people were emphasising only pollution; "I'm not in any way trying to minimize the problem of pollution", he argued. "At the moment, it is at least as serious as, or possibly more serious in the United States than population growth" [16].

Yet in 1973, in a surprisingly off-hand dismissal of the pollution issue, he observed that "from the point of view of an ecologist . . . [air pollution is] one of the relatively trivial problems . . . it's amenable to rather rapid technological cure and is just a symptom of some of the things we're doing, rather than something eco-logically serious" [17]. Ehrlich argued that the one difference between himself and Malthus was that Malthus overlooked the possibility of technological advances, while Ehrlich had not [18]. Yet Ehrlich's contention that the earth was producing as much food as it could has since been shown to be wrong, and by the early 1980s it was increasingly widely accepted that the root cause of hunger was not a shortage of food so much as an imbalance between supply and demand. Ehrlich's argument made no allowances for the inefficiency of food production techniques, falling production rates, or poor land management, and his suggested solutions made no mention of the need to use existing resources more efficiently, or to reduce waste. He never alluded, for instance, to the potential for land reform and agricultural intensification.

Ehrlich also criticised Commoner for being preoccupied with pollution to the virtual exclusion of other forms of environmental deterioration, yet was himself preoccupied with the single issue of population, and looked at *that* from a limited perspective. As a cause of resource depletion, population growth has since been joined – if not eclipsed – by the inefficient and unsustainable use of resources. In other words, it is less a question of sheer numbers of people than of how resources such as food are used and distributed. Both Commoner and Ehrlich were guided more by what they saw happening in Western industrialised countries, and less by what was happening – or has since been shown to have been happening – in centrally planned systems and poorer countries.

If anything, subsequent events and scientific and demographic evidence have proved both men largely correct in their central theses (as far as they went), but suffering in similar proportion from obsessions, inaccuracies and misconceptions. Ehrlich himself pinpointed one of the dangers to which he had fallen prey, when he noted that scientists were often criticised either for being too narrow or for stepping out of their field of speciality; but he often felt moved to go beyond the boundaries of his formal training to seek solutions to human problems, and saw "no other course than for scientists in all fields to do the same – even at the risk of being wrong" [19]. Similarly, in 1973 he observed that "most of the criticism of environmentalists implies that they should never make errors. But there are going to be continuing errors in the statements of environmentalists because they are dealing with systems that we don't understand completely and where there is a great deal of uncertainty" [20].

The tragedy of the commons

A similarly controversial doomsday thesis was the essay on the "tragedy of the commons" [21] written by Garrett Hardin, a biologist on the faculty of the University of California at Santa Barbara. It was first presented as a presidential address to the Pacific Division of the American Association for the Advancement of Science in December 1967. As Hardin himself pointed out, the commons theme was not new, and was well known in social science circles [22]. What were new – and what generated the controversy – were his conclusions. He argued that there were no "scientific" solutions to problems such as overpopulation. The "tragedy" lay in the inevitability of the destruction of communally owned resources; Hardin suggested that the inevitability of global destruction predetermined the choices that mankind should make to ensure its survival.

He used the parable of a commons on which a number of cattle herders grazed their cattle. A particular number of cattle at a particular time ate grass at the same rate as it grew – supply and demand were in perfect balance. Then one herder concluded that he could add one more cow and reap the benefits while the costs were spread among the other herders, whose cows had to settle for less. He also concluded that if he did not add an extra cow, the other herders might and they would then reap the benefits at his expense. The only rational solution was to add a cow. But every other herder reached the same conclusion and decided that they must introduce additional cows.

Thus "each man is locked into a system that compels him to increase his herd without limit – in a world that is limited. Ruin is the destination towards which all men rush, each pursuing his own best interest in a society that believes in the freedom of the commons. Freedom in a commons brings ruin to all" [23]. Hardin suggested that pollution was the reverse of the tragedy of the commons in that humans were not taking from but were giving to the commons in the form of noxious waste. "The rational man finds that his share of the cost of the wastes he discharges into the commons is less than the cost of purifying his wastes before releasing them. Since this is true for everyone, we are locked into a system of 'fouling our own nest", so long as we behave only as independent, rational, free-enterprisers".

How, Hardin asked, could we "legislate temperance" in, for example, human procreation? Prohibition was easy to legislate, but temperance not so, and he took issue with the view of the Universal Declaration of Human Rights that "any choice and decision with regard to the size of the family must irrevocably rest with the family itself, and cannot be made by anyone else". Temperance could not be achieved by appeal to conscience, but only through "mutual coercion, mutually agreed upon by the majority of the people affected", especially where applied to controlling population growth. In other words, people needed to be coerced into a sense of communal responsibility because they would never adopt it voluntarily.

Global models and the limits to growth

Overpopulation was not the only old theory revived by New Environmentalism. An idea with an even more impressive intellectual pedigree – the limits to exponential growth – was dusted off and revisited with even greater controversy. Thomas Malthus, David Ricardo, John Stuart Mill, W Stanley Jevons, Karl Marx and Friedrich Engels had all at one time or another looked at related issues [24]. As recently as 1953, the lawyer Samuel Ordway had outlined his own (largely ignored) "Theory of the Limit to Growth" which anticipated many of the sophisticated and expensive computer simulations of the 1970s [25].

The main product of the 1970s revival was *The Limits to Growth*, published in 1972. The roots of the report went back to the late 1940s, when Jay Forrester, a professor of management at the Massachusetts Institute of Technology (MIT), pioneered the application of the digital computer, tactical military decision-making, and information-feedback systems to studies of the interacting forces of social systems [26]. During the late 1950s, he refined his theories of industrial dynamics as a management technique. The system dynamics method argues that models are needed to describe the organisation of systems, their internal relations, and assumptions about external contacts across the system boundaries. Components of relationships can then be changed in order to simulate alternative outcomes. The method holds that mental models are inferior because only computer models enable relationships and their consequences to be made explicit [27].

During the mid-1960s, Dr Aurelio Peccei, an Italian management consultant and president of Olivetti, had begun to reflect on the problems of the world. He saw them as embodied in a set of interconnected relationships and felt they could only be understood through an overview that showed the links between seemingly unrelated occurrences and conditions. He outlined his thoughts in *The Chasm Ahead* [28]. In 1968, he convened a meeting in Rome of a group of 30 economists, scientists, educationalists and industrialists. Out of this meeting emerged the Club of Rome, a loose association of scientists, technocrats and politicians. By 1970 the Club had 75 members from 25 countries. Its goal was to foster understanding of the interdependent economic, political, natural and social components of "the global system", and to encourage new attitudes, policies and institutions capable of redressing the problems, of which environmental degradation was just one. Others included urban sprawl, loss of faith in institutions, rejection of traditional values, and economic disruption, all of which the Club saw as so complex as to be beyond the competence of conventional institutions and policies.

Forrester's system dynamics method had been widely criticised [29], but the Club saw in it considerable potential for its own interests. In 1970 it launched a Project on the Predicament of Mankind (PPM), and invited Forrester to Switzerland to outline his method. The "predicament" was that human society, despite its knowledge and skills, did not understand the "origins, significance, and inter-relationships of its many components and thus is unable to devise effective responses" [30]. The failure had occurred because society continued to examine single issues without understanding that the whole was more than the sum of its parts.

Meanwhile, during their study of the preparations being made for the 1972 UN Conference on the Human Environment to be held in Stockholm (see Chapter 5), a group at MIT concluded that a Study of Critical Environmental Problems (SCEP) would help the conference planners. During July 1970, 70 scientists and professionals and 45 observers met in Williamstown, Massachusetts, to study and discuss the effect on global climatic and terrestrial conditions of specific atmospheric, terrestrial and marine pollutants, and to examine research and monitoring procedures.

"The existence of a global problem", SCEP emphasised, "does not imply the necessity for a global solution" [31]. Corrective action, it concluded, was often best taken at national, regional or local levels, but the potential for international cooperation in research and monitoring was high. SCEP's general recommendation was for new methods of standardised global data gathering. The report made two particularly important points: that the available data, especially at the international level, were fragmentary, contradictory, sometimes unreliable, and often unavailable (because of inconsistent reporting and lack of standardisation); and that environmental problems had to be considered from the different perspectives of rich and poor countries. "There is little reason to believe that the developing countries can be diverted from their preoccupation with the first-order effects of technology to a concern about the side effects upon the environment. Currently, and in the foreseeable future, the advanced industrial societies will have to carry the load of remedial action against pollution" [32]. The MIT report called for a more complete study of such issues as marine oil pollution, atmospheric carbon dioxide build-up, and the potential effects of supersonic airliners on the atmosphere; the formulation of new priorities; and the abandonment of the assumption that the environment must bear the costs of industrial and technological development.

The Club of Rome project was launched at a meeting in Cambridge, Massachusetts, in late July 1970. Forrester had outlined a global model – called World I – identifying specific components of the problem and suggesting techniques for analysing the most important of these components. He argued that the human mind was incapable of understanding, predicting or controlling the activities of very complex problems, and that human intuition often misled people into pursuing remedies which had either no effect, or the opposite effect to that desired [33]; computer simulation was thus vital to helping society cope with macropolicy questions.

Forrester developed his model into World 2, outlined in his book *World Dynamics*. Looking only at the broad aspects of the world system, he neither addressed the difficulties of implementing changes in human attitudes, nor allowed for changes in human aspirations and values brought on from recognition of the predicament facing mankind [34]. He set up a team under the direction of 28-year-old Dennis Meadows (then assistant professor of management at MIT) to make a yet more detailed and polished version – World 3. Five basic factors were identified as determining and ultimately limiting growth: population, agricultural production, natural resources, industrial production and pollution.

Using the Forrester model, the team reached three main conclusions:

1) If existing trends in world population, pollution, industrialisation, food production and resource depletion continued

unchanged, the limits to growth on the planet would be reached within one hundred years. The most likely result would be a sudden and uncontrollable decline in both population and industrial capacity.

2) It was possible to alter these growth trends and to establish a condition of ecological and economic stability that was sustainable far into the future. The state of global equilibrium could be designed so that the basic material needs of each person on earth were satisfied and each person had an equal opportunity to realise their individual human potential.

3) If the world's people decided to strive for this second outcome rather than the first, the sooner they began working to attain it, the greater would be their chances of success [35].

The essential thesis of the MIT model, released in March 1972 as *The Limits to Growth*, was that the roots of the environmental crisis lay in exponential growth. Catastrophe was inevitable by the end of the century, brought on by the exhaustion of resources, and rising death rates from pollution and food shortages. Increased food supply, the discovery of new sources of energy, and technological advances to control pollution could reverse the trend. Ultimately though, there was an urgent need to achieve global equilibrium through recognising the limits to economic and population growth. "Technological optimism", the team argued, "is the most common and the most dangerous reaction to our findings from the world model. Technology can relieve the symptoms of a problem without affecting the underlying causes . . . [and] can thus divert our attention from the most fundamental problem – the problem of growth in a finite system" [36]. The authors recommended, among other things, a 40 percent reduction in industrial investment, a 20 percent reduction in agricultural investment, a 40 percent reduction in the birth rate, and a massive transfer of wealth from rich to poor countries.

Drawing on the findings of Worlds 2 and 3, the Club of Rome reached a number of its own conclusions [37], many of them remarkably perceptive:

1) It was essential that the quantitative restraints of the world environment be realised; population pressure alone was enough to compel society to seek a state of global equilibrium;

such equilibrium could only be achieved if the lot of the poor countries was substantially improved.

2) Global development was so closely interlinked with other issues that an overall strategy needed to be developed to tackle all major problems, particularly humanity's relationship with the environment.

3) If society was to embark on a new course, concerted international measures and joint long-term planning on an unprecedented scale were needed; imposing a break on population and economic growth should not lead to a freeze on economic development; rather, the MDCs should take a lead by decelerating their growth and helping LDCs advance their economies more rapidly. (These views were to gain wider currency in the late 1970s and early 1980s (see Chapter 9).)

The authors of World 3 did not claim infallibility. They admitted that their model was "imperfect, over-simplified, and unfinished", and that much further study was needed. Yet they felt it important to publish the findings when they did because decisions with far-reaching global physical, economic and social implications were constantly being made, and could not await perfect models and total understanding. The purpose of publishing *The Limits to Growth*, a non-technical summary of their findings, was to open the debate on accelerating global trends to a wider community than that of scientists alone; in this they succeeded. Meadows and his team positively welcomed constructive criticism and discussion, as indicated by their association with the Sussex team (see below).

One of the motives behind the Club's work was the belief that scientists and politicians had become too complacent and willing to believe that people could always pull a solution out of the air when things seemed to be on the point of going too far. The Club hoped to shock people out of their complacency, "to provide warnings of potential world crisis . . . and thus offer an opportunity to make changes in our political, economic, and social systems to ensure that these crises do not take place" [38], and to shock society into shifting from growth to global equilibrium. The Club of Rome saw Worlds 2 and 3 as means to their ends, and hoped that by quantifying the human predicament, the models would encourage people to look for solutions. Unlike Hardin, the Club believed that the improvement of the lot of the LDCs was essential to the achievement of equilibrium. But like Hardin, who believed that "no technical solution can rescue us from the misery of over-population" [39], the Club believed "technological solutions alone" [40] could not extricate humanity from the vicious cycle of growing population and the overexploitation of natural resources. The Club concluded that redressing the global imbalance was a challenge for the present generation, not the next, and that this demanded concerted international measures and long-term planning on an unprecedented scale.

Across the Atlantic, meanwhile, a second "doomsday hypothesis" – *A Blueprint for Survival* [41] – had been published as a radical response to what was regarded as the staid attitudes of the British conservation establishment. The spark came from an August 1971 article in *The Observer* by its environment correspondent, Gerald Leach. In it he observed that while the main lines of the changes needed to move towards the spaceship economy were becoming clear, no-one had sketched out the details. Edward Goldsmith, editor of *The Ecologist*, organised a conference at which it was decided to build a model for Britain. The *Blueprint*, which drew heavily on the SCEP model and was influenced by *The Limits to Growth*, was published in *The Ecologist* in early 1972.

It started from a similar premise to that of the MIT model, that "if current trends are allowed to persist, the breakdown of society and the irreversible disruption of the life-support systems on this planet . . . are inevitable" [42]. Population growth and resource consumption demanded radical changes in attitudes and practices; indefinite growth could not be sustained by finite resources. Among the recommendations were the use of fewer pesticides and fertilisers, efficient disposal of sewage and reduction of industrial waste, protection of genetic resources, social accounting (e.g. making polluters pay), the stabilising of population growth, and the creation of a new decentralised social system. Like MIT, the *Blueprint* team acknowledged their debt to John Stuart Mill. To implement its ideas, the team proposed a Movement for Survival, a (still-born) coalition of environmental organisations working to persuade governments to take measures leading to the stable society.

The theme of non-growth was taken further in 1973 by the British economist E F Schumacher. In his book *Small is Beautiful* [43], he criticised the waste and squandering of resources and the over-reliance of Western industry on capital- and energy-intensive technology. Criticising the value system that allowed such a state of affairs to continue, he challenged people to re-examine their values and lifestyles, and to make a transition from the belief that "more is better" to "small is beautiful". Schumacher's thesis was given special significance by the decision of the Arab members of OPEC in October 1973 to impose an oil embargo, contributing to a quadrupling in the price of oil. It also became one of the bibles of the green movement (see Chapter 9).

Apocalypse tomorrow

By the beginning of the 1970s, many Western Europeans and North Americans were thoroughly alarmed by the apparently dismal prospects for the future. Despite the lack of complete scientific data, speculation became a popular pastime. In the wake of the prophets came a flood of often fantastic apocalyptic predictions, many of which later came back to haunt their authors. For example:

- Paul and Anne Ehrlich warned that "mankind itself may stand on the brink of extinction" [44]. Ehrlich often warned of the prospect of "eco-catastrophe", worldwide plague and nuclear war if population growth continued.
- Barbara Ward and René Dubos predicted that by 1985 all land surfaces other than the coldest and highest would be occupied and utilised by people [45].
- Predictions were made that by 1985, a fleet of 300 Concordes, together with an expanded fleet of Boeing supersonic airliners, would be burning 2.2 billion barrels of oil per year, or one-ninth of world demand in 1971 [46].
- In 1970, *Life* made a number of predictions for which scientists claimed "solid experimental and theoretical evidence": air pollution combined with a temperature inversion would kill thousands in a US city in the early 1980s; urban dwellers would be wearing gas masks to survive air pollution; air

pollution would halve the amount of sunlight reaching the earth by 1985; and a major ecological system would have broken down somewhere in the United States [47].

In 1969, Paul Ehrlich correctly predicted the failure of the Green Revolution, the incompetence of aid programmes to poor countries, and the collapse of the Peruvian anchovy industry (it collapsed in 1972, three years earlier than Ehrlich predicted). However, he also incorrectly predicted:

1) The collapse of the whaling industry in 1973 (it did not collapse).
2) The reduction of the annual ocean fish catch to 30 million tonnes by 1977 (in the event, it was more than twice that figure, although the possibility of a collapse in world fisheries persisted as catches continued to be unsustainable).
3) An annual rate of deaths from malnutrition of 50 million (it is impossible to reach more than an approximate figure of deaths from malnutrition in any given region or period, but mortality figures from countries experiencing famine between 1960 and 1983 indicate that just over 12 million people died [48]. Even the most pessimistic projections of annual deaths from all forms of malnutrition would fall well short of Ehrlich's prediction. Of course, whatever the estimates, 12 million deaths was a tragedy of gigantic proportions).
4) Diatom blooms in the oceans and the extinction by 1979 of all important marine animal life (marine life was to prove considerably more resilient than many scientists expected).

What these and other predictions emphasise is that the environmental crisis seemed much worse in 1968 than it was to seem 10 or 15 years later. By then, some action at least had been taken that may have allowed the world to avoid an apocalypse; even so, it is questionable whether some of the predictions would ever have come true. Much of the alarmism was created and fed by the prophets of doom. When Ehrlich wrote *The Population Bomb*, the population of the United States was growing at nearly 1.5 percent annually, enough to double the American population in about 60 years. Given the high average per capita consumption of natural resources by American consumers, the implications of this growth seemed serious. By the late 1970s, however, the American population growth rate had fallen below 1 percent annually. In 1978 [49], Ehrlich admitted that no-one had anticipated the rapid change of reproductive behaviour which occurred in the early 1970s. But he was still only marginally more optimistic. Those who claimed that there was no population problem, only a problem of distribution, were wrong, he argued; the only sensible strategy remained that of ending population growth as rapidly and humanely as possible.

Responses to The Limits to Growth

As the number of doom-mongers proliferated, so too did the number of their critics. In his review of these critics, Sills [50] suggests that there were two analytically distinct positions concerning the nature of the environmental problem: pessimism and optimism. Environmentalists by this definition were pessimists, and their critics were optimists. The two sides differed over projections on natural resources, food, pollution and population. The most common criticism of the environmentalists was that they were alarmists, a view encapsulated in a review of *The Limits to Growth*, published under the title "The Computer That Printed Out W*O*L*F*" [51].

The Limits to Growth itself became the subject of debate and criticism. Particular invective was directed at the recommendation for massive non-growth; not only would this produce a major industrial slump in MDCs, charged the critics, but it would put a brake on development in LDCs. The World models began with a recipe of doom, argues O'Riordan, "and one can only assume that this enormously complicated computer programme was produced to estimate the timing of the cataclysmic result that was so pre-determined"; Peccei's "evangelical passion for an earth-awakening 'commando operation'" furthermore threw a certain amount of scientific caution to the winds. The report interested hard-line conservative politicians, who "sought a politically respectable rationale for blocking what they regarded as exceptionally progressive social reform" [52]. In his review of the third Conference in the Countryside in 1970 series, the British environmentalist Robert Boote said, "If we underestimated the task in

1963, this is no cause to accept the clamour of the neo-Malthusians that we face impending doom" [53]. The Marxist view was that *The Limits to Growth* ideology was aimed at breaking working-class resistance to authority [54]. *The Limits to Growth* (and the "doomsday syndrome" generally) was also criticised [55] for suggesting the hopelessness of taking reasoned action and for ignoring the ability of humans to make social and political adaptations (see also the Kahn and Simon debate in Chapter 10).

Forrester probably had an interest in promoting the system dynamics methodology, comment the authors of *Global 2000*, while the members of the Meadows team "probably had less well-defined aspirations. They were relatively young (average age below 30) and for the most part at the start of their careers. Meadows and his wife had just returned from a year in Asia, during which they had become concerned about problems of development and the environment, and were eager to explore the causes and possible cures of such problems. Most of the team members were formally trained in science, engineering or system dynamics, rather than the social sciences" [56]. Significantly, the 17-member team consisted of ten Americans, three Germans, a Norwegian, a Turk, an Iranian and an Indian; in other words, it was heavily weighted towards Western industrialised countries.

The most comprehensive critique of *The Limits to Growth* was that undertaken in 1972 by 13 essayists associated with the Science Policy Research Unit of the University of Sussex in Britain [57]. Their report focused on the weaknesses in the methodology of the MIT analysis, the technical value of the model, and the ideological values of the modellers. The Sussex authors stressed that they did not underestimate the positive importance of the MIT work, and acknowledged that as a result of reading *The Limits to Growth*, many people were thinking about and discussing the problems; "in particular, they are discussing once again whether or not the world is likely to run up against physical limits". The open public debate surrounding the MIT work was its most important achievement, argued the Sussex team. (By the late 1970s, about four million copies of *The Limits to Growth* had been sold in 20 languages [58].)

The team argued that the social sciences could benefit from the use of computer modelling, but models had their limitations. The MIT team had set itself the task of drawing up a model in which relationships were an accurate representation of the real world as it was in 1970, but their model fell short of needs. The basic problem lay in a lack of data (for which the MIT team could not be blamed, and which it indeed admitted), the assumptions made about relationships, the choice of assumptions, and the relative neglect of economics and sociology. Hence the dangerous self-deception of the assertion by Meadows in the introduction to *The Limits to Growth* that "the basic behavior modes we have already observed in this model appear to be so fundamental and general that we do not expect our broad conclusions to be substantially altered by further revisions". It was, the Sussex team argued, "essential to look at the political bias and the values implicitly or explicitly present in any study of social systems. The apparent detached neutrality of a computer model is as illusory as it is persuasive" [59]. Stressing that subjective values and attitudes influence forecasts (and indeed admitting that its views on *The Limits to Growth* reflected its own political biases and subjective limitations), the Sussex team identified a second major weakness – "computer fetishism, [which] . . . endows the computer model with a validity and an independent power which altogether transcends the mental models which are its essential basis".

The views of the Sussex team differed in three fundamental respects from those of the MIT team:

1) The Sussex team put much greater emphasis on the political and social limits to growth than on the purely physical limits (poverty, they argued, was a major problem, in the light of which the MIT goal and zero growth was not ideal); "the Growth versus No Growth debate has become a rather sterile one . . . because it tends to ignore the really important issues of the *composition* of growth in output, and the *distribution* of the fruits of growth". The problem was one of stimulating more equitable distribution.

2) The MIT group was underestimating the possibilities of continued technical progress. The Sussex team argued that "the inclusion of technical progress in the MIT model in sectors from which it is omitted has the effect of indefinitely

postponing the catastrophes which the model otherwise predicts". Studies made 100 years before the MIT study (which made forecasts 130 years ahead) could not have foreseen the dependence on oil and the growth of nuclear power, the Sussex team argued.

3) The Sussex team was not fully convinced that world models based on systems dynamics could develop into satisfactory tools of forecasting and policy-making. Robert Golub, a physicist at Sussex, argued that the MIT approach was inherently dangerous because it gave the false appearance of precise knowledge of quantities and relationships which were unknown (and often unknowable), stimulated gross over-simplification, and encouraged the neglect of factors difficult to quantify, such as policy changes or social values [60].

There was no question that exponential growth could not continue indefinitely, but the Sussex team took exception to the MIT contention that existing growth should end within the lifetime of many people then alive, and that unless drastic steps were taken, global disaster would occur. *The Limits to Growth* has also been criticised by Sandbach [61] and O'Riordan [62] for basing all its predictions on known reserves of resources (although the MIT team was careful to point out that new discoveries "would only postpone shortage rather than eliminate it" [63]). Sandbach cites the example of a 1945 American study [64] where, if the predicted reserves of 41 commodities had remained static, 21 would by 1980 have been exhausted. Technological progress has repeatedly shown that resources have become easier to extract and substitute, that the efficiency of industrial processes has grown [65], and that the volume of known exploitable resources has often grown with demand.

It is now clear that the MIT models were designed at a time when understanding of environmental processes and resource issues was incomplete (it remains incomplete today), when computer modelling was in its infancy, and when perceptions were likely to have been influenced by the prevailing Malthusian gloom of the times. The weaknesses of *The Limits to Growth* lay not so much in its broad conclusions (although many of these were disputed) as in its methodology. Some critics felt the method to be too simple, and thus insufficient to provide policy guidelines. Still others felt that since *The Limits to Growth* was basically a "sensationalised" version of *World Dynamics*, publication of *Limits* could have been delayed until some of its structural problems had been resolved [66].

The Sussex team was not itself immune to misconception. In criticising the MIT model pollution sub-system, it argued that "most disasters caused by material pollutants are likely to be local . . . or to be caused by one pollutant or class of pollutants". By aggregating all pollutants, the Sussex team argued, "and assuming that they behave in some composite way, attention is drawn away from what are urgent, and still soluble problems, and diverted into speculation upon an imaginary race against time between 'Life' and 'Global asphyxiation'". Even as the team wrote, there was growing evidence of the emerging problem of acid pollution (the MIT team had touched on sulphur dioxide pollution), which has gone on to disprove the Sussex contention; it may be caused by one class of pollutants, but the paths to acid damage are enormously complex, and the problem is neither entirely local nor always capable of local solution [67].

A decade later, the authors of *Global 2000* criticised the Worlds 2 and 3 models on a number of counts. "They are general, strategy-oriented models and make no attempt to develop specific, detailed analyses. They familiarize one with the basic tendencies in population–resource–environment systems but do not speak to the problems of specific regions" [68]. Further problems identified by *Global 2000* were that the models were based on a series of controversial assumptions (including the inability of technology to alleviate natural limits to growth); they focused on metal resources without giving attention to fossil fuels; they omitted social factors, such as income distribution and the international order, which "may pose limiting problems well before actual physical limits are encountered"; they suffered from a weak database and an aggregation of items with dissimilar behaviour in the pollution sub-system; and they failed to allow for qualitative changes in the nature of economic growth that could make it less demanding on limited resources. *Global 2000* concluded that while the World models helped clarify the nature of long-term global problems, "their limitations render them unsuitable as primary tools of analysis or as tools for detailed analysis of global problems and their solutions". For Hecox, the lasting contribution of *The Limits to Growth* lay more in the questions it raised than in the answers it provided, and more in focusing public attention on crucial issues of global futures than in specific descriptions of those futures [69]. (The Club of Rome sponsored a more optimistic follow-up to *The Limits to Growth*, entitled *Mankind at the Turning Point* [70]. Dividing the world into sub-regions, it offered a gaming technique by which policy-makers could actually test their strategies. Deliberately low-key, the report was all but ignored.)

The doomsday syndrome

If the prophets of doom elicited reasoned scientific rebuttal and scholarly analysis, they also drew passionate and occasionally reactionary attacks on their alarmism. If the doom-critics had a standard-bearer, it was probably John Maddox, the editor of the British science journal *Nature*.

The opening line of his 1972 book *The Doomsday Syndrome* reads: "This is not a scholarly work but a complaint" [71]. He objected to the models and essays ignoring the ways in which "social institutions and human aspirations can conspire to solve the most daunting problems". He felt that the doomsday debate was too dogmatic – you were either far-sighted and for the preservation of the environment, or you were heartless and against it. By spreading gloom and alarm, he argued, the doomsday syndrome could undermine the capacity of the human race to look out for its survival, and "be as much a hazard as any of the conundrums which society has created for itself".

Maddox viewed with scepticism the values and the history of the entire environmental movement: the environmental argument in support of the Test Ban Treaty of 1963 was acceptable to the signatories only because they had by then achieved the strategic objectives of the test programmes; Rachel Carson had, to an extent, seriously misled her readers, and the influence of *Silent Spring* depended much on Carson's "technique of calculated overdramatisation"; and the claim that the decision of the US Congress in 1971 to abandon its supersonic airliner project was an environmental victory was misplaced – far more important was the unwillingness of Congress to be coerced into agreeing to a development project of questionable economic benefit.

Other doom-critics were less guarded in their attacks, and while their arguments were often of doubtful merit, they do give a taste of the extremes to which the debate went. Few were more indignant than Thomas R Shepard Jr, the publisher of *Look* magazine. In his 1973 book *The Doomsday Lobby*, co-authored with Melvin Grayson, he described *Silent Spring* as an attack on scientific and technological progress, an attack on the United States, and an attack on humanity. Rachel Carson had become a standard-bearer for the "left-wing academic brigade". Millions of Americans had bought the book "as avidly as the buxom hausfraus of Bavaria had bought the garbage of Adolf Hitler, and for much the same reason". In 1961, they related, there were 110 reported cases of malaria in Sri Lanka (then Ceylon), and no deaths; in 1968 there were 2.5 million cases, and 10 000 deaths. There were many who believed – wrote Grayson and Shepard – that these new cases and deaths could be attributed in large measure to the impact of *Silent Spring* on producing a ban on DDT. It was, they wrote, "The Book That Killed" [72].

Shepard may have been upset, but his views paled beside those of Petr Beckmann, an electrical engineer at the University of Colorado. In his book *Eco-hysterics and the Technophobes* [73], he expressed himself unobliged to observe the niceties of scientific etiquette because – he wrote – he was not arguing with scientists but with "benighted fanatics" preaching "vicious nonsense". For him, *The Limits to Growth* was "one of the major cripples begotten by the philosophy of apocalypse", the word ecology had lost all meaning, and the prophets of doom were ignorant about demography, economics and science. He had no quarrel with the idea that the environment should be protected and preserved, but felt that "econuts" and the "ecocult" had come to dominate the environmental movement to the point where the movement was beginning to degenerate into blind technophobia. Science itself was under attack, he wrote; environmentalists were curtailing scientific activity and reducing new enrolments in schools of physics and engineering.

The fray was finally joined by the Nobel laureate Norman Borlaug (the father of the Green Revolution), who denounced "hysterical environmentalists" for attempting to block the use of agricultural chemicals. "If agriculture", he continued, "is denied the use of agricultural chemicals because of unwise legislation that is now being promoted by a powerful group of hysterical lobbyists who are provoking fear by predicting doom for the world through chemical poisoning, then the world will be doomed not by chemical poisoning but from starvation" [74].

Beyond these views, there was growing evidence of the emergence of what Killian calls a "counter-social movement" [75]. At one level, environmentalism raised the ire of those who believed in the sanctity of "traditional values", such as the right to determine the size of one's own family. At another level, attempts were made to relate the environmental movement to a larger conspiracy. The Daughters of the American Revolution felt Earth Day was subversive; a state administrator from Georgia mounted a small campaign to draw attention to the fact that Earth Day fell on Lenin's birthday [76]; the president of the American Coal Association warned that the environmental movement could be radicalised to the point that it could weaken the United States by denying it necessary minerals and other resources [77]. Finally, there was the issue of "pollution versus payroll", in which many threatened industries argued that they would no longer be able to operate if forced to meet stringent environmental controls, and thus many of their employees would lose their jobs [78].

There is no longer any doubt that the prophets did, to some extent, overstate the problem. More traditional environmentalists may have feared that the doomsday syndrome would do more harm than good to the environmental cause. Robert Allen, one of the authors of *A Blueprint for Survival*, observed that most ecologists cast themselves as moderates [79]. Maddox warned that the environmental movement could find itself "falling flat on its face when it is most needed, simply because it has pitched its tale too strongly" [80]. Daniel Luten, president of Friends of the Earth, reflected in 1985 that the prophets predicted immediate crisis "because they were afraid that the public's attention span wasn't long enough to look at the deeper issues they felt needed attention. When there was no immediate crisis they were discredited" [81].

In fairness, most of the prophets were outlining scenarios which illustrated what *could* happen, not what necessarily *would* happen. The authors of *The Limits to Growth* emphasised (clearly to little effect) that "our posture is one of very grave concern, but not of despair" [82]. The models and essays drew bleak pictures, and made some prophecies that proved false; yet they made people think. It may have been crude to use such shock tactics, but the intense interest generated in the environment, if often lacking the support of credible scientific data and relying too heavily on postulation, nevertheless cleared a path for change in social and political attitudes.

Like Smith, Malthus, Mill, Marx and Keynes before them, the new prophets of doom touched off heated debate, so that their arguments became less important than the effects of the arguments. Marx once observed of Malthus' book on population that "in its first edition it was nothing but a sensational pamphlet and plagiarism from beginning to end into the bargain. And yet what a stimulus was produced by this libel on the human race!" [83]. Whatever inaccuracies or delusions marked the writings of Ehrlich, Commoner, Hardin, Meadows and others, their contribution to New Environmentalism was that they challenged people to think about the issues. To that extent, they succeeded in their stated aims. The events and the debates of the 1960s placed increasing pressure on governments to act in a more concerted way to address the real and potential problems of the global environment. The way was now cleared for the first of the major global summits on the environment, the Stockholm conference of 1972.

5

The Stockholm Conference (1970–1972)

In 1968 and 1972, two international conferences met to assess the problems of the global environment, and – more importantly – to suggest corrective action. The first was the Biosphere Conference, held in Paris in September 1968. Concentrating on scientific aspects of the conservation of the biosphere, it was partly a product of the growth in the coordination of ecological research encouraged by the International Biological Programme (see Chapter 3). The second was the United Nations Conference on the Human Environment, held in Stockholm in June 1972.

Stockholm was the pivotal event in the growth of the global environmental movement. It was the first occasion on which the political, social and economic problems of the global environment were discussed at an inter-governmental forum with a view to actually taking corrective action. It aimed to "create a basis for comprehensive consideration within the United Nations of the problems of the human environment", and to "focus the attention of governments and public opinion in various countries on the importance of the problem" [1]. It resulted in the creation of the United Nations Environment Programme (UNEP), and it marked an important transition: from the emotional and occasionally naive New Environmentalism of the 1960s to the more rational, political and global perspective of the 1970s. Above all, it brought the debate between poor and rich countries – with their different perceptions of environmental priorities – into the open, and caused a fundamental shift in the direction of environmentalism.

The Biosphere Conference

The Biosphere Conference picked up the theme of international cooperation in ecological research that had first been explored at UNSCCUR in 1949. At the 1962 National Parks Conference in Seattle, a meeting on endangered species was proposed [2]. This was discussed at the IUCN 1963 General Assembly, and plans drawn up in 1965–66 by a multi-NGO steering committee. UNESCO then suggested that a more general conference on the rational use and conservation of the biosphere was needed if emerging states were to be persuaded of the virtues of conservation. The Biosphere Conference (the Intergovernmental Conference of Experts on the Scientific Basis for Rational Use and Conservation of the Resources of the Biosphere) was held under the auspices of UNESCO in Paris from 1 to 13 September 1968. The biosphere was defined as "that part of the world in which life can exist, including . . . parts of the lithosphere, hydrosphere and atmosphere" [3]. The conference discussed human impact on the biosphere, including the effects of air and water pollution, overgrazing, deforestation, and the drainage of wetlands.

Several themes emerged from the debate on the national reports distributed at the conference:

1) Although some changes in the environment had been taking place for decades or longer, they seemed to have reached a critical threshold.
2) In industrialised countries this was "producing concern and a popular demand for correction".
3) Parallel with this concern was a realisation that traditional ways of developing and using natural resources had to be changed, with careless development giving way to development which recognised that the biosphere was a system, the whole of which could be affected by activities in any one part of it.
4) A new interdisciplinary approach to the planned use of natural resources was needed; the natural sciences and

technology alone could not solve resource management problems – the social sciences too needed to be considered.

5) A vast amount of new research was needed, in rich and poor countries; since there was no universal solution to the problems of the biosphere, understanding and techniques would have to be adapted to areas within countries and to regions of two or more countries.

The conference agreed a list of 20 recommendations. The first eight were based on the need for more and better research on ecosystems, human ecology, pollution, and genetic and natural resources, and on the need for an inventory and monitoring of resources. Recommendations 9–13 argued the need for new approaches to environmental education. A proposal had by then been adopted by the UN Economic and Social Council (ECOSOC) for a conference on the human environment; delegates at Paris welcomed this, noting that the rational use and conservation of the human environment depended on understanding not only the scientific problems but the economic, social and political dimensions as well, which were outside the purview of the Paris conference. Recommendation 19 noted the need for taking ecological impact into account in large-scale development projects. Delegates feared that industrialisation and the intensive exploitation of natural resources in poor countries could cause irreparable damage to ecologically fragile environments, and so inhibit socio-economic development.

An important outcome of the Biosphere Conference was the emphasis on the interrelatedness of the environment. Delegates concluded that the deterioration of the environment was the fault of rapid population growth, urbanisation and industrialisation. A massive rural exodus had led to the disappearance of traditions and customary rights, and changes in lifestyles, resulting in particularly serious problems in poorer countries. The world "lacked considered, comprehensive policies for managing the environment. It is now abundantly clear that national policies are mandatory if environmental quality is to be restored and preserved".

Recommendations 1 and 20 argued the case for a new international research programme on humans and the biosphere. "Many of the changes produced by man affect the biosphere as a whole", the conference noted, "and are not confined within regional or national boundaries . . . these problems cannot be solved on a regional, national or local basis, but require attention on a global scale" [4]. The International Biological Programme was due to close in 1974; it had made a valuable start, but it was a non-governmental endeavour, and so had only limited abilities. UNESCO believed that the IBP put too little emphasis on studying the areas where neighbouring ecosystems met, and that because it was run solely by natural scientists, took little account of social and economic data in the study of ecosystems [5]. A successor to the IBP was discussed, and the Man and the Biosphere programme (MAB) was eventually launched in November 1971 (see Chapter 10).

Preparations for Stockholm

The significance of the Biosphere Conference is regularly over-looked, mainly because of the much greater public and political impact of the 1972 Stockholm conference. Yet initiatives credited to Stockholm were in some cases only expansions of ideas raised at Paris. Some of the intellectual foundations of Stockholm reflected those of Paris, and some of the recommendations were common to both. The real difference lies in the fact that while Paris addressed the scientific aspects of environmental problems, Stockholm looked at the wider political, social and economic questions. This not only gave NGOs (i.e. the citizens' movement) greater involvement in the discussions, but it made for more dramatic news headlines.

If there was any single issue that spawned Stockholm, it was acid pollution. Research during the late 1960s had revealed a disturbing increase in the acidity of rain falling in Sweden (see Chapter 10), prompting Swedish scientists to demand preventive action. Sverker Astrom, the Swedish Ambassador to the United Nations, submitted a proposal for an international conference in a resolution put before ECOSOC in July 1968. The resolution was rapidly adopted by the General Assembly the following December, probably reflecting the impact of New Environment-alism [6].

The resolution emphasised the environmental work already being undertaken by inter-governmental organisations, NGOs, and UN specialised agencies (it actually listed ILO, FAO, UNESCO, WHO, WMO, IMCO and IAEA, which suggests a very loose definition of what constituted "environmental activity"). The conference – it went on – was needed to provide a framework within which the UN could comprehensively assess the problems of the human environment, and focus the attention of governments and public opinion. It should also identify those aspects of environmental problems which could only or best be solved through international cooperation [7]. This was the critical point. It was no coincidence that acid pollution – a transnational issue – had sparked off the conference; American and European environmentalists were preoccupied at the time with pollution.

But the most significant outcome of the pre-conference discussions was the tenacious new role of LDCs in the environmental debate. Pollution – mainly an industrialised country problem – may have been the spark for the conference, but poorer countries used their General Assembly voting power to make sure that their perspective was appreciated from the outset. The General Assembly resolution expressed the hope that LDCs would "derive particular benefit from the mobilisation of knowledge and experience about the problems of the human environment, enabling them . . . to forestall the occurrence of many such problems". Subsequent UN General Assembly and ECOSOC resolutions reflected LDC wariness of the non-growth philosophy underlying *The Limits to Growth*. A July 1970 progress report on conference preparations warned that the popularisation of environmental problems "raised the danger of a concentration on the more spectacular aspects of environmental deterioration (such as pollution) in a few advanced countries, to the neglect of less obvious aspects of a cultural and economic nature". An information programme aimed at legislators, policy-makers, and leaders of industry and agriculture was needed to put issues such as pollution in perspective, and to draw attention to the environmental problems of poorer countries [8].

LDCs were clearly worried that environmental safeguards and restrictions imposed by industrialised nations would retard development, that trade restrictions might follow as MDCs prohibited imports of food contaminated by pesticides, and that

LDCs might not benefit from the management of shared natural resources. "Debates on doomsday theories, limits to growth, the population explosion, and the conservation of nature and natural resources", noted UNEP, "were thought of as largely academic, of no great interest to those faced with the daily realities of poverty, hunger, disease and survival" [9]. Of much greater urgency was short life expectancy, the shortage of basic necessities such as shelter, clean drinking water and adequate sanitation, and, above all, the need to feed and employ rapidly growing numbers of people.

There was a strong temptation for LDCs to concentrate all their energy and resources on the short-term resolution of these problems, and to worry about any resulting environmental problems later. On the other hand, a number of LDC governments felt that they might learn from the environmental mistakes of the industrialised world. In December 1971, the UN General Assembly passed a resolution devoted largely to outlining the reservations of LDCs. It stressed that the Stockholm action plan must recognise that "no environmental policy should adversely affect the present or future development possibilities of the developing countries . . . [and that] the burden of the environmental policies of developed countries cannot be transferred . . . to the developing countries". Britain and the United States were the only two countries to vote against this resolution [10].

Many of the LDC concerns were raised at two preparatory meetings held during 1971: the Panel of Experts on Development and Environment (Founex, Switzerland, 4–12 June), and the SCOPE/UNCHE (Scientific Committee on Problems of the Environment/UN Conference on the Human Environment) working party on environmental problems in less developed countries (Canberra, Australia, 24 August–3 September). The Founex panel tried to assure LDCs that environmental protection would not go against their interests; it would not affect their position in international trade, and they could maintain their industrial development plans while avoiding the pitfalls experienced by MDCs. Rather than a confrontation between developers and conservationists, observes Rodgers, "what emerged was a consensus forged under the leadership of [LDC] development economists which identified the environment as a critical dimension of successful development" [11]. It has been argued that Founex began to clarify the links between environmental protection and economic development, destroyed the idea that these concepts were necessarily incompatible, and began to convince LDCs that environmental concerns were more widespread and more relevant to their situation than they had appreciated, and that they should not be a barrier to development, but should be part of the process [12].

The Founex meeting had been convened by Maurice Strong, then director-general of the Canadian External Aid Office; he was now appointed secretary-general of the Stockholm conference, and headed a 27-nation Preparatory Committee set up to make plans for Stockholm and to draw up an agenda. The reservations of the LDCs, he later recorded, "made it clear that they thought under-development and poverty constituted the most acute and immediate threat to the environment of their peoples". As a result, the agenda of the conference and the very concept of environment were broadened to include issues such as soil loss, desertification, tropical ecosystem management, water supply and human settlements. LDCs, Strong noted, had "forced a clear recognition of the relationship between environment and development" [13]. A conference agenda was agreed at the February 1971 meeting of the Preparatory Committee. It included the management of human settlements, natural resource management, control of pollutants, education and information, and environment and development.

Attention now turned to the question of the institutional arrangements to follow the conference. It was agreed that some new structure was needed, but there was no agreement on the form it should take. At its third session in July 1971 the Preparatory Committee had before it a report from outgoing UN Secretary-General U Thant outlining criteria for these arrangements. This included the proviso that "all functions that can best be performed by existing organizations should be assigned to those organizations, both international and national, most capable of carrying them out effectively. *No unnecessary new machinery should be created*" (my emphasis) [14]. The report further suggested that it would be more logical to think in terms of separate sectoral organisations linked by "switchboards" rather than in terms of a global "super agency". This was in marked contrast to an earlier proposal made by U Thant for just such a "super agency", which had clearly met with the active opposition of existing UN agencies [15]. Any policy centre, warned the report, "that is expected to influence and co-ordinate the activities of other agencies should not itself have operational functions which in any way compete with the organizations over which it expects to exercise such influence" [16].

In a barely disguised marketing exercise, the existing UN agencies put their case in a subject paper prepared for governments before the conference. Drawn up by a committee of the UN agencies, the paper amounted to a defence of existing UN environmental protection activities. They were systematic, noted the report, and they had dealt with a variety of problems related to the environment. Considering the complexity and variety of issues, the cooperative arrangements among UN organisations had provided "an effective and dynamic mechanism" [17]. The UN's sectoral pattern was still the best approach to dealing with a large number of environmental problems, both nationally and internationally, because it could "provide the flexibility required to combine . . . these sectoral activities" on an ad hoc basis [18]. Admittedly, there were gaps (notably in research, data exchange and the provision of technical assistance), there was new ground to be broken, and many issues had received inadequate attention; the multi-disciplinary approach had been applied only in a limited number of instances. But recognition that many of the problems of the human environment were intersectoral had led to greater coordination in such areas as water resource development, population, and environmental research.

The report went on to outline existing UN activities in the areas of human settlements, natural resource management, and pollution. This would help Stockholm delegates fully appreciate the potential offered by the UN system for "broadened worldwide efforts toward a better human environment". The UN system had not been designed for many of the tasks it now regularly and effectively undertook; however, "new responsibilities do not automatically require new institutions and mechanisms, but do mean an adaptation of existing mechanisms and arrangements . . . the institutions, the experience and a large measure of expertise

needed, exist" [19]. The specialised agencies were clearly concerned that any changes agreed at Stockholm might threaten their
future independence [20]. This disquiet was not raised in open
forum at Stockholm, but there were apparently enough private
discussions during the conference to move Maurice Strong to
make a public declaration to the conference that the ultimate
authority for programmes was with each of the specialised
agencies [21].

A parallel paper prepared by the conference secretariat offered the
opposite view to the UN report, arguing that decentralisation was
not the most effective form of management. It recommended the
establishment of a new inter-governmental body within the UN,
backed by a small secretariat and a limited budget. Population
would not be on its agenda since the UN had recently set up the
UN Fund for Population Activities (UNFPA). Both Britain and the
United States had actively promoted the idea of limited institutional arrangements, but while Britain had suggested that no
new funds at all be provided for UN environmental work, an
Advisory Committee of the US State Department had recommended a Voluntary Fund for the Environment, with a minimum
annual budget of $100 million (of which half would be designated
for human settlements). This should be administered by a "strong,
high-level executive (i.e. a single officer supported by a small
staff) for environmental affairs" established in the office of the
UN secretary-general [22]. The committee also recommended the
creation of a UN Inter-governmental Body for the Environment as
a subsidiary of the General Assembly, to advise and support the
executive. Funding might be worked out through national
assessments based on each country's rate of energy consumption.
In February 1972, President Nixon had proposed a fund to be
contributed voluntarily by UN members, with a five-year target of
$100 million [23].

A panel had meanwhile been set up in the United States by the
National Academy of Sciences (at the request of the State
Department) to examine the US mandate at the conference. It
recommended that, given the diffuse aims of the conference, and
the breadth of environmental problems, "we envisage not a choice
between the principal existing structure for international cooperation, the United Nations, or a new international structure,

but the emergence of flexible federations of networks of institutions – public and private, global and regional, ongoing and ad hoc – to deal with international environmental problems" [24]. The panel recommended that the United States promote a single focal point in the UN system for environmental problems, an independent research and advisory board, a global monitoring system, an environmental fund, and support for the work of transnational or regional organisations to address common problems where national capabilities were inadequate. The conference secretariat ultimately agreed that the form of the new institution could not be decided until the functions to be performed by the UN had been decided.

National reports were submitted to the Preparatory Committee by 80 countries, regional seminars were held to air the reservations of LDCs, and meetings were held to negotiate the publication of three new environmental conventions: making illegal the dumping of wastes at sea, conserving sites of cultural or natural heritage value, and preserving wetlands and islands as sites of special ecological significance (see Chapter 10). Preparations like these made the going at Stockholm itself much smoother. What happened at the conference was just the tip of the iceberg, notes Sohn; "a whole mountain of arduous preparatory labor was the necessary prerequisite of the final success" [25]. The reports ultimately gave Stockholm a sense of direction, concentrated the minds of delegates, and avoided much time-wasting preliminary discussion.

What Landsberg calls the "patient missionary work" [26] of Maurice Strong had also helped avoid major disagreement between MDCs and LDCs. Strong had constantly emphasised the compatibility of development and environmental quality in his preparatory talks with LDC governments. Landsberg believes that the discussions about development and environment at Founex, Canberra and other meetings had helped reduce what otherwise could have been "a great deal of rhetoric and sharp controversy at Stockholm. In a way, the impression had taken hold that all these problems had been talked about, and with exceptions, there was almost a reluctance to go over the familiar ground once again" [27]. Differences of opinion remained, but they did not polarise the conference irretrievably. Fears that the LDCs would discount environmental concerns were not borne out [28].

In May 1971, Maurice Strong commissioned the British journalist Barbara Ward and the French-born American biologist René Dubos to prepare an unofficial report that would provide Stockholm delegates with the intellectual and philosophical foundation for their deliberations; Strong described it as providing "a conceptual framework" [29]. The report, later published as *Only One Earth* [30], was reviewed by a committee of 152 consultants with backgrounds in industry, scientific research, planning, international relations, economics and development. All this reviewing and editing produced a document that was often bland and rhetorical, and occasionally alarmist, and that provided general guidance rather than specific proposals (which, it was assumed, would come out of the conference itself).

The book summed up by outlining three very broad requirements for future progress: a "collective international responsibility" for learning more about natural systems and how they were affected by human activity and vice versa; the adoption of global (rather than national) and coordinated policy on questions of global proportions, such as climate and oceans; and unity of purpose based on "loyalty to the earth", a belief in the need to protect and enhance the environment, and recognition of the concept of the interdependence of life on earth.

Ward and Dubos criticised existing international institutions for lacking "any sense of planetary community and commitment". They assessed the characteristics of environmental problems in LDCs and MDCs separately. Pollution, the waste and misuse of land, urban growth, the consumer society, and pressure on resources were listed as "problems of high technology", i.e. rich country problems. Population pressures, the potential problems of the Green Revolution, industry and pollution, and urban growth were assessed in the context of LDCs.

Despite its sweeping nature, *Only One Earth* was well received, and provided a useful philosophical peg for the conference. It was published by a new research institute, the International Institute for Environmental Affairs (IIEA), set up in 1972 under the sponsorship of the Aspen Institute for Humanistic Studies of

Colorado. IIEA was to help prepare for Stockholm and then to follow up its findings and to some extent to act as a bridge between LDCs and MDCs [31]. It would concentrate on the social and political impact of environmental management and on the international implications of environment/society relationships, acting as a source of reliable information and as a communications focal point for institutions, people and ideas [32].

A memorandum on a proposed structure for IIEA noted that Stockholm was a pressing political opportunity to begin encouraging increased international cooperation in the environmental field, yet a "real danger exists that the outcome could be more divisive than anything else. Almost inescapably, the Stockholm Conference will bring to a head an incipient but necessary political collision between environmental goals and development goals . . . it will at least impinge upon questions of international standards and enforcement procedures and thus upon international law" [33].

The philosophical foundations of IIEA lay in the results of a four-month feasibility study conducted in February–May 1970 by the Anderson Foundation. The study found that national and international governmental institutions were concerned almost exclusively with the physical symptoms of environmental problems, rather than the implications for social or institutional change; that public interest (at least in the United States) was focused almost entirely on domestic environmental problems; and that while there were strong pressures to halt environmental degradation, there were few pressures to "help guide the 'environmental movement' along constructive, dynamic paths of reform in traditional attitudes, values and institutions" [34].

IIEA began by hosting a series of workshops at Aspen on the international management of environmental problems, and passed on its recommendations to the Stockholm organisers. IIEA's co-chairman, Robert O Anderson (chairman of Atlantic Richfield and the seed funder of the Institute), believed that the institute should "steer a steady mid-course between doom and gloom alarmists and those who resist acknowledging the clear danger to which the human environment is being subjected" [35]. In January 1973, Barbara Ward became full-time president of the Institute, moved the headquarters to London, and renamed it the International Institute for Environment and Development (IIED), reflecting the outcome of the discussions on LDC/MDC priorities at Stockholm. IIED subsequently functioned as a policy research group, investigating the theme that development without proper regard to environmental constraints was both unsustainable and wasteful (see Chapter 8).

The Stockholm Conference

The United Nations Conference on the Human Environment was held in Stockholm, Sweden from 5 to 16 June 1972. It was attended by representatives from 113 countries, 19 inter-governmental agencies, and 400 other inter-governmental and non-governmental organisations. Although China was represented, notable for their absence were all the East European countries but Romania, which boycotted the conference because of an argument over the voting status of East Germany. They had all, however, taken part in the preparatory discussions.

Maurice Strong opened the conference by noting that it would launch "a new liberation movement" to free humans from environmental perils of their own making, that the "no-growth" concept was not viable, and that the traditional concepts of the basic purposes of growth needed to be rethought [36]. The conference would be concerned mainly with "the characteristics of the environment which affect the quality of human life – a very subjective and ill-defined concept" [37]. Though the concept of the "human environment" had emerged before the conference, it was the emphasis on this theme that distinguished Stockholm from previous international gatherings at this level.

Many reports of the conference reflect a prevailing feeling of excitement and anticipation. Lee Talbot, who attended as a member of the US Council on Environmental Quality, believes this was partly because many of the participants were new to the UN system, partly because of the hope that lofty declarations would be converted into action, and partly because Stockholm was the first UN theme conference [38]. (Later theme conferences focused on population (1974), habitat (1976), desertification (1977), and new and renewable sources of energy (1981).) There was also an air of youthfulness about the conference; it followed closely on the heels of New Environmentalism, and was seen by many as official UN sanction that the problems identified during the 1960s deserved government attention (although some national governments had already begun to address them – see Chapter 7). Holdgate recalls that "the dominant feeling, certainly among delegates with a professional background in the environmental sciences, was that environmental issues had 'broken through'. For the first time the environment was being discussed by the world's governments as a subject in its own right" [39]. Barbara Ward noted in her speech to the conference that it was impossible to be taking part "without wondering whether we may not be present at one of those turning points . . . when the human race begins to see itself and its concerns from a new angle of vision" [40]. She later recalled: "Those of us who were there experienced . . . a feeling that at last we were getting going" [41].

The enthusiasm was by no means universal. Although IUCN, along with other major conservation organisations, had taken part in Preparatory Committee meetings, it was lukewarm towards the conference. It recorded rather dismissively in its annual report for 1971 that "few who had worked closely with the [organising] programme held out hope that Stockholm would produce any basically new approach to the problems of the environment". It did concede that there had been a recent awakening in political concern, and that existing organisations would most likely "find their environmental programmes strengthened as a result of the conference" [42]. At the conference itself, Gerardo Budowski, who attended as director-general of IUCN, conceded only that "the time and place were favourable" [43]. In its annual review for 1972, the Union noted that while there had been general recognition at Stockholm that the conservation of nature and natural resources should be an integral part of sound development and environment programmes, "the theme of wilderness and the need to maintain and enhance diversity was given little attention" [44]. While it enthused about the achievements of the Second National Parks Conference and the adoption of the World Heritage Convention, IUCN was reserved in its judgements on Stockholm.

The major breakthrough at Stockholm was the new perception of the position of LDCs. Despite the earlier attempts to allay their concerns, many had remained sceptical. The publicity given to pollution-related incidents in the years before Stockholm had encouraged LDCs to equate environment with pollution. Because many in turn saw pollution as external evidence of industrial development, efforts to control it were seen as efforts to limit development. Ambassador Keith Johnson, the Jamaican rapporteur-general of the conference, observed that many LDCs had "a lingering fear that Stockholm was merely another ploy by the developed countries to avoid supporting the development revolution" [45].

A theme running through many LDC speeches was that environmental factors should not be allowed to curb economic growth. The point was well taken; Aaronson noted that, following Stockholm, it would be "difficult for Western environmentalists ever again to view 'the environment' in a parochial way" [46]. The view of LDCs dominated the discussions, and forced Western environmentalists to abandon their parochialism and begin to see environmental problems in a global perspective. MDCs had gone to the conference determined to discuss their own definitions of critical environmental problems, and found the discussions leading them to a compromise position on the relative priorities of LDCs and MDCs.

The role of the Chinese delegation deserves special mention. The Chinese had agreed to come to Stockholm only at the last minute, and there was some concern over their plans for the conference sessions, particularly that they would assume the leadership of the less developed countries [47]. In the event, the positions taken by many LDCs were strengthened by China's presence [48]. In a major address to the conference, Tang Ke, the chairman of the Chinese delegation, argued that China supported the LDCs in exploiting their natural resources in accordance with their own needs; "each country has the right to determine its own environment standards and policies in the light of its own conditions, and no country whatsoever should undermine the interests of the developing countries under the pretext of protecting the environment" [49].

Otherwise, the delegation played a passive role. Its main interest appeared to be in the Declaration on the Human Environment, a draft of which had been developed in the 18 months prior to the conference by the Preparatory Committee. A motion by China led to renewed discussion, tempered by concern that a text be agreed by the end of the conference; Maurice Strong argued that it would be one of the key measures of the success of Stockholm. The Chinese initially took an extreme view, arguing that the preamble should state that the environment was, in some places, endangered by "plunder, aggression and war by the colonialists, imperialists and neocolonialists", that overpopulation was caused by "plunder, aggression and war", and that "the notorious Malthusian theory is absurd in theory and groundless in fact" [50]. Towards the end of the discussions they suggested that all principles on which consensus had not been reached should be omitted. But when the Declaration came to a vote on the final day of the conference, the Chinese were the only delegation not to receive it with acclamation.

The United States delegation found itself in a curious position. One of the strongest advocates of the Stockholm conference from the outset, it opposed many of the principles or amendments proposed or supported by less developed countries, tried to weaken the proposed International Register of Potentially Toxic Chemicals, abstained from voting on a resolution condemning nuclear weapons tests (especially those in the atmosphere), and opposed the expansion of the proposed governing council of the new UN environmental programme. It was also consistently criticised – by, for example, Sweden, India, China, Iceland and Tanzania, and by activist American groups outside the conference hall – for the human and environmental costs of the war in Indochina. By contrast, the United States won popular acclaim for sponsoring a ten-year moratorium on commercial whaling, an issue that attracted wide attention among delegates, NGOs and the media.

A significant factor in the quality of Stockholm was the role of NGOs. More than 400 were officially represented, mainly international and MDC NGOs. The presence of many unaccredited groups had raised fears for security at the conference, but these were dispelled by the arrangements made for NGO involvement, which included an Environment Forum (Miljöforum), the official arena for accredited NGOs at Stockholm, sanctioned by the UN. The sceptics felt that rather than offering NGOs the opportunity to express their view, the Forum was designed to divert their attention away from the official conference, thereby minimising the attention drawn to controversial issues [51]. The Forum was handicapped by funding limitations and fears that it would either be too radical or too conservative, but it was nevertheless able to arrange a series of useful briefings and meetings, albeit away from the conference hall itself. *The Ecologist* and Friends of the Earth collaborated on the publication of *Stockholm Conference Eco*, a newsletter designed to provide a constructive appraisal of conference sessions. An alternative People's Forum (Folkets Forum) was set up on the initiative of PowWow, a group formed in Stockholm in 1971 which argued that the problems of the environment could not be solved by governments.

The more radical groups were concerned that the conference had no plans to deal with issues such as chemical and biological warfare, population, and the "ecocidal" activities of the United States in Indochina. Some felt that the conference was inadequate because government representatives would be bound to promote the vested interests of their governments, whether or not these interests coincided with those of improving the human environment as a whole [52]. Strict security over admission to the conference sessions initially caused some ill-feeling among NGOs, but Barbara Ward arranged briefing sessions, tickets, documents, and access to the conference for the groups [53].

Talbot recalls the excitement among NGOs and citizen groups, who believed that they were finally attracting the attention of governments. But, he notes, it was clear to most in the government delegations that the NGO activities were "separate from and had little discernible effect on 'the real action'", and that there was subsequently real disillusionment on the part of many NGOs as they came to realise how little a role they actually played [54]. NGOs initially played an active role in UNEP affairs, but financial constraints and a falling interest in the global solution ("or at least", argues Sandbrook, "a falling interest in UNEP providing one" [55]) had by 1980 resulted in diminishing NGO attendance at the annual UNEP Governing Councils. In

1974, more than 150 NGOs had registered to attend the Governing Council; by 1980 the number had fallen to less than 20. At the 1980 Governing Council, Sandbrook found very little evidence of governments from any region having consulted with NGOs about their position before attending the Council; many complained that the interest was not there even when sought. The most consistent link between UNEP and NGOs has remained the Environment Liaison Centre (ELC), a coalition NGO which regularly provides information and material on UNEP activities to more than 3000 NGOs.

In spite of the limited NGO role in UN affairs, the post-Stockholm era saw renewed growth in the formation of new NGOs. By 1982, the ELC estimated that there were 2230 environmental NGOs in less developed countries, of which 60 percent had been formed since Stockholm, and 13 000 in more developed countries, of which 30 percent had been formed since Stockholm [56]. New forms of NGO had also emerged. Noting that pressure groups in Western liberal democracies play a complementary role to government institutions, helping keep governments informed, responsive and in check, Lowe and Goyder argue that it is logical to assume that as governments agree to form levels of decision-making higher than those within the nation state, non-governmental groups would similarly regroup to meet the new level [57].

This would appear to be the case with the European Environmental Bureau (EEB), the origins of which can be traced directly to Stockholm. The conference not only put national NGOs in touch with one another, but emphasised that they faced common problems demanding a concerted response. The first suggestion for an umbrella group for European NGOs came from Julian Lessey of the Conservation Society in Britain. At a meeting in Brighton in 1974 between 20 representatives of groups from Western Europe and North America, including IIED and the Sierra Club, it was agreed that the European Community was "progressively becoming more important for environmental matters" [58], and that closer cooperation was needed between Community NGOs. The EEB was created in December 1974 to offer those NGOs a channel of access to the European Community, whose first Environmental Action Plan had been published in 1973. The creation of the EEB suggested that after many previous false starts, when international NGOs had lacked authorities which they might lobby, the creation of international governmental organisations had given international NGOs contextual relevance and permanence [59].

Despite the sceptics, there was optimistic expectation among many of the participants at Stockholm that the conference offered a real opportunity to begin dealing with the dangers of environmental degradation. Under these circumstances, Holdgate argues, it was inevitable that "some of the euphoria . . . would not survive the harsh reality of making the action plan work" [60]. Within a year of the conference, the energy crisis of 1973–74 had altered the international economic climate. Declining economic growth rates and political instability further diverted interest away from the environment, which was widely regarded as a long-term concern. Much of the optimism and euphoria of Stockholm was based on political naivety, but Ward notes that high expectations were a characteristic of many conferences, where the build-up of interest and excitement tended to overwhelm participants with their own importance. Yet, she felt, the creation of a new UN body and of a focus-point where interests could be expressed, and the dissipation of LDC unease, were major achievements [61].

Stockholm was largely agreed on both the problems and the solutions, but, Ward noted, the "action [of governments] rarely matched their promises. For an increasing number of environmental issues the difficulty is not to identify the remedy, because the remedy is now well understood. The problems are rooted in the society and the economy – and in the end in the political structure" [62]. The true significance of Stockholm was that it was part of a process which brought the environment to the attention of governments, encouraged subsequent international agreements and conventions on key environmental issues, and resulted in the creation of the United Nations Environment Programme [63]. As Holdgate et al. observe, the Stockholm conference was "a focus for, rather than the start of, action on environmental problems" [64]. Barbara Ward argued that people found it very much easier to identify needed changes than to actually begin implementing them. The difficulties were heightened if, in addition to identifying a new approach, the new approaches had to be linked with new institutions, methodologies and perceptions [65].

Declaration, Principles and Action Plan

The Stockholm conference produced a Declaration, a list of Principles, and an Action Plan. The Declaration was not intended to make legally binding provisions, but to be "inspirational", to put on record the essential arguments of environmentalism, and to act as a preface to the Principles, outlining broad goals and objectives. It was remarkable that so many countries – with such different political, economic and social systems – should have been able to agree such a broad-ranging and philosophical exercise. The Declaration did not attempt to define the term "human environment", partly because it was felt that it would be difficult at that stage to achieve a definition that was not unduly restrictive.

The 26 Principles can be broken down into five main groups. These stated that:

1) Natural resources should be conserved, the earth's capacity to produce renewable resources should be maintained, and non-renewable resources should be shared.
2) Development and environmental concern should go together, and less developed countries should be given every assistance and incentive to promote rational environmental management. (This group was designed to reassure LDCs.)
3) Each state should establish its own standards of environmental management and exploit resources as it wished, but should not endanger other states. There should be international cooperation aimed at improving the state of the environment.
4) Pollution should not exceed the capacity of the environment to clean itself, and marine pollution should be prevented.
5) Science, technology, education and research should all be used to promote environmental protection.

There were only minor disagreements on most Principles; the one exception was the Principle concerning the provision of information on national activities which might have adverse consequences beyond their borders. The UN General Assembly discussed the issue and concluded that information exchange should not be seen as enabling one state to interfere with the development of natural resources in another. Principles 21 and 22 ultimately recommended that states had the right to exploit their own resources and the responsibility to ensure that they did not cause damage to other states, and that states should cooperate to develop international law on liability and compensation [66]. Principle 11 argued that the environmental policies of all states "should enhance and not adversely affect the present or future development potential of developing countries". Landsberg notes that the breadth of the agenda and the cumbersome nature of the processes that were involved in discussing and agreeing recommendations posed potential threats to the success of the conference [67]. But a frenetic pace of discussion and amendment was maintained throughout, and the final business was compressed into the last three days. This gave the proceedings a sense of urgency which may have discouraged delays.

Sandbrook has summarised the general intent of the Action Plan as launching "a set of internationally coordinated activities aimed first at increasing knowledge of environmental trends and their effects on man and resources, and secondly, at protecting and improving the quality of the environment and the productivity of resources by integrated planning and management" [68]. The Action Plan consisted of 109 separate recommendations, ranging from the specific to the general, and falling into one of three broad groups: environmental assessment, environmental management, and supporting measures. Almost half dealt with the conservation of natural resources, while the rest covered issues relating to human settlements, pollution and marine pollution, development and the environment, and education and information.

The legacy of Stockholm

The Stockholm conference was the single most influential event in the evolution of the global environmental movement, and of a global environmental consciousness. It had four major results.

First, the conference confirmed the trend towards a new emphasis on the *human* environment. "Before Stockholm", Barbara Ward observed, "people usually saw the environment . . . as something totally divorced from humanity . . . Stockholm recorded a fundamental shift in the emphasis of our environmental thinking" [69]. Thinking had progressed from the limited aims of nature protection and natural resource conservation to the more comprehensive view of human mismanagement of the biosphere. The nature of environmentalism itself changed – from the popular, intuitive and parochial form which had emerged in MDCs in the late 1960s, to a form that was more rational and global in outlook, and which placed emphasis on working towards a full understanding of the problems and agreeing effective legislative action. New Environmentalism was transformed into terms that encouraged more governments to develop national policies on the environment.

Second, Stockholm forced a compromise between the different perceptions of the environment held by MDCs and LDCs. This is somewhat ironical, because the conference was initially a product of concern in industrialised countries in the 1960s. But the conference organisers were never allowed to let the conference concentrate solely on MDC interests. During the early UN debates on the conference, LDCs used their UN General Assembly voting power to encourage MDCs to recognise the need to balance environmental management priorities with the aims of economic development. MDCs were at least encouraged to begin to reinterpret the priorities of environmentalism, to take a broader view of the global interrelatedness of many problems, and to begin to understand how many of these problems were rooted in social and political problems, particularly in LDCs. Under any circumstances, it was perhaps inevitable that many of Stockholm's recommendations would be compromises; the concerns of the LDCs injected a much-needed note of realism into the proceedings of the conference itself, and led ultimately to a much wider view being taken of the roots and causes of the environmental crisis. Before Stockholm, environmental priorities had been determined largely by more developed countries; following Stockholm, the needs of less developed countries became a key factor in determining international policy.

Third, the presence of so many NGOs at the conference – and the part they played – marked the beginning of a new and more insistent role for NGOs in the work of governments and inter-governmental organisations. The NGOs had little influence at the conference itself, and have not always since achieved as much influence at UN meetings as they might have, but there was a rapid growth in the number and quality of NGOs in the post-Stockholm decade. The conference not only put national NGOs in contact with one another, but emphasised that they faced common problems demanding a concerted response.

Finally, the most tangible outcome of Stockholm was the creation of the United Nations Environment Programme. It had limitations and deficiencies, but it was probably the best form of institution possible under the circumstances, and it became the focus of a new interest in global responses to global problems.

6

The United Nations Environment Programme (1972–1992)

For all their merits and for all the significance attached to the process of simply reaching agreement on their content, the Stockholm agreements would remain paper exercises until they had some practical result. Their true effectiveness would depend on the institutional arrangements made for turning principles into actions. Against the background of concerns raised by UN specialised agencies and of recommendations submitted by national governments, the decision was made to leave the institutional arrangements to the conference itself.

The arrangement eventually confirmed by the UN General Assembly in December 1972 was not for the creation of a new specialised agency, but of a cross-cutting policy coordination body; the United Nations Environment Programme (UNEP) [1]. This was created as recognition that "environmental problems of broad international significance" fell within the province and competence of the UN network. The headquarters of every existing UN specialised agency were in North America or Europe, so when it came to the question of a secretariat for the new body, there was a campaign to have it set up in a less developed country [2]. Several MDCs argued that, given UNEP's coordinating role, it should be sited closer to the existing UN agencies [3]; despite this, the LDC option prevailed, and UNEP was located in Nairobi, Kenya. It was hoped that this would further appease those in the LDCs who doubted the benefits of environmental planning. Liaison offices were also set up in New York and Geneva, and regional offices in Bangkok, Beirut, Mexico City and Nairobi. Maurice Strong was appointed first Executive Director of UNEP.

Implementing the Action Plan

The new organisation had four parts: a Governing Council for environmental programmes; a small Secretariat that would be the "focal point for environmental action and coordination within the UN system"; a voluntary Environment Fund to which governments could contribute; and an Environment Co-ordination Board made up of members of all relevant UN bodies. The Governing Council would meet annually, promote international environmental cooperation, provide "general policy guidance for the direction and coordination of environmental programmes within the United Nations system" [4], and ensure that governments gave emerging international environmental problems appropriate attention.

The blueprint for UNEP was the Stockholm Action Plan, which was to be implemented in three ways: environmental assessment, environmental management, and supporting measures.

Global environmental assessment

This materialised in the form of Earthwatch, a UN-sponsored network of channels of information designed to research, monitor and evaluate environmental processes and trends, provide early warning of environmental hazards, and determine the status of selected natural resources.

Earthwatch in turn had three disparate components. The first was the International Referral System (INFOTERRA), a decentralised "switchboard" for the exchange of information. Environmental surveys were to be put into effect by the second component, the

Global Environment Monitoring System (GEMS). This would collect information from governments and build a picture of regional and global environmental trends. The third component was the International Register of Potentially Toxic Chemicals (IRPTC), which became operational in 1976. Based in Geneva, it was to build up a databank on potentially toxic chemicals for the use of governments; they would be notified of any changes and advised on appropriate action. IRPTC was an ambitious exercise; to make it worthwhile, a great deal of time had to be taken to keep up the quality of its data [5]. The siting of the Register in Geneva however, along with the Regional Seas Programme (see below), gave it better access to other UN agencies and greater freedom from the bureaucracy of the UNEP headquarters [6]. A fourth component – the Global Resource Information Database (GRID) – was added in 1985 to computer-generate environmental data for use by planners.

Earthwatch had broad and often sweeping goals. Its credibility was most obviously undermined by the lack of an adequate organisational structure and adequate funding [7]. The head of Earthwatch had a coordinating rather than an executive role; the programme began with only two or three professional staff; much of the money allocated to Earthwatch was spent on individual programmes rather than on Earthwatch per se; the programme structure of UNEP did not relate sufficiently to Earthwatch; and few governments even seemed to be aware that Earthwatch existed. It was supposed to be an activity of all relevant UN agencies, coordinated by UNEP, but its lack of personnel and money meant that there was virtually no environmental assessment activity within the UN, and the work undertaken by the individual agencies was not properly coordinated or evaluated [8]. An independent assessment of INFOTERRA in 1980 concluded that it had fulfilled the mandate outlined at Stockholm, but that it was under-used [9]. The position had improved by 1992, however, by which time it was receiving nearly 22 000 queries each year and had become the world's biggest environmental information system.

GEMS early faced three major problems: the lack of evaluation and assessment within Earthwatch as a whole, reliance on the cooperation and work of others, and a general pessimism about the value of global monitoring [10]. Many of the monitoring systems set up after Stockholm did not live up to expectations, largely because of a lack of clearly defined objectives. Such monitoring as had existed before Stockholm tended to concentrate on pollution. The World Meteorological Organisation was supposed to provide a foundation for GEMS by setting up a network of ten baseline atmospheric stations in remote areas, and 100 regional stations removed from centres of major environmental contamination. But in the first five years of GEMS, only 12 air monitoring stations were established, giving some indication of the size of the undertaking.

Within two years of its creation, the GEMS agenda had broadened to become a system that would give warning of threats to human health and impending natural disasters, a concept so broad that as late as 1977 most of GEMS was still in the design phase. At the 1979 UNEP Governing Council, several governments expressed concern about the apparent lack of progress in Earthwatch, which led to a hasty meeting of experts to review developments. Their resulting report [11] was descriptive rather than critical, but did suggest that one of the major limits on environmental assessment was the variable quality, comparability, timeliness and representativeness of data. This, UNEP argued, together with the minimal resources given to Earthwatch, explained why there had been so few comprehensive assessments [12].

Environmental management

The information gathered by Earthwatch was supposed to help with the implementation of the second part of the Action Plan, environmental management. The aim here was to develop a comprehensive planning structure that would support environmental protection. Treaties would be drawn up, action would be taken to preserve biological diversity and genetic resources, and a number of specific goals – including a moratorium on commercial whaling – would be promoted.

This was generally a workable plan with identifiable goals, but progress was uneven. UNEP felt that many governments lacked the political will to take the advice of their own experts, and that some of the Stockholm recommendations touched on delicate issues relating to state sovereignty and economic development [13]. UNEP did, however, work with other UN agencies, IGOs and NGOs in drafting and agreeing new international treaties, notably the Convention on International Trade in Endangered Species (CITES), the Bonn Convention on migratory species, and the Convention for the Protection of the Mediterranean Sea against Pollution (Barcelona, 1976). A moratorium on whaling was agreed in 1982 and went into effect in 1986, but was not enough to stop "scientific" whaling by countries such as Japan, Iceland and Norway. On development aid, UNEP helped encourage bilateral and multilateral aid agencies to make environmental assessment part of their agendas (see Chapter 8).

Supporting measures

These included education, manpower training, public information, and financial assistance. In 1975 a joint UNEP/UNESCO Environmental Education Programme was created, and in 1977 the UNEP/UNESCO Inter-governmental Conference on Environmental Education was held in Tbilisi, USSR; both events resulted in a series of training workshops and seminars, the creation of an information network, and the training of environmental specialists. But education was ultimately a national issue, and the work of UN specialised agencies was to be less significant than the work of national NGOs.

In Britain, the United States, and other MDCs, education had long been an important element in the work of NGOs, and this continued during the 1970s and 1980s. On public information, UNEP was less than successful. In 1972 it established 5 June as World Environment Day, but this had little effect; outside environmental NGOs, almost no-one knew it existed. To complicate matters, UNEP was unable to decide between running its own modest information programme, and devolving responsibility to outside agencies. In 1975 it provided the funding to set up Earthscan, a news and information service within IIED, which went on to produce a substantial body of information for media and NGOs. By 1986, when most of Earthscan's staff left to form The Panos Institute, its networks included media, journalists and NGOs in 130 countries. It worked closely with UNEP, but the proportion of funding it received from UNEP steadily fell.

UNEP: The first 20 years

UNEP experienced mixed fortunes in its first two decades. Its prospects were made no easier by the fact that it had one of the most difficult jobs in the entire UN system [14]. It was not designed as an executive body with the same kinds of powers as FAO or UNESCO, but had instead to coordinate the work of some UN agencies, promote policy initiatives with others, and provide information to others. It had a huge constituency (effectively the entire natural environment) and limited finances. It had to involve itself in many different activities, and often had to take action based more on opportunity than on any carefully considered long-term plans. It had no power to interfere in the domestic affairs of countries, and so had little chance of encouraging national governments to agree regional environmental policies. Broadly speaking, its problems fell into four main categories: financial, managerial, political and constitutional.

Money has been a continuing problem. UNEP made a promising start, with $60 million pledged to the Environment Fund in just six months (the target was $100 million in five years). Governments (a total of 96 in 1983 had fallen to 81 by 1989) made a voluntary contribution to the Environment Fund. During UNEP's first eight years, the United States contributed $40 million (36 percent of the Fund), while 64 countries (such as Zambia, Jordan and Paraguay) made no contributions at all between 1978 and 1981. (The United States continues to be the major source of UNEP funding, and the strongest influence on the decisions of both the Secretariat and the Governing Council [15].) In its first five years, UNEP planned to raise $20 million per year, a target that it very nearly achieved. In the period 1978–81 it raised about $31 million per year (as against a planned $37.5 million per year).

The target for the period 1982–83 was $60 million per year, but funding targets proved increasingly unrealistic and elusive, and

UNEP had to settle for an average annual income of $30 million in 1979–87. Set against inflation, this was worth less and less. The complications of shortfalls in income were aggravated by contributions arriving late, or at the end of the financial year, or in non-convertible currency (currency that could only be spent in the donor country). All these problems made planning difficult. Nearly 23 percent of UNEP's spending in 1989 went to other UN agencies, while 51.1 percent went to other institutions, and 26.3 percent to projects directly implemented by UNEP [16].

UNEP's second major handicap was its own management. It was accused by its critics of having a blinkered view of global problems, of being inefficient, of failing to outline its priorities, of being too centralised in the person of the executive director, and of biting off more than it could chew. The fault was seen to lie partly in UNEP's own management policies and partly in the limitations inherent in UNEP's constituency. Maurice Strong, despite his role in Stockholm and in the foundation of UNEP, was new to environmental matters, so when he became first executive director, he appointed senior staff from the areas he knew best: business, politics and international public service [17]. The long-term result was that UNEP suffered management systems based on bureaucratic procedures rather than on professional approaches to the problems of the environment.

There has been little improvement during the tenure of Strong's successor, Egyptian microbiologist Dr Mostafa Tolba, who has often taken a hands-on approach to UNEP's work. By 1980, personnel issues had reached such a low ebb that the permanent representatives to UNEP of the European Community countries compiled a report outlining what they saw as the key problems: autocratic management with no delegation of authority, and all decisions, no matter how small, taken by the executive director; low staff morale and high turnover (one in three staff positions was vacant in 1980, and about one in five in 1989); and the unhealthy state of the Environment Fund, caused by dissatisfaction with the performance of UNEP and Dr Tolba [18]. (An unsuccessful attempt was made in 1980 to replace Tolba at the end of his first term in office with the Ghanaian scientist Dr Ernest Boateng; Tolba began his fifth four-year term in office in 1992.)

Staff numbers were by no means large; in 1975, UNEP employed 99 staff (85 in the headquarters and 14 in regional offices) on an annual budget of $30 million. By 1980 it had 180 professional staff positions, and by 1989 it had 274 – but all on roughly the same budget. The impermanence of its headquarters arrangements and the postponement in 1980 of new building plans made the management problems no easier. Only in 1983 – after being based temporarily in several different offices – did UNEP finally move into permanent office buildings on the outskirts of Nairobi.

The third source of problems was UNEP's location in Nairobi. It helped redress the imbalance in the location of UN agency headquarters, and it probably helped broaden the minds of European and North American environmentalists by drawing attention to the problems of LDCs. But it has also tended to isolate UNEP from the industrialised countries where many of the key decisions affecting the global environment are taken. UNEP itself felt that the location made it difficult to recruit highly qualified staff, and made it necessary for UNEP to create a new infrastructure from very little; if it had been located within an existing UN agency, it would have been able to draw from a common pool and direct more of its resources at substantive action [19].

The location in Kenya also tended to leave UNEP divided between MDCs, which supported an emphasis on global problems such as pollution, and LDCs, which adopted UNEP as their own UN "agency", wanted emphasis given to environmentally sound development, and hoped that UNEP would be sympathetic to the needs of LDCs in any conflict of interest with MDCs. This reached a point where the Governing Council was accused of rejecting project suggestions from the Secretariat because they were not sufficiently LDC-oriented [20]. By the late 1980s, several LDCs had begun to criticise Tolba for focusing too much on issues such as climate change and ozone depletion, and wanted him to focus on issues of more direct relevance to LDCs, such as air and water quality. In 1990 the LDC-dominated UN General Assembly took negotiations on climate change out of the hands of UNEP and the WMO, and put them in the hands of a new ad hoc body over which it had more control [21].

The fourth source of problems was constitutional. From the outset, UNEP headquarters was divided between the Programme proper and the Fund. The former was responsible for devising programmes, which may or may not have been put into effect in the form of projects. The latter was responsible for managing finances for these projects. This division demanded that all UNEP activities be approved by both the Fund and the Programme, and involved staff from both sides in formulation and execution. The division between the Secretariat and the Governing Council caused additional problems. The Council was drawn from 58 member governments, representatives of which were voted onto the Council for three-year terms by the UN General Assembly. The Council met annually for two weeks to discuss and decide overall policy. It was supposed to promote international environmental cooperation, guide policy and review progress in UN agencies, draw the attention of governments to emerging global environmental problems, ensure that development in LDCs was not handicapped by environmental management policies, and manage the Environment Fund.

Critics charged that the Council was successful in the last of these responsibilities, but not in the others. It was often accused of being too cumbersome and too obsessed with procedure, in common with the rest of the UN system. Martin Holdgate, President of the 1984 UNEP Governing Council, was concerned that procedural matters had come to take up so much time that they tended to obscure UNEP's real goal of addressing global environmental needs, and that too much time was spent by the Plenary Session on discussions "that were unlikely to help resolve these appalling problems" [22].

The most critical constitutional problem lay in the nature of UNEP's relationship with other UN agencies. Lacking executive powers, it had little scope for carrying out its own projects, and had instead to work through the other UN specialised agencies. Its job of persuading other agencies to execute programmes was hampered by the fact that it had few incentives to offer and no powers of enforcement [23]. Furthermore, some of UNEP's slow progress reflected the fact that the environment had proved more complex, and more costly to monitor, than Stockholm delegates realised [24]. The Action Plan was widely regarded as too broad, too vague about priorities, and – above all – too lacking in means of implementation. The job of assessing UNEP's effectiveness was complicated by the difficulty of assessing its precise role in a given project. Unlike WHO or FAO, observed Dr Tolba, UNEP could not "say at the end of the day [that it had] eradicated a disease here or planted so many thousand hectares of rice fields there" [25].

In 1976, the UN General Assembly reviewed its institutional arrangements for the environment and concluded that they were adequate. But UNEP itself admitted their shortcomings [26]. The incompatibility between the desire for a small secretariat and the need to maintain the wider-ranging aims of the programme was a problem that had still not been resolved as late as 1982. Perhaps the most fundamental problem of all was that UNEP's role was consistently and widely misunderstood [27]. UNEP was never intended to be a full UN specialised agency, but simply the environmental programme of the UN system. It was designed to be able to take a comprehensive view of the global environment and to develop an environmental programme that could be carried out by all relevant agencies – its role was catalytic.

As Holdgate observes, existing UN agencies – notably FAO, WHO, WMO and the World Bank – were already addressing environmental questions (as they had been at pains to emphasise before Stockholm) and the environment could not be isolated, but instead needed a coordinated approach [28]. Well-established and powerful organisations were bound to be doubtful about any outside attempts to coordinate their work; Maurice Strong and the UNEP Council responded by developing a series of activities that met a real need and did not conflict with those of the established bodies [29]. The first three of these – GEMS, INFOTERRA and marine pollution – were agreed before Stockholm. As its own activities evolved, so UNEP's credibility and capacity to do the job of coordination and compilation of a truly system-wide programme increased [30].

UNEP's relations with other UN agencies were a key determinant of its influence. In its first few years, these relations were poor, for three main reasons. First, the novelty of the situation made existing UN agencies distrustful of UNEP. Second, UNEP – disregarding its limited powers – tended to try to influence the activities of other agencies more than its constitution allowed. Tolba was not discouraged by the complaints this attracted: "We will never stop interfering in everyone else's business", he argued, "as long as it involves the environment. That is our mandate" [31]. Third, the Environment Co-ordination Board (ECB) – through which UNEP was supposed to coordinate and influence the activities of other UN agencies, and through which those agencies could influence UNEP – was not up to the task. The ECB concluded in 1976 that the cycle of its meetings needed to be planned to allow prompt responses to Governing Council decisions, that the concept of joint programming needed more work (involving all agencies concerned), and that there needed to be more multi-agency programming rather than bilateral discussions between UNEP and the other agencies [32]. The joint programming that had taken place by February 1976 amounted to a series of meetings between UNEP and other UN agencies which really did no more than identify areas of common interest and agree ways of keeping each other informed.

At the 1977 UNEP Governing Council, the ECB was charged with drawing up Memoranda of Understanding with other specialised agencies [33], which it subsequently did, without success. In 1982, the System-Wide Medium-Term Environmental Programme (SWMTEP) was introduced to define exactly what each UN agency would do in the period 1984–89. Most of the descriptions of action to be taken by each agency were bland and generalised; SWMTEP outlined areas of interest but spoke only in broad terms of appropriate action [34]. It was so broad that nearly every initiative on the environment could be fitted into one or another of its proposals; rather than allowing UNEP to do a few things well, it ran the danger of further diluting the UNEP agenda. Yet ten years after Stockholm, UNEP confidently believed that its relations with other agencies had improved as the joint programming had grown [35]. A second SWMTEP was agreed in 1988 to cover the period 1990–95.

A UNEP success: The Regional Seas Programme

Often described as one of UNEP's major successes – if not its only real success in its first decade – was its Regional Seas Programme

(RSP), in which UNEP successfully brought nearly 140 countries and 14 UN agencies together to confront pollution and coastal degradation in shared seas. Stockholm ambitiously recommended action to end all significant marine pollution within three to four years, particularly in enclosed and semi-enclosed seas. The idea for the RSP was born at a June 1971 meeting of experts held in London in preparation for Stockholm. Reviewing the position of marine pollution, they concluded that a sea-by-sea approach to the problem was more realistic and attainable than a broad-ranging global programme [36]. (The principle of a regional approach to marine management was not new; the International Council for the Exploration of the Seas, for example, had been active in the North Atlantic and Baltic from 1902.)

The RSP was launched in 1974 with a strategy carefully designed to respect national sensitivities, particularly over data on pollution, and to leave the actual implementation of each regional plan firmly in the hands of the coastal states concerned. The RSP involved most of the major UN bodies, and illustrated exactly the kind of part-catalytic, part-executive role that UNEP could play [37]. Under the Programme, surveys of each region were carried out and a plan of action drafted. UNEP then arranged a meeting between relevant governments to have them agree an action plan. This was followed by monitoring and information exchange, with national institutions meeting to discuss action. UNEP acted as the initial catalyst, and as each programme grew, the states themselves took over funding and management, and national scientific bodies undertook monitoring and research, drawing on UN agencies for specialist advice. In this way an international body was bringing a number of nations together on a shared problem.

The model for the RSP was the Mediterranean Action Plan (MAP), adopted by 16 Mediterranean states in 1975. The first component of the Plan was the Barcelona Convention for the Protection of the Mediterranean Sea against Pollution, and two protocols (one to prevent dumping from ships and aircraft, the other to encourage emergency cooperation in the event of pollution by oil or other substances). The Convention was signed in 1976 and came into force in 1978. In 1980 a third protocol was added, concerned with pollution from land-based sources. The Convention and the protocols were agreements of honour – there were no means of enforcing them.

The second component of MAP was monitoring and research, carried out by the national laboratories of coastal states. The third component was environmental management, consisting of a long-term programme of study and research into development and environment (the Blue Plan) and a Priority Actions Programme concentrating on selected priority areas. The final component was the small secretariat set up to oversee the action plan. Using a similar blueprint, but allowing variations for specific needs, action plans were subsequently drawn up for ten regional seas, including the Red Sea (1976), the Kuwait region (1978), the West and Central African coastal seas, the Caribbean, the East Asian seas, the southeast Pacific seas (all 1981), and the southwest Pacific seas (1982).

Unfortunately, the Programme's success was limited by a number of problems, several of which were outlined in the UNEP-commissioned Portmann report of 1982 [38]:

1) Other UN agencies were reluctant fully to support the Programme.
2) Financial support, because it was voluntary, was unpredictable, which made UN agencies even less willing to become involved. UNEP spent $8 million on the Mediterranean Action Plan in its first five years; when the governments involved took over responsibility, they reduced the budget by a quarter. Three countries – France, Italy and Spain – between them subsequently supplied 80 percent of governmental contributions [39]. Late payments meant that funds for the Mediterranean almost dried up in 1981–82.
3) In many regions, the level of expertise and the facilities available for the implementation of the action plan were inadequate.
4) A clear deficiency affecting all regional plans was the scarcity of information on pollutants, and the limited amount of reliable data on pollution levels. As of 1985, there was only one completed report on the state of a regional marine environment: that for the Mediterranean. Although the Mediterranean Action Plan was well progressed, problems

with financing and disagreements over standards limited the improvement that actually occurred.

Despite these problems, the Regional Seas Programme is widely regarded as one of UNEP's major success stories. UNEP attributed the Programme's success to the fact that it was regional rather than global, involving nations in urgent common problems which could only be solved by mutual action [40]. As a regional endeavour it also had more easily manageable proportions and more easily achieved aims. Other problems (such as acid pollution or pollution of shared rivers) have been proven to be best tackled by countries bilaterally or regionally, or where there are identifiable shared interests, economic costs or political implications. By 1992, nearly 140 countries, 14 UN agencies and 12 other international organisations were involved – to varying degrees – in the RSP, which had produced eight international conventions and 18 protocols and agreements.

UNEP foiled: The problem of desertification

An indication of how more broad-ranging schemes can fail, even where national or regional provisions are included, lies in one of UNEP's major failures, and an area to which it devoted considerable time and resources: the campaign against desertification. "Desertification" describes human degradation of land that causes it to lose its fertility and its capacity to provide economic returns under cultivation or grazing [41]. Desertification does not imply the spread of natural deserts so much as the increased incidence of desert conditions in semi-desert areas.

One-third of the earth's land area is semi-desert, and supports more than 600 million people. About half this area – supporting 60 million people – was thought to be threatened by desertification in the 1980s [42]. According to the UN Desertification Map of the World, more than 40 percent of non-desert Africa was at risk of desertification; half the world's people most menaced by desertification live in the West African Sahel [43]. The causes are complex, but they include deforestation, overcultivation (brought on by a combination of increased food demand from growing populations and an increase in cash crop cultivation, and leading to declining soil fertility, wind and water erosion, sand dune encroachment and falling crop yields), overgrazing, and poorly designed and managed irrigation. The incidence of these phenomena in turn strikes at the heart of the resource management dilemma of many of the poorer LDCs.

Drought and famines are commonly perceived as acts of God; until perhaps 20–25 years ago, much of the literature on famine concentrated on the link between absolute food supply and starvation. Sen rejects this notion, observing that while famines involve often widespread acute starvation, not all groups in famine-affected areas go without [44]. They may lack purchasing power, political power or access to transport. Timberlake argues that while drought may be a natural precursor of famine (i.e. an act of God), the Sahelian famine of 1984–85 was a direct result of unsound economic, agricultural and environmental strategies (i.e. an act of humans). African peasants, in their efforts to survive, were compelled to draw increasingly upon their "capital stock" of forests, soils and rivers; this process "bankrupted" Africa's environment by undermining the ability of African nations to feed themselves [45].

The 1968–73 drought in the Sahel illustrated some of the dangers associated with the spread of human settlement into marginal arid lands. Drought in the area is not unusual (there were major droughts in 1910–14, 1927–30 and 1940–44 [46], and again in 1984–85), but the circumstances of the 1968–73 drought gave cause for particular concern. The ultimate cause, argues Murdoch, "was the destruction of a complex pattern of living arrangements that had previously allowed quite large numbers of people to live in a difficult environment" [47].

Over a period of centuries, Sahelian nomads had created an agricultural, economic and trading system designed to account precisely for the limitations of their environment. They raised mixed herds of camels, cattle, sheep and goats; they staggered breeding patterns in order to have milk throughout the year; they moved their herds according to the incidence of rain, moving them during dry seasons to areas of permanent vegetation; they kept larger herds than they immediately needed, thereby assuring food security in times of drought; they took to hunting and gathering in times of extreme drought; and they maintained complex trading patterns with the savanna regions to the south, ensuring a regular supply of grain.

Colonialism brought taxes and export demands, forcing peasants into cash crop production, undermining indigenous agricultural systems, reducing soil fertility, increasing soil erosion, and impoverishing peasants. Land was worked more intensively to make up for lost fertility, and peasants moved into marginal lands to produce food and cash crops (meanwhile reducing fallow periods). The changes this wrought in the economic and agricultural systems of the Sahel persisted, accounting in large part for the significantly decreased resistance to drought which made the famines of 1968–73 and 1984–86 so disastrous. Murdoch concludes that the poverty of the peasants was "a causal mechanism in the vicious circle of underdevelopment that has prevented the sustained growth of an integrated economy, which would in turn provide more income, greater employment, and more capital for investment". He further notes the effect of the collapse of traditional nomadic trading in destroying the long-term strategy of the nomads [48].

Years of good rain during the 1960s had encouraged the spread of rainfed cropping and livestock pasturing into marginal lands on the edges of the Sahara. When the rains failed in 1968, the herds of livestock were deprived of pasture (but not water) and began dying in large numbers. The rains failed again in 1970 and the harvest was quickly exhausted, leaving an estimated three million people in six countries in need of emergency food aid. By 1973, when the full extent of the drought became clear, it was estimated that between 100 000 and 250 000 people and 3.5 million head of cattle had died.

Under normal circumstances, nomadic pastoralism makes optimal use of drylands; moderate sustainable grazing can actually increase the productivity of pastures. But increases in the sizes of herds and decreases in the areas of pasture available to them led to overgrazing. In Niger, for example, between 1938 and 1961, the number of donkeys increased by 200 percent, sheep and goats by 300 percent, cattle by 480 percent, and camels by 700 percent [49]. The growing numbers of livestock were partly a function of human population growth. Herds are regarded as an insurance against dry years. During years of good rainfall, the numbers are allowed to increase. When drought first appears, however, herders are reluctant to reduce stock numbers, thereby placing greater pressure on drought-stressed pastures. Improved veterinary care has further increased stock numbers, and the policy of governments to encourage nomads to settle offers the land little relief from grazing. The building of wells has further tended to concentrate nomads, often attracting many more animals than the wells were designed to support, and intensifying the use of surrounding land.

The 1968–73 drought was one motive behind the convening of the 1977 UN Conference on Desertification (UNCOD), held in Nairobi. The goal was to provide a forum for the discussion of the problem, which was seen to be reaching crisis proportions, and to plan action. The convening of the conference implied clear recognition that desertification was a primary element in the reduction of Africa's ability to feed itself; it also succeeded in firmly establishing the role of human activity in desertification. The conference resulted in a Plan of Action to Combat Desertification (PACD), which recommended – among other things – national plans of action, improved livestock raising, the monitoring of desertification trends, transnational projects aimed at linking countries in integrated anti-desertification measures, and the creation of green belts to physically halt the spread of deserts. Emphasis too was placed on curbing population growth and learning to understand the social, economic and political factors associated with desertification. The UN Sudano-Sahelian Office (UNSO) was made responsible for coordinating follow-up action in the Sudano-Sahelian region, and UNEP for the rest of the world.

Tolba argued that there was general agreement that UNCOD was "one of the best scientifically prepared UN conferences of the 1970s" and that the recommendations, if effectively applied, "would have put the international community in a position to have halted desertification by the year 2000" [50]. As executive-director of UNEP, his assessment was obviously not disinterested, but there is much evidence to back up his conclusion. Unlike many other environmental problems, there was certainty about the causes and the necessary corrective action. But in May 1981, Tolba reported that progress on the implementation of the Plan of Action had been slow. A May 1984 meeting of the UNEP Governing Council confirmed that the objectives of the UNCOD Plan of Action were still sound and viable, but Tolba now admitted that the goal of stopping desertification by the end of the century had been unrealistic [51].

The meeting concluded that desertification had continued to extend and intensify, rates were unlikely to change in grasslands and irrigated lands, and would grow to critical proportions in rainfed croplands, and that the cost of losses in production due to desertification amounted to five times the estimated cost of halting desertification ($4.5 billion per year for 20 years). The countries worst affected were LDCs in tropical drylands, particularly those beset by low incomes, drought and political unrest. Continuing drought in the Sudano-Sahelian belt, and an economic recession which had cut the available funding, had not helped. Four-fifths of the investment in desertification-related projects had been in the form of "preparatory or supportive" action such as building roads, supplying drinking water, providing housing and extending irrigation. Only 20 percent of spending had been in the form of corrective action of the kind recommended by UNCOD. The transnational projects were stillborn, and little was done to monitor the situation or increase understanding of the process. Only 22 percent of all aid to the Sahel went into agriculture and about 1.4 percent into forestry. Few countries had agreed national plans of action or tried to assess the extent of desertification. Few corrective measures had involved the local community.

While the technical solutions to desertification were well known and understood, the economic, social and political means to apply them had not yet been found [52]. There were three levels of approach to the problem: national, regional and international. At the national level, the UNCOD Plan of Action had recommended that coordinating national machinery be established to combat desertification and draw up national plans of action. In all but three cases, responsibility had, in the event, been given to existing agencies.

In many cases, failure to establish national machinery reflected the low national priority given to combating desertification [53]. Tolba pointed out that this had been encouraged by the lack of political power among the rural poor most immediately affected. LDCs had also felt that there were more immediate short-term problems that needed to be addressed, and were reluctant to plan for the long term. As for MDCs, aid agencies consistently preferred to finance visible "showcase" projects such as dams, roads and factories, which used experts and equipment from donor nations, creating jobs and profits in those nations. Rural projects were harder to identify, plan and implement, and less visible [54]. There was also a prevailing lack of awareness in MDCs – many of them far removed from the immediate causes and effects – about the extent of the problem.

At the regional level, four UN regional commissions organised meetings and began collecting data, but none drew up regional plans of action. UNEP blamed the failure on civil strife and warfare, strained political relations between the countries involved, and a lack of money, rather than on the inadequacy of regional machinery [55]. One of the most effective regional agencies was UNSO, which helped produce a strategy on desertification for the Sudano-Sahelian region, raised $40 million in 1978–83 for anti-desertification programmes in the 19 countries it served, and helped establish two regional study centres. But it also had its problems. One criticism was that the office, based in New York, had more experience of technical assistance than of desertification problems, and might have classified a project as "anti-desertification" only because it was politically expedient so to do [56].

At the international level, all UN agencies were encouraged to support anti-desertification activities, and two ad hoc agencies were set up to encourage this: the Desertification Branch of UNEP, and the Inter-Agency Working Group on Desertification (IAWGD). UNEP believed that this system had "generally operated effectively" [57], but financial constraints meant that the Desertification Branch had not had its full complement of pro-fessional staff, leaving it little opportunity to function effectively. "It is the key UN desertification unit", concluded UNEP, "and yet to date it has never had the resources to fulfil its functions" [58].

IAWGD by contrast, was moderately successful in bringing UN agency representatives together to coordinate research, training and information exchange within the UN.

Of all the obstacles to progress, none was more serious than the sheer lack of money. At UNCOD, Tolba had said that $2.4 billion would need to be spent annually for 20 years to halt desertification in the South. A Special Account was set up within the United Nations to finance anti-desertification projects, but between 1977 and 1984 it attracted a paltry $48 524. The Consultative Group for Desertification Control (DESCON) – a hybrid of representatives from UN agencies and aid agencies – was set up to identify sources of finance and priority projects, and bring the two together. In 1978–83 it reviewed 48 projects, arranging full finance for 12 and partial finance for seven. The amount actually secured by DESCON was $26 million, or about a quarter of the total needed.

UNEP believed that both MDCs and LDCs alike had been confused about DESCON's aims, and had not fully used its services. UNEP offered two explanations for the parlous financial situation: LDCs suffering from desertification had seemed unable (or perhaps unwilling) to give priority to anti-desertification measures, and activities to combat desertification were generally not competitive in terms of short-term economic cost-benefit ratios. Mohammed Kassas, president of IUCN and an authority on drylands, pointed out, for example, that Egypt spent $13 800 per hectare reclaiming desert land. Invested in a bank, this sum could earn $1700 a year in interest, far more than the land could return [59].

In 1982, Grainger warned that ten years after the climax of the 1968–73 Sahelian drought, the Sahel was moving steadily towards another disaster; experts disagreed whether the next crisis was just around the corner or some years away, but past experience dictated that it must come [60]. Despite the urgent need to increase food production, less than a quarter of aid to the region had been invested in agricultural development. Population in the Sahel was growing at 2.5 percent annually, crop yields were falling (rainfed cereal production was down to 75 percent of its 1968 level), and many countries had come to rely on food aid (much of which reached only the towns). Drought did indeed return to sub-Saharan Africa, and famine followed.

In May 1984, a group of 25 journalists visited Ethiopia, under the aegis of the environmental information service Earthscan, to be shown the effects of desertification. It was immediately apparent that Ethiopia was already in the early stages of a major famine. All 25 journalists filed stories to their newspapers and journals, reporting that five million people faced starvation, but there was little interest and few were printed. In October 1984, a BBC television crew filmed a report on refugee camps in rural Ethiopia. The screening of the film resulted over the next 18 months in a worldwide public awareness and fund-raising campaign of unprecedented proportions.

British rock artists led by Bob Geldof and Midge Ure formed Band Aid, and in November recorded a best-selling single – "Do They Know It's Christmas" – to raise funds for famine relief. They were followed by an American counterpart – USA for Africa with "We Are the World" – and simultaneous Live Aid concerts in Britain and the United States. By 1986, a total of $150 million had been raised by Band Aid and Live Aid, and $51 million by USA for Africa [61]. By 1984–85, famine afflicted 20 countries (the Sudan, Ethiopia, Niger, Mozambique, Somalia, Chad and Mali were the worst affected). An estimated one million people died from malnutrition and related diseases, ten million were forced to abandon their homes and lands in search of food, water and pasture, and 30 million in 20 countries had insufficient food on which to live.

Very little of the media publicity given to the famine in the West talked about environmental degradation as a root cause. Yet the famine/drought led to the realisation among government officials, aid agencies and development planners that African development policies over the preceding 20 years had failed. In 1984, the normally cautious World Bank concluded that "the economic and social transformation of Africa, begun so eagerly and effectively in the early years of independence, could be halted or reversed" unless development policies changed [62]. Timberlake observes that the famine had the positive effect of starting "a painful reappraisal among those responsible for Africa's 'development', and brought a new willingness to admit mistakes" [63]. The causes of the famine vindicated many of the warnings made before, during and since Stockholm about the nature of the relationship between development planning and environmental management.

UNEP: A mixed record of achievement

UNEP was the most tangible result of the Stockholm conference. Although imperfect and, two decades later, still insufficient in many ways, it was probably the best form of institution possible given the limitations imposed by other UN specialised agencies, the low level of funding from governments, and the nature of international relations. But it had severe obstacles placed in its path from the outset. It had too little money, too few staff, and too much to do, it had the thankless task of coordinating the work of other UN agencies against a background of inter-agency jealousy and suspicion, and national governments were unwilling to grant UNEP significant powers. Ten years after Stockholm, UNEP itself could claim only "a mixed record of achievement . . . [with] fair-to-good progress . . . in implementing some of the elements of the Action Plan . . . [while] for other elements, progress has been very slow" [64]. By 1989, Mostafa Tolba was lamenting the gap between political word and deed, and could only conclude that while the world was no cleaner or healthier than it had been in 1972, it was not as bad as it might have been without UNEP's efforts [65].

Apart from the Regional Seas Programme, UNEP's most notable success was its involvement in promoting agreement on the 1985 Vienna Convention for Protection of the Ozone Layer and the 1987 Montreal protocol limiting the production and consumption of CFCs and halons (see Chapter 10). The UNEP-sponsored Coordinating Committee on the Ozone Layer meanwhile helped build consensus on the dimensions of the threat to the ozone layer. UNEP also helped promote research on global climate change through the UNEP/WMO Inter-governmental Panel on Climate Change (created in 1988) and the 1990 Second World Climate Conference, and played a key role in negotiations leading to the 1992 Framework Convention on Climate Change (see Chapter 11). It also helped develop the Tropical Forest Action Plan and create the International Tropical Timber Organisation, supported research on plant genetic resources (see Chapter 10), provided the secretariat for CITES and the Migratory Species Convention, helped draw up the 1989 Transboundary Hazardous Waste Convention and the 1992 Convention on Biological Diversity, and was responsible for planning and organising the 1992 Rio summit (see Chapter 11). Through GEMS, UNEP also promoted the development of monitoring programmes, and through IRPTC it made a start on coordinating data on toxic chemicals.

But the failures have outnumbered the successes. At its 1977 session, the UNEP Governing Council set out 21 specific goals to be met by 1982. In 1982, the Sierra Club and the Agesta Group of Sweden made separate assessments of progress; the results are compared in Table 6.1. The Governing Council reviewed progress in 1982, and by 1989 had agreed to focus on more specific issues, listing eight areas of concentration (including regional seas and desertification).

UNEP itself believed that it would never have been possible to set out immediately to implement the recommendations of the Stockholm Action Plan for three reasons: the small secretariat and limited funding, the immensity of its task, and the nature of the recommendations themselves, which varied from the specific (in terms of goals and necessary actions) to the general (in terms of necessary action rather than goals) [66]. Under the circumstances, it can be credited with having achieved more than it was in reality empowered to do; a distinction must be made between what UNEP actually *could* do and what outsiders felt it *should* do.

On balance, Tolba believed that UNEP's most important overall achievement was to raise the general level of environmental awareness in decision-making circles [67]. UNEP could claim to have helped draw the attention of governments both to their own national environmental problems and to shared global problems. But its principal handicaps remain: it is rarely in a position to back up its warnings and advice with either money or technical

Table 6.1 The performance of UNEP, 1972–1982

	Sierra Club	Agesta Group
Good progress	Regional Seas conservation conventions/protocols INFOTERRA global monitoring	Regional Seas conservation conventions/protocols periodic reports
Fair progress	IRPTC microbiology rural technology industries inter-state relations education periodic reports	IRPTC microbiology rural technology industries inter-state relations global monitoring INFOTERRA
Limited progress	advice to governments development planning communications desertification	advice to governments development planning communications education
Slow progress	health disaster warning system technical assistance management	health disaster warning system technical assistance management desertification

Sources: Robinson, Nicholas A, Prepared statement before the Subcommittee on Human Rights and International Organizations, Committee on Foreign Affairs, US House of Representatives, 20 April 1982; The Agesta Group, *Twenty Years After Stockholm: Summary of Comments Received* (Farsta, Sweden: Agesta Gammelgard, April 1982)

assistance, and it is less an executive agency than a coordinating programme; hence its successes and failures will continue to depend on its abilities to encourage governments and other agencies to take action.

7

The North: Politics and Activism (1970–1986)

As the following for New Environmentalism intensified, public concerns were increasingly reflected in changes in public policy at the national level. In 1956–60, only four major pieces of national environmental legislation were passed in OECD member states; by contrast, ten were passed in 1961–65, 18 in 1966–70, and 31 in 1971–75 [1]. As of August 1971, 12 countries (Australia, Britain, Canada, France, West Germany, India, Japan, Kenya, New Zealand, Singapore, Switzerland and the United States) had either planned or implemented reorganisation of their environmental programmes [2]; by June 1972, the number had reached 25 (11 of them in LDCs); by 1985, more than 140 countries had created national environmental agencies [3].

While the creation of these new agencies and the passage of new legislation might have helped allay the fears of environmentalists, the policy changes were often more quantitative than qualitative. Many Western European centre-left political parties began to develop environmental policy platforms in the early 1970s, but their responses were poor enough to stimulate the growth of green political parties, notably in Germany, Switzerland, Belgium and The Netherlands (see Chapter 9).

To make matters worse, few governments gave their new environmental agencies adequate powers. Some restructured the divided responsibilities of existing departments, some created entirely new departments, and some created new regulatory agencies with cross-cutting powers; whichever option each state chose, the solutions rarely proved sufficient to deal with the problems. There were three main reasons for this.

First, the environment as a policy issue proved almost impossible to compartmentalise. A problem common to almost all attempts to create new government machinery has been that of deciding the delineation of responsibilities, and of providing the necessary legal authority. The environment really impinges on almost every other area of public policy. In theory, a true "department of the environment" would have to be armed with an awesome array of laws and powers. In practice, the new national environmental agencies rarely had enough power to deal with their responsibilities.

Second, the creation of new departments often caused conflict with existing departments unwilling to give up their powers, resulting all too often in new agencies with mismatched, inadequate, or incomplete duties, or with much responsibility but little power. In the United States, nearly 30 different agencies have regulatory responsibilities for different aspects of environmental management [4]. In Britain, the misnamed Department of the Environment probably has less real influence over environmental policy than the Department of Agriculture (and no British government department does as much in real terms as the private environmental movement itself) [5].

Third, many of the new agencies lacked adequate human, technical and financial resources; they tended to be junior members of government, their directors often had to operate at middle levels without access to senior policy-makers, and the monitoring and enforcement of legislation varied from close control to none at all [6]. The OECD concluded in 1985 that even among its member states, several countries were unable to give their environmental programmes the resources they needed [7].

Six elements in particular determined the nature of the response of most governments to the environmental issue in the 1970s and 1980s: (1) the level of public political activism; (2) the degree of faith in the administrative ability of national government (much greater in Britain, for example, than in the United States); (3) the role of law and the division of powers between central and local government (greater centralisation in Britain than in the United States); (4) the degree of public consultation and of public access to the policy-making process (overt lobbying in the United States, private consultation in Britain); (5) the degree of public access to information (greater in the United States than in Britain); and (6) the nature of existing institutions.

The responsibilities given to the new environmental agencies revealed much about the political and economic priorities of different political systems. Because most LDCs wanted to plan natural resources in the interests of economic development, they often combined responsibility for natural resources, tourism, wildlife, population and land-use under one or two agencies. In industrialised countries, by contrast, pollution control was usually the major focus (as it was in some of the more industrialised LDCs, such as India, Brazil and China). The MDC priority was to "anticipate and prevent", while LDCs were still in the "react and cure" phase [8].

In MDCs there was also an interest in addressing transboundary problems such as acid pollution, toxic chemicals, hazardous wastes, shared fisheries and river basin management. There was the beginning of a true weighing of national with international interests, for example in the issue of acid pollution (see Chapter 10). In most cases, environmental policy initiatives were driven by national responses to national problems, but the fact that many different countries began addressing environmental problems at about the same time suggests that national initiatives were influenced too by wider trends: advances in scientific knowledge, the findings of global models, events in other countries (such as environmental disasters), and membership of international treaties or inter-governmental organisations.

Nationally and internationally, an important influence in the making of environmental policy came from non-governmental organisations, which both drew attention to issues and monitored the implementation and effectiveness of law. As the number of state environmental agencies and pieces of legislation grew, so did the number of – and support for – NGOs. Most groups shifted away from a focus on nature protection and towards wider environmental questions, and away from purely charitable concerns and towards political activism and lobbying. Most NGOs still gave priority to domestic issues, but many (especially the larger NGOs and NGO coalitions) began paying more attention to issues that had to be addressed at the regional or global level. This to some extent influenced the perception of national movements towards the issues. A 1974 survey of 635 local amenity societies in Britain, for example, revealed that 83 percent saw their work as connected with universal problems of pollution, overpopulation and shortages of natural resources, e.g. local traffic schemes linked to global oil consumption [9].

The contrasting responses of Britain and the United States to environmental policy-making give some idea of the different issues at stake, the different national styles of regulation, and the inherent complexity of the environment as a political issue.

Britain: Nanny knows best

On the face of it, Britain has an impressive record in recognising and responding to environmental degradation. In 1273 it passed what may have been the world's first piece of anti-pollution legislation (a decree prohibiting the burning of sea coal). In 1863 it created the first pollution control agency (the Alkali Inspectorate). In 1947 it passed one of the most comprehensive planning acts in the world, the Town and Country Planning Act. In 1956 it was the first major industrialised nation to pass a Clean Air Act. In 1970 it created the world's first cabinet-level "environment" department.

Yet, paradoxically, successive post-war governments have proved slow to respond to trends in public opinion on the environment. Britain's position on acid pollution provides an example. The problem was first identified in Britain, Battersea power station in London (opened 1929) was the first power station in the world to fit anti-pollution scrubbers, and London was one of the first cities in the world to respond successfully to smog problems. Yet Britain consistently lagged behind other West European nations during the 1980s in agreeing to international action to curb acid pollution. The answers to such paradoxes must be sought in the nature of the British political system.

British policy-makers have traditionally viewed themselves as custodians of the public interest, and have felt sure they could understand this interest with minimal reference to the public itself. The British political system also places limits on public access to information, and encourages the belief that a passive public will accept what is thought to be in its interest. This in turn has meant that much policy-making in Britain has been executed by selective consultation with interest groups, with no requirement to inform the public [10].

Voluntary compliance with "decent" standards of behaviour has been a key element of pollution control, an attitude described by Jon Tinker in 1972 as the "Nanny knows best" syndrome, in which the government appeals to the sense of fair play of polluting industries [11]. Some of Britain's pollution rules, he argued, were better suited to an Edwardian girls' school than to an advanced industrial society. Offenders, he noted, "are taken quietly on one side by the prefects and ticked off for letting the side down. There is no need for prosecutions: the shame of being found out is reckoned to be punishment enough". The non-coercive approach to pollution control was reflected in the fact that the Alkali Inspectorate prosecuted just three cases between 1920 and 1967 [12]. Stanley Johnson argued that Britain's approach to pollution control tended towards conservatism in believing in innocence until guilt had been proven [13]. In 1972, the Royal Commission on Environmental Pollution concluded in its second annual report that there was a need for more public openness in the environmental policy process [14].

A second source of problems lies in the fact that although Britain is often held up as a model of democracy, the process of government is limited by the domination of an elitist bureaucracy. British civil servants are commonly criticised for failing to adopt modern methods of management, for not being sufficiently systematic, for not planning ahead, and for being obsessed with procedure.

A third problem lies in the inadequacies of local government, which has considerable control over the environment. There is relatively little public interest in local politics, yet local government has much of the authority for ensuring public health. In the industrial heartlands of the Midlands, south Wales and Scotland, the weaknesses of local government were reinforced by a prevailing public unwillingness to acknowledge pollution as a problem, or – in coal mining areas – to accept less pollutive alternative energy sources such as natural gas. As happened so often elsewhere, fears that environmental controls would undermine existing industry and drive away new industry at a time of economic hardship discouraged the implementation of pollution controls [15].

Until 1970, authority for environmental policy in Britain was divided between a disparate group of agencies; for example, air pollution control was divided between the Ministries of Housing and Local Government (Alkali Inspectorate), of Technology, Transport and of Agriculture, the Department of Social Services, the Board of Trade, and the secretaries of state for Scotland and Wales. Harold Wilson first proposed an amalgamation in 1969, and created both the Ministry for Local Government and Regional Planning [16] and the Royal Commission on Environmental Pollution. There was much discussion about environmental issues both within the Labour government and the Conservative opposition in 1969–70, but the 1970 election still focused on more familiar issues.

Following the Conservative victory, however, the word "environment" appeared for the first time in the Queen's Speech in July 1970. A Government White Paper in October noted that it was "increasingly accepted that maintaining a decent environment, improving people's living conditions and providing for adequate transport facilities all come together in the planning of development . . . Because these functions interact, and because they give rise to acute and conflicting requirements, a new form of organisation is needed at the centre of the administrative system" [17].

The Ministries of Housing and Local Government, Public Building and Works, and Transport were now amalgamated into a new Department of the Environment (DoE) responsible for "the whole range of functions which affect people's living environment". The department was given four objectives, but only two – those relating to developing a "practical and positive approach" to pollution in all its forms, and developing a positive approach to planning – were strictly policies on the environment (the others related to reforming local government and housing). One of the DoE's earliest activities in pollution control was a reorganisation of water services. Under the 1973 Water Act, responsibility for water supply, sewerage and water conservation in England and Wales was taken from local and regional agencies and given to ten new Regional Water Authorities. The 1974 Control of Pollution Act addressed several environmental problems, including waste disposal, and water, air and noise pollution. Bennett sees it as "the first formal recognition of the environment as a single entity" [18].

The creation of the Department of the Environment – the first so-named department in the world – is often given greater significance than it deserves. The event was more a reorganisation of government machinery than the creation of a new department with new powers. Environmental policy remains a small (and not very important) part of its responsibilities; it has always given much greater weight to its responsibilities in local government and housing. By 1985, it had become obvious that the structure of the department was unsatisfactory, and the Labour party followed the lead of the now defunct Liberal–SDP Alliance in suggesting the need to reorganise the government structure relating to environmental management.

For Britons, the most controversial and widely debated environmental issue of the 1970s and 1980s – and perhaps of the 20th century – was the countryside. The rural ethic holds a place in the British psyche that is equivalent to the position of forests in Germany or wilderness in the United States. Social and economic change over a period of six thousand years has produced the characteristic British landscape which has long inspired writers, artists and poets: small fields and meadows divided by hedgerows and sprinkled with copses and small areas of woodland. It has also removed all but 7 percent of the natural forest cover of the British Isles. Very little, if any, true wilderness remains, and only the vestiges of once great natural forests remain in locales such as Sherwood, the New Forest and the Forest of Dean. For the rest, wildlife must co-exist with agriculture. In England alone, 70 percent of the land area is farmed.

During the Second World War, the need to become self-sufficient in food encouraged agricultural intensification, a process which continued through the post-war years, encouraged by tariffs on imports and subsidies to farmers – particularly those made available under the European Community's Common Agricultural Policy. One result was the removal of hedgerows and forests and the reclamation of wetlands at an unprecedented rate in order to create bigger fields and bigger yields. Between 1946 and 1974, a quarter of the hedgerows in England and Wales – about 120 000 miles (193 000 km) in all – were removed [19]. Deciduous forests were steadily replaced by commercial conifer plantations or converted to arable land, and between 1947 and 1980, half the ancient woodlands in Britain were lost [20]. Grasslands, bogs, marshes, heaths, downs and moorlands were similarly converted.

In 1980, Marion Shoard criticised the changes in her book *The Theft of the Countryside*. Noting that Britain's planning system was widely considered the most sophisticated and effective mechanism in the world for curbing the inherent tendency of powerful private interests to override public interest in land, she asked what it was doing to safeguard landscape from the systematic onslaught of modern agriculture. "The answer", she wrote, "is almost nothing. The planning system does not attempt to reconcile the different priorities of food production and landscape or wildlife conservation in cases where the two interests conflict . . . [Farming and commercial forestry] are effectively above the law as it applies to other activities which affect the environment" [21].

Much of the conflict between conservationists and farmers came to a head during the formulation of the 1981 Wildlife and Countryside Act, which attracted a record 2300 amendments before it was finally passed. Among the many anomalies in the Act was the fact that landowners whose land contained so-called Sites of Special Scientific Interest were given no incentive to maintain such sites, and plenty of incentive to develop them. Within months of the passage of the Act, it became clear that it was insufficient, and there was strong support among conservationists for its replacement.

Private environmental bodies are a key element in British policy-making. Where most other industrialised countries make and implement environmental policy through government agencies, many functions in Britain are carried out by private groups: the National Trust, for example, does much more than the government in acquiring and maintaining historic buildings and scenic landscape, and most nature reserves are run by local naturalist groups, which are coordinated in turn by the Royal Society for Nature Conservation. Many environmental groups receive direct government funding, and nearly half have representatives on one or more official advisory committees.

Until the 1970s, most British groups relied on private negotiations with government officials; thereafter, many became more involved in direct lobbying, political activism, and mobilising public opinion. The change is exemplified by the comment of one senior official of the Council for the Protection of Rural England (CPRE), who pointed out that under the leadership of Sir Herbert Griffin, secretary-general from 1926 to 1965, the CPRE did not seek attention and fastidiously avoided embarrassing those whom it influenced or sought to influence. "Nowadays", the official noted, "we are not reluctant to go public. Indeed, we are very media-conscious. This is better suited to the general style of environmental politics which has become more conflict-oriented" [22]. Members of both houses of parliament hold official or honorary positions in many environmental organisations, and increased interest in environmental issues has been reflected in parliamentary debates and questions.

Silent Spring, Aberfan, *Torrey Canyon* and the rise of the global environmental movement all influenced British environmentalism, and the membership of environmental groups surged during the 1970s. Between 1967 and 1980, for example, the membership of the CPRE and of the Ramblers Association more than doubled, that of the Royal Society for Nature Conservation more than quadrupled, and that of the National Trust (whose interests go beyond nature protection) grew by 530 percent. The number of local amenity societies increased sixfold between 1958 and 1975;

Table 7.1   Membership of selected British and US environmental groups 1968–1993 (in thousands)

	1968	1972	1976	1980	1985	1989	1993
Britain							
National Trust	177	346	548	950	1323	1750	2200
Royal Society for the Protection of Birds	41	108	204	321	390	433	860
Greenpeace	–	–	na	10	50	320	350
Royal Society for Nature Conservation	35	75	109	140	165	205	215
Friends of the Earth	–	na	na	12	27	120	200
Ramblers Association	14	26	30	36	50	73	76
Council for the Protection of Rural England	16	25	28	27	27	45	46
TOTAL	283	580	919	1496	2032	2946	3947
United States							
National Wildlife Federation	364	524	620	4100	4200	5100	5600
Greenpeace	–	–	na	na	na	850	2300
Sierra Club	68	136	164	270	390	450	565
National Audubon Society	66	164	269	415	500	550	550
Wilderness Society	39	67	91	70	65	220	390
Izaak Walton League	56	56	50	52	50	50	50
TOTAL	593	947	1194	4907	5205	7220	9455

na = not available

Sources: Sandbach, Francis, *Environment: Ideology and Policy* (Oxford: Basil Blackwell, 1980), 12; Fox, Stephen, *John Muir and His Legacy: The American Conservation Movement* (Boston: Little Brown & Co, 1981), 315; McCormick, John, *British Politics and the Environment* (London: Earthscan, 1991), 152; National Wildlife Federation, *Conservation Directory* (Washington DC: National Wildlife Federation, 1980, 1981, 1985 and 1989); Hoyle, Russ (Ed) *Gale Environmental Almanac* (Detroit, MI: Gale Research Inc, 1993); information from groups

by 1977 they had a total membership of 300 000 [23]. Growth of membership continued through the 1980s, notably among more activist groups such as Greenpeace and Friends of the Earth, which saw their membership grow by 3400 percent and 1600 percent respectively between 1980 and 1993 (see Table 7.1). By 1990, it was estimated that the British environmental movement had 4.5 million members, or 8 percent of the total population [24]. This made it the largest mass movement in British history.

As in the United States, members of British environmental groups are generally more affluent and better educated than the average. Because class is still a major social division in Britain, and because it is in turn tied to labour and employment, amenity organisations are more active in the predominantly white collar and professional south of England than they are in the predominantly manual and industrial Midlands and in the north. The class identification of environmentalists is nowhere more marked than in the support given to many environmental groups by peers, and by the active role of the House of Lords in initiating, debating and amending much environmental legislation.

The United States: Checks and balances

As in Britain, the United States had until 1970 no single national agency responsible for pollution control; responsibility lay with a confused coalition of separate agencies in the Department of Health, Education and Welfare. Air and water pollution were generally considered state and local matters, so the role of the federal government in environmental policy-making was limited. Environmental organisations had, however, begun pressing for more vigorous action on the environment, and in his 1970 Message to Congress, Richard Nixon spoke of the "inadequacy of our institutions for dealing with problems that cut across traditional political boundaries" [25]. The pressures of New Environmentalism promoted a new approach to environmental policy.

Despite attempts to rationalise environmental policy-making and implementation, the stratified nature of the US political system has complicated attempts to address an already complex policy problem. Public policy in the United States is shaped by the dispersal of government power through federalism and through checks and balances, which often makes it impossible to differentiate responsibilities. Further complexity is added by the fragmentation of environmental responsibilities among many institutions, and attempts to apply federal environmental policies through state and local governments. The final layer of complexity is added by the division of powers for making and implementing policy among the White House, Congress, the bureaucracy and the courts.

Bureaucratic problems (particularly the lack of coordination within and between departments) are illustrated by the example of the Department of the Interior: two of its agencies – the Fish and Wildlife Service and the Bureau of Land Management – are in direct competition. The one preserves wildlife on public lands, while the other has been traditionally inclined to protect the rights of those who want to graze livestock or extract minerals [26]. Apart from the Interior, Agriculture and Energy Departments, no less than 27 different organisations – from the Army Corps of Engineers to the Federal Aviation Administration, the Food and Drug Administration, the National Park Service and the US Coast Guard – are involved in overseeing environmental regulation [27].

Despite all these jurisdictional claims, the Environmental Protection Agency (EPA) is the most important of the major regulatory agencies. The history of the EPA dates from 1969, when a President's Advisory Council on Executive Organisation (the Ash Council) was set up to examine federal natural resource policy and pollution control programmes. Among its recommendations was one for a huge new department of natural resources and the environment, replacing the Department of the Interior (long regarded as the unofficial department of natural resources), and drawing off relevant responsibilities from other departments. (Similar proposals had been made by the 1949 Hoover Commission, and again in a 1965 Senate bill [28].) The Ash Council wanted to minimise the number of federal agencies reporting to the president [29]. It initially favoured consolidating existing pollution programmes under the proposed new Department of Natural Resources, but recanted when some of its members argued that this would submerge pollution control programmes and result in decisions favouring resource development at the expense of improved environmental quality [30].

On 1 January 1970, the National Environmental Policy Act (NEPA) was signed into law after rapid passage through Congress, and despite White House opposition. It drew the attention of all government agencies to the environmental consequences of their activities, and required an environmental impact statement (EIS) of all major federal programmes "significantly affecting the quality of the human environment". More than 12 000 such EISs were prepared in the first decade of operation [31]. The Act also created the Council on Environmental Quality (CEQ) – based in the Executive Office of the President – to draw up an annual environmental quality report and to advise the president on national policies for improving environmental quality. (Nixon had pre-empted Congress by creating in May 1969 his own Cabinet-level advisory Environmental Quality Council. The Council met only a few times and accomplished little [32].)

The CEQ was given no real powers, and Davies and Davies suggest that it derived what influence it had solely through its location in the Executive Office; it was doubtful, they noted, that the CEQ could "withstand the blows of a hostile president" [33]. (This was confirmed in 1981, when President Reagan first considered abolishing the CEQ, and then settled on dismissing almost all the staff and halving its budget.)

The compromise reached on pollution programmes was the establishment in December 1970 of the EPA, an independent pollution control agency with consolidated responsibility for regulating and enforcing federal programmes on air and water pollution, environmental radiation, pesticides and solid waste, and, to a lesser extent, for research. The agency reported directly to the president. The decision to create EPA was a compromise; the original proposal for a new department of natural resources would likely have met terminal Congressional opposition [34].

The EPA became – in personnel and budgetary terms – the biggest regulatory agency in Washington DC. It began with a staff of 8000 and a budget of $455 million; by 1981 it had a staff of nearly 13 000 and a budget of $1.35 billion [35], and by 1992 those figures had risen respectively to 18 000 and $6.5 billion, making the EPA the largest regulatory agency in the world [36]. It is responsible for major pieces of legislation, such as the Clean Air Act, the Clean Water Act, the Resource Conservation and Recovery Act, and the Toxic Substances Control Act. In addition to regulation, it also has powers of disbursement, notably through the administration of Superfund, a multi-billion dollar programme for cleaning up the nation's waste dumps. EPA's first decade saw an impressive outpouring of federal environmental legislation. Despite pressures imposed on the Nixon administration by business interests, congressional support for environmental reform ensured the passage of key legislation on air and water pollution control, solid waste recovery, and pesticide regulation.

The new toxic waste legislation was put to the test by a major public controversy in 1979 in a suburb of Niagara Falls called Love Canal. The manufacture, consumption and disposal of chemicals, especially those used in fertilisers and pesticides, had often given cause for concern. In 1976, following several years of unusually heavy rain and snow, chemicals began seeping into the basements of homes near Love Canal, an uncompleted and abandoned 19th century waterway in New York State. The canal had earlier been used as an industrial dump, and then sold to the Niagara Falls Board of Education, which built a school and playing field on the site. Some of the land was sold off to a developer, who built several hundred homes alongside the site of the canal. Studies now identified 82 different chemical compounds, including trichlorophenol, which contained dioxin.

In August 1978, pregnant women and children under two years of age were advised to leave the area. By July 1979, 263 families had been evacuated and their homes bought by the state, 1000 additional families had been advised to leave the area, and nearly $27 million had been spent by municipal, state and federal authorities to provide temporary housing, close off the contaminated area, and contain the seepage of chemicals [37]. Love Canal was only the most publicised of many such potential incidents; a 1979 report to the EPA estimated the number of disposal sites containing hazardous wastes in the United States at between 32 000 and 50 000, of which 1200–2000 could pose significant risks to human health or the environment [38].

White House attitudes to the environment underwent a dramatic transformation under the early Reagan administration. The change says much about the relationship between conflicting pressures for regulation and for deregulation in a capitalist society. Vig and Kraft suggest that the Reagan environmental agenda was based on (1) regulatory reform, (2) reliance as much as possible on the free market to allocate resources, and (3) the shifting of responsibilities for environmental protection to state and local government [39]. Two Reagan appointments exemplified the attitude of the new president: that of James Watt as Secretary of the Interior, and that of Anne Burford (née Gorsuch) – a Watt protégé – as administrator of the EPA.

Watt had served at the Interior Department for six years during the Nixon administration. Prior to his appointment as secretary, he had run the Mountain States Legal Foundation, an organisation devoted to legal action to curb or repeal federal actions in Colorado and other western states. Watt believed that most resource problems could be solved by opening them to the market. Watt's outspokenness soon became as big an issue as his policies. In a January 1982 speech, he said he never used the words Democrat or Republican – "it's liberals and Americans". A year later he compared his environmentalist critics to Nazis and Bolsheviks [40]. His policies included the opening up of wilderness areas to oil and gas leasing, the privatisation of lands owned by the Forest Service and the Bureau of Land Management, and an increase in the availability of federally owned coal, oil and gas.

Anne Gorsuch was an attorney and one-term state legislator from Colorado; her previous clients had included many industries opposed to federal environmental regulation. Environmentalists interpreted her appointment as a signal that the White House intended to move the EPA's sympathies away from environmentalists and towards business and other regulated interests [41]. Of the 15 subordinates named by Gorsuch, 11 had been connected with industries regulated by EPA. President Reagan early made it clear that he proposed to reduce the power of the EPA, instituting budget and personnel cuts (of 30 percent and 23 percent respectively [42]) between 1981 and 1983.

Under Gorsuch's tenure, most of the agency's major programmes were near-paralysed, and staff morale at the EPA collapsed. Suggestions that the EPA administration was involved in political chicanery became a political embarrassment. In December 1982, Gorsuch was cited for contempt of Congress for refusing – on presidential orders – to deliver subpoenaed documents on alleged mismanagement of Superfund. In March 1983, she resigned (the month before, she had married Robert Burford, head of the Bureau of Land Management). The appointment of William Ruckelshaus (who had been first administrator of the EPA) seemed to augur well for the agency, but continued personnel and budgetary cuts continued to interfere with EPA's effective operation.

The principle implicit in American politics that the interests affected by public policies should have an active input into making and assessing those policies has meant that the environmental lobby, like all other lobbies on Capitol Hill, has had a major role in policy-making. Organisations such as the Sierra Club and Friends of the Earth formed their own political action committees (through which money could be directly contributed to political candidates); the League of Conservation Voters became increasingly active in presidential and congressional elections; and a number of organisations – notably the Environmental Defense Fund and the Natural Resources Defense Council – increased the size of their scientific and technical staffs in order to provide expert testimony and reduce their dependence on studies provided by government agencies or regulated interests [43].

Those who, in the 1960s, had talked of the faddishness of environmentalism had cause to revise their opinions a decade later. Not only did environmental issues retain their prominence on the policy agenda, but alarm at the anti-environmentalist stand of the Reagan administration led to a surge in membership for environmental groups in 1981–82. A 1980 CEQ poll suggested that about 7 percent of the American population (17 million people) might be involved in one environmental organisation or another, and a further 55 percent were sympathetic to the environmental movement [44]. The average member tended to be strongly liberal, and sympathy for the movement was greatest among whites, those with at least some college education, and those with higher incomes [45].

Activism and the international environment

As noted earlier, New Environmentalism had largely bypassed the established conservation movement. Although some of the older, established groups ultimately adopted new activist tactics, new politicised environmental groups were needed to both feed on and service the new priorities. The change in the United States began with the creation of new organisations such as the Environmental Defense Fund and Friends of the Earth (FoE), and was then transposed to international questions through the efforts of FoE and Greenpeace, both overtly activist organisations.

The very creation of Friends of the Earth was symptomatic of the change in priorities. FoE was established in 1969 following a disagreement between the Sierra Club and its executive director, David Brower. Brower had been executive director of the Club since 1952, during which time the Club had come to be regarded as the most influential of the traditional conservation groups [46], and Brower among the best known conservationists. He set out to involve the Club in critical public issues, such as the building of a dam that threatened the Dinosaur National Monument on the Colorado–Utah border, and support for the 1964 Wilderness Act.

Partly as a result, Sierra Club membership grew from 7000 to 70 000; polls revealed that Brower's policies had the support of 85 percent of Sierra Club members [47]. His critics, however, argued that his independence of mind and his determination to follow through pet projects meant that he often let Sierra Club administrative work fall overdue. Although authorised to carry out as much political lobbying as the tax-exempt status of the Club allowed, his campaigning against plans by the Bureau of Reclamation to build two dams in the Grand Canyon was instrumental in the loss of the Club's tax-exempt status. In addition, his alleged dereliction of duty to the Club had been associated with heavy annual deficits in 1967–69. He was removed from office in 1969.

Upon his removal, Brower founded Friends of the Earth, whose philosophy was a direct reflection of New Environmentalism: that the solution to environmental problems lay not in temporary remedies but in fundamental social change. It adopted vigorous campaigning methods aimed at achieving maximum publicity and drawing attention to activities and ventures that threatened the environment. It has subsequently drawn its support from young, well-educated, middle-class discontents [48]. It was conceived from the outset both as an organisation that would be "blatantly active" and as an international organisation. The FoE "formula", according to Brower, was "to find people in other countries who share our own ideas about the limits to growth . . . and who have a respect for biological diversity. Then these people become the Board of Directors for their own country. They run their own show" [49].

The first FoE office was opened in San Francisco in 1969, followed by offices in Paris (July 1970) and London (October 1970). Initially, Brower simply appointed friends as his overseas representatives, but the recruitment process was later formalised. Two meetings in 1971 (in France and Sweden) resulted in the establishment of an international office nominally based in San Francisco. Burke notes that the primacy of self-determination and consensus decision-making was a defining characteristic of FoE International; "if this has, at times, resulted in a slowing down of the rate of development of FoE as an effective force internationally, it has also meant an absence of destructive divisions within the organisation" [50].

Autonomous groups were subsequently set up in most Western European countries and further afield (e.g. Malaysia and South Africa), with often different methods and patterns of organisation, but all pursuing the aim of promoting "more rational use of our natural resources by all constructive means, and to work against those who are destroying those resources" [51]. The issues FoE addressed included alternative sources of energy, wildlife issues, transport, pollution, and changes in legislation.

It was pollution – specifically that created by fallout from atmospheric nuclear tests – which led to the creation of Greenpeace. Since the Second World War, the United States, Britain, France and China had all conducted nuclear tests in and around the Pacific. American plans to explode a nuclear device on Amchitka Island (off the coast of Alaska) in 1971 encouraged a group of American environmentalists, the Don't Make a Wave Committee, to protest by sailing a fishing boat into the area, thereby contributing to the postponement of the test and the eventual cancellation of all tests on Amchitka [52]. Similar tactics were used again in June 1972, when a crew of volunteers led by a Canadian, David McTaggart, sailed a yacht towards a French test site at Mururoa Atoll, southeast of Tahiti; a bomb was detonated with the yacht only 80 km (50 miles) away.

In August 1973, the yacht again sailed into the French test site, and this time its crew was physically assaulted by French commandos. Smuggled photographs of the attack attracted considerable publicity; partly as a result, France announced a short moratorium on tests in November. Australia and New Zealand maintained diplomatic pressure on France throughout the 1970s, and McTaggart went on to found Greenpeace. Greenpeace continued its public protests, but France carried out regular tests throughout the 1970s. Greenpeace protest activities against the French tests took their most serious turn in July 1985, when the Greenpeace ship *Rainbow Warrior* was blown up in the harbour at Auckland, New Zealand, by members of Direction Général de la Sécurité Extérieur, the French intelligence service. One member of the Greenpeace crew died in the incident. The subsequent controversy seriously compromised Franco-New Zealand relations, and led to the resignation of the French Defence Minister, Charles Hernu.

Greenpeace has also campaigned against whaling, sealing, nuclear power and radioactive waste disposal. In many cases it has adopted the same tactics of direct action, such as attempting to obstruct the disposal at sea of nuclear waste, or sealing in the Arctic. The key to its activities is always the generation of often graphic and visually effective media publicity. As Greenpeace grew, so autonomous groups rejecting the control of the original headquarters in Vancouver were set up in Britain, France, and The Netherlands. By 1985 there were Greenpeace offices in 17 countries, with a total membership of 1.2 million [53]; by 1994, the global membership figures for Greenpeace were close to four million.

Nuclear power? No thanks

Of all the new issues addressed by the new activists, few proved so confrontational as the movement against nuclear power. The advent of nuclear power in the 1950s had been widely – but not universally – welcomed. It was portrayed as a source of energy cheaper and cleaner than traditional sources, and with the potential to reduce dependence on fossil fuels. During the period of greatest optimism, it was predicted that over 100 nuclear power plants would be built each year by the 1980s. In the event, the world's nuclear power generating capacity in 1983 was less than half that projected; there were 282 commercial nuclear plants in 25 countries, with about 174 000 megawatts of generating capacity, or enough to produce 9 percent of the world's electricity [54].

Four main factors contributed to the change of heart: public opposition based on safety and environmental concerns (especially concerning the disposal of nuclear waste); operating problems (for example with advanced gas-cooled reactors); disagreement within the industry about the relative merits of different reactor designs; and – perhaps most important – the fact that nuclear power was by the early 1980s no longer economically attractive. The building of new nuclear power stations frequently ran over budget, and it was finally revealed that nuclear power was not cheaper than coal-fired power. This had always been a contentious claim anyway.

The first major reactor accident occurred in Canada in 1952, when operator confusion and technical problems combined to produce an explosion inside the core of a research reactor. There were no injuries nor excessive radiation [55]. Public concern about the safety of nuclear power stations did not emerge until development of the nuclear power industry was further advanced. The accident at Windscale, Cumbria, in October 1957 (see Chapter 3) was more public, and was instrumental in causing a short-term cutback in British government plans for nuclear power development (other factors included the resilience of the world oil market, falling oil prices, expansion of the coal industry, and the expense of building nuclear power stations). The first accident in the United States – resulting in the deaths of three operators – occurred at a reactor in Idaho in January 1961. The exact cause of the accident has never been established, but it may have been human error [56].

The earliest public opposition to the building of power stations came from local residents. In Britain, opposition to nuclear power arose initially because of fears about the safety of stations. The need to site stations well away from population centres and near a ready source of water meant that many were built in areas of outstanding natural beauty, such as Snowdonia in Wales. This elicited protest and opposition from local residents and national pressure groups. Hall argues, however, that these protests were not symptomatic of a widespread desire by communities to reject nuclear power. He suggests that British opposition groups were far less successful than they were to become in the 1970s, when there was growing public perception that the nuclear power programme was not a success, and plans to introduce American pressurised water reactors aroused greater and more widespread intellectual indignation than previous schemes [57]. There was considerable ignorance about nuclear power, a legacy of the secrecy which had surrounded the early research into nuclear weapons; there was also a residual naive faith in the ability of science to benefit society.

Public opposition to nuclear power was much more vocal, and often violent, in Germany, France and Switzerland. In 1971, for example, plans were announced to build a reactor at Whyl in southwest Germany. Despite the opposition of local people, construction began in February 1975. Several hundred protestors immediately occupied the site, to be dispersed by police a few days later. Within days, the site was reoccupied, this time permanently. There followed several years of confrontation, and by 1982 construction had still not begun. Similar opposition met plans to build a station at Kaiseraugst in Switzerland. Mass demonstrations against plans to build a reactor at Creys-Malville in France in July 1976 were countered by forceful action by riot police, during which a demonstrator was killed [58]. Riot police were also used at Brokdorf and Grohnde in Germany in 1976 and 1977, and at Kalkar in The Netherlands in 1977.

In the United States, safety was a more important issue for nuclear power opponents than it had been in Britain. Non-violent opposition was adopted by protesters at a site in Seabrook, New Hampshire, in October 1976; more than 1400 were arrested. Public suspicion was raised in 1974 by the unexplained death in a car crash in November of that year of Karen Silkwood, an employee at the Kerr-McGee plutonium plant in Oklahoma. She had been en route to a meeting with a union official and a reporter, at which she intended to produce evidence of malpractice at the plant. The plant was subsequently closed.

The accident in March 1978 at the Three Mile Island power station in Harrisburg, Pennsylvania, encouraged the opponents of nuclear power. The accident, involving both mechanical failure and human error, was triggered by the failure of a valve and the closure of a pump supplying water to a generator, leading to shutdown of the reactor. This was exacerbated by the failure of a pressure relief valve to close (leading to reactor coolant being released), by the fact that auxiliary feedwater pumps were not operating (in violation of regulations), by the failure of operators to respond promptly, and by faulty instrument readings.

Conflicting reports about the release of radioactivity led to the evacuation of pregnant women and young children within an 8 km (five mile) radius [59]. The incident raised many questions about the safety of reactors and the adequacy of safety regulations, and led directly to a series of cancellations of orders for new reactors. The public effect of the accident was compounded by the release, just two weeks before, of the film *The China Syndrome*, with Jane Fonda and Jack Lemmon, based on a fictional malfunction at a nuclear power station. In May 1979 a demonstration – the largest against nuclear power – was held in Washington DC, involving 75 000 people. Three Mile Island also had repercussions outside the United States. Two days before, the Swedish government had refused a public referendum on the Swedish nuclear programme; within a week this decision had been reversed, and a referendum was held a year later.

The international scope of the anti-nuclear movement was emphasised in May 1977 by the convening of the non-governmental "Conference on a Non-Nuclear Future", held alongside an International Atomic Energy Authority conference in Salzburg, Austria. An international information exchange network – the World Information Service on Energy (WISE) – was founded, subsequently deriving its funding from licensing arrangements on the copyrighted symbol of the movement: a bright red smiling cartoon sun on a yellow background, surrounded by the slogan "Nuclear power? No thanks". By 1983 the symbol was available in 40 languages [60]; its success seemed to symbolise the growing presence of a new and more activist environmental movement unconstrained by national frontiers.

The environmental movement – and specifically the anti-nuclear movement – had often been criticised for overstating its case, and for using scare tactics to garner sympathy and support. Yet Three Mile Island had shown how close catastrophic environmental disaster might be. Confirmation of the extent to which the global environment could be contaminated by human activity was finally provided on 26 April 1986, when a reactor exploded at the Chernobyl nuclear power station, 50 miles (80 km) from Kiev in the Ukraine. The accident was caused by an experiment involving the deliberate switching off of safety systems; at least 32 deaths were ascribed to the blast, to the fire, and to radiation in the aftermath of the explosion. More than 200 people suffered severe radiation sickness, and about 135 000 had to be evacuated from the Chernobyl area. Winds carried the radiation across to Scandinavia and to parts of eastern and northwestern Europe, contaminating milk products and vegetables, and compelling farmers in some areas to keep their livestock under cover. Although there is little agreement on the precise scale of the long-term threat to health, many scientists believe that the number of people likely to suffer radiation-related illnesses in the coming decades will run into thousands.

The accident at Chernobyl was a spectacular example of how technology – if mismanaged or misdirected – could bring sudden and extreme environmental contamination. However, it is clear that most human-made environmental change is much slower, much less obvious and more difficult to detect and measure. In most cases, it has been a function of the rate of technological development and economic growth. Where growth and development are relatively rapid and widespread, so is environmental change. Hence the problems evident in the environment of industrial society.

In less developed countries, growth and development have often been rapid, but have also been unequal. In their haste to provide their populations with the supposed benefits of industry, the governments and planners of LDCs have often put short-term benefits before long-term costs. The frequent result has been a creeping and insidious form of environmental change which has discriminated against the rural poor, bringing gradual rather than rapid degeneration: soil erosion, deforestation, siltation, the spread of desert conditions, and – ultimately – hunger, famine and death. If industrialised nations have witnessed environmental change as a consequence of overdevelopment, LDCs are witnessing change as a consequence of unequal development. The result is that the problems and the policy responses of low-technology society are often very different from those of high-technology society.

8

The South: Environment and Development (1972–1987)

Before Stockholm, many environmentalists in industrialised countries had questioned – and rejected – the growth ethic. They saw economic growth as the primary threat to the environment, rejected the economic and social values of capitalism, and sought to change those values outside established political and economic institutions. Meanwhile, many LDC governments saw environmental management as an unacceptable burden, and an obstacle to economic development, and saw the "limits to growth" debate as completely inappropriate to their own needs and priorities.

A decade after Stockholm, attitudes in both arenas were more conciliatory. The interests of economic development and environmental management were no longer seen as incompatible, and it was widely agreed that compromise between the two was both possible and essential. The new environmental slogan was "sustainable development".

Like so many "new" environmental concepts before and since, there was little new about sustainable development. It was almost indistinguishable from the conservation espoused by German and Indian foresters, and by Theodore Roosevelt and Pinchot. Delegates to Lake Success in 1949 and Bukavu in 1952 had talked of the need to manage natural resources rationally. IUCN had argued the need to reconcile conservation and development policies as early as 1956. At Arusha in 1961 it was noted that "only by the planned utilisation of wildlife as a renewable natural resource . . . can its conservation and development be economically justified in competition with agriculture, stock ranching and other forms of land use" [1].

IUCN had launched the African Special Project largely because it felt that foreign aid was "prone to overlook conservation and the value of wildlife and habitat as a continuing economic, scientific, and cultural asset" [2]. At the First World National Parks Conference in Seattle in 1962 it was resolved that conservation was an important element of development and that international agencies should incorporate ecological studies into their planning [3]. Also in 1962, the UN General Assembly adopted a resolution on economic development and nature conservation, which endorsed an earlier UNESCO resolution that, to be effective, measures to preserve nature and natural resources "should be taken at the earliest possible moment simultaneously with economic development" [4].

For all the debate, there is still no generally agreed definition of sustainable development. It is usually applied to LDCs and to the kind of economic and social development needed to improve life for the world's poor without destroying or undermining the natural resource base. IIED attempted a definition in 1982: "the process of improving the living conditions of the poorer majority of mankind while avoiding the destruction of natural and living resources, so that increases of production and improvements in living conditions can be sustained in the longer term" [5]. While it may be an approach to the problems of LDCs, it is equally applicable to MDCs. A simpler and more appropriate definition might be economic development that takes place within the carrying capacity of the natural environment.

Before Stockholm, the preoccupation among European and American environmentalists with the limits to growth had led most to overlook LDC problems. The change of emphasis following Stockholm was marked and rapid. The links between environment and development were raised so often that, at the 1976 UNEP Governing Council, several delegations questioned the need apparently felt by the UNEP secretariat to continue to defend the notion. The idea was well understood and well established, they protested; it could stand restatement, but no further elaboration was needed [6]. Yet elaboration of the issue has been at the core of the environmental debate since Stockholm. Environmental problems in MDCs had been portrayed as a result of overdevelopment (the reckless and profligate exploitation of natural resources), and in LDCs as a result of underdevelopment (unequal access to national wealth, lack of economic opportunity, and the unequal exploitation of natural resources) [7]. A 1976 UNEP executive-director's report argued that the worst environmental problems were occurring "at the two extremes of the scale of wealth" [8].

The new emphasis of the post-Stockholm environmental movement came out of four broader developments: changes in international economic and political relations, the growth of a new global view of the environment, the desire of many Northern environmentalists to accommodate the different priorities of LDCs, and the growing self-confidence and sophistication of environmental NGOs. Where the environmentalists of the 1960s had promoted their cause as an alternative view for those who rejected conventional economic wisdom, those of the 1970s worked to incorporate new values into the policies of existing institutions, notably industry and government.

Environment and development

Following Stockholm, UNEP and the UN Conference on Trade and Development (UNCTAD) suggested the need for meetings to discuss the implementation of the ideas raised at Founex and Canberra in 1971. The meetings would bring together social and natural scientists in an attempt to discuss collaboration, and could be followed up with a series of regional seminars and conferences on environment and development. This would all lead to a proposed (but still-born) Stockholm II conference to be held in 1977.

Two meetings – sometimes confusingly called "Canberra II" and "Founex II" – were held. "Canberra II" (the UNEP–UNCTAD Expert Group on the Impact of Resource Management Problems and Policies in Developed Countries on International Trade and Development Strategies) met in Geneva in April 1974. The meeting agreed that the physical availability of natural resources would not be a serious problem in the foreseeable future. Rather, the problem was one of the "implications of making sufficient quantities of natural resources available and of using them rationally for economic development" [9]. The meeting concluded that, given the complexity of international economic relations, future development was likely to be constrained by problems in the distribution of natural resources well before any problems of finite quantities arose. This was a very different conclusion from those of Paul Ehrlich and the Club of Rome. Closer and more equitable economic cooperation between countries, the group noted, could form an important prerequisite for more rational resource management on a global scale.

The meeting also noted (not surprisingly, since it was held against the background of the 1973–74 energy crisis) that natural resources were destined to play a much more important role in international affairs, and that LDCs, frustrated in their efforts to negotiate changes in the world economic order, were likely to use natural resources as bargaining chips. MDCs, for their part, were growing increasingly aware of the importance of a continuance of supply, and had made greater efforts to decrease their dependence on imported raw materials and energy. The oil crisis had given LDCs a new sense of commodity power, leading to a new phase in North–South relations [10]. In May 1974, the UN General Assembly adopted a declaration calling for the establishment of a New International Economic Order that would provide a more balanced global economic structure.

That same month, a small UNEP–UNCTAD meeting on Alternative Patterns of Development was held to discuss further the agenda for Founex II. Among its conclusions were the following:

1) The development of LDCs was governed by the availability of natural resources to a far greater extent than in MDCs, where skills, capital resources and technological capabilities were more influential.
2) The capacity to cope with environmental disruption was more limited in LDCs, which had fewer technological and capital

resources than MDCs. Hence environmental degradation could have a more immediate and more rapid impact on economic development.

3) A fundamental rethinking of planning and development strategies was needed to give higher priority to social structures, more equitable distribution of income, and environmental issues. At the local level, far greater consideration should be given to local needs and conditions before – for example – using techniques, crop varieties, agricultural methods, etc., that had worked elsewhere.

"Founex II" (the Symposium on Patterns of Resource Use, Environment and Development Strategies) was held in Cocoyoc, Mexico, in October 1974. It was chaired by Barbara Ward, and drew together a small group of delegates from 22 countries (eight MDCs, 14 LDCs). It was held to discuss the relationship between environment and development in the light of the experience of the previous few years, to analyse the impact that environmental issues – and specifically the growing awareness of the limitations to natural resources – were having (or should have) on development strategies and international economic relations, and to provide input into the rethinking on development and international economic problems then taking place in the United Nations [11].

A Declaration, drafted largely by Barbara Ward, was issued at the end of the symposium, summing up the points raised. It noted that more people were hungry, shelterless and illiterate than when the UN was founded. The world had yet to emerge from the consequences of nearly five centuries of colonialism, which had concentrated economic power in the hands of a small group of countries. Much of the pressure on natural resources was due to the high consumption of resources in MDCs: "Pre-emption by the rich of a disproportionate share of key resources conflicts directly with the longer term interests of the poor by impairing their ultimate access to resources necessary to their development and by increasing their cost. All the more reason for creating a new system of evaluating resources which takes into account the benefits and burdens for the developing countries". The lack of resources for full human development was a continuing cause of population growth, and unequal economic relationships contributed directly to environmental pressures. Any process of growth which did not lead to the fulfilment of basic human needs (food, shelter, clothing, health and education) was a travesty of the idea of development.

The Declaration recommended that:

1) policies should be implemented aimed at satisfying the basic needs of the poorest, while ensuring adequate conservation of resources and protection of the environment;
2) governments and international organisations should promote the management of resources and the environment on a global scale;
3) strong international regimes should be set up for the exploitation of the global commons, this exploitation to be taxed so as to benefit the poorest countries;
4) new priorities were needed in scientific and technological research and development;
5) new development priorities should aim at curbing over-consumption in the North and stepping up the production of essentials for the poor.

The Declaration ended by challenging the assumptions of New Environmentalism. The way forward did not lie through "the despair of doom-watching nor through the easy optimism of successive technological fixes", but through careful and dis-passionate assessment of the "outer limits" of the earth's physical resources and through a search for ways to achieve the "inner limits" of fundamental human rights.

Development aid policies and the environment

Following Stockholm, bilateral and multilateral aid agencies began thinking more carefully about the environmental viability of their programmes. The pre-Stockholm concerns with popu-lation, pollution and flawed technology now gave way to the role and effects of poverty. The World Bank estimated in the early 1970s that about 800 million people, or one in five humans, were so deprived of income, goods and basic needs as to be members of the "absolute poor". World Bank President Robert McNamara defined absolute poverty as "a condition of life so degraded by disease, illiteracy, malnutrition, and squalor as to deny its victims basic human necessities; a condition of life so limited as to prevent realization of the potential of the genes with which one is born; a condition of life so degrading as to insult human dignity" [12].

During the 1950s and 1960s, the conventional view in the development community was that economic growth was the most effective way of eradicating poverty. The best way to help the poor was to build the capital, infrastructure and productive capacity of an economy; the gains of economic growth would "trickle down" to the poor through market forces creating jobs, raising productivity and wages, and lowering prices. But growth did not always reduce inequality, nor did income automatically trickle down to the poor. If anything, it promoted a dual economy – a modern, urban sector alongside a stagnant traditional sector. To make matters worse, much aid was being spent on non-essential prestige projects, such as new highways, airports and office buildings. In the 1970s, attention turned to the notion of economic growth with income redistribution [13], and finally to the idea that the provision of basic needs (such as food, health, education, shelter, water and sanitation) was more important to the poor than the more nebulous question of equality.

By the late 1960s, several development aid agencies had become aware that the benefits of their aid were often undermined by the lack of environmental impact assessments. Much aid was wasted because it either resulted in, or was undermined by, environmental degradation: soil erosion, desertification, siltation of dams, failure of irrigation systems, and so on. The Conservation Foundation in the United States had already begun thinking in the 1960s about the need to take ecological factors into account in development planning; in 1968 it sponsored a conference at Airlie House, Virginia, on the ecological aspects of international development. The main conclusion reached was that development economists, planners, engineers and ecologists should work more closely with each other in the design of development projects.

More meetings followed Airlie House, involving the World Bank, FAO, UNDP, IUCN, the International Biological Programme (IBP) and the Conservation Foundation. A meeting was held at FAO in Rome in 1970 involving all these groups and the aid agencies of Canada and the United States. It was decided that IUCN and the Conservation Foundation should prepare a guidebook for development planners. This was published in 1973 [14]. It examined the ecological principles that needed to be considered in instances where economic development threatened major modifications of natural systems, and argued that the UNESCO/FAO definition of conservation as "the rational use of the earth's resources to achieve the highest quality of living for mankind" could equally well be used to define the goals of economic development.

The book argued that there should be growing convergence rather than conflict between the aims of conservation and development, and that the ecological limitations on natural systems had to be taken into account if development was to succeed. It set out in general terms the ecological and development needs of humid tropical areas and of pastoral lands in semi-arid and semi-humid regions, and assessed the impact of the development of tourism, agricultural development projects, and river basin projects. It explored general ideas rather than laying down comprehensive principles. IUCN subsequently pursued some of these ideas through the publication of a series of guidelines on development planning.

In 1977–79, IIED undertook a series of studies of the environmental policies of bilateral and multilateral development aid organisations [15]. Four major problems were identified in financing institutions generally: (1) the lack of any clear procedures for the environmental assessment of projects (with the exceptions of the World Bank and the Organization of American States), (2) a general lack of criteria for assessing environmental impact (stemming in large part from the lack of conceptual definitions of what constituted environmental concerns), (3) the lack of alternative forms of analysis and accountancy which included the long-term social and environmental effects of development projects, and (4) a lack of personnel with appropriate training.

The first of the IIED studies focused on multilateral aid agencies. It concluded that, of the nine agencies studied, the World Bank had the most advanced environmental policy and practices and "undoubtedly exerts intellectual leadership on environmental matters in the whole international development community". This was thanks in large part to the personal influence and interest in environmental matters of Robert McNamara [16]. The Bank had established a new post of Environmental Advisor in 1970 (a move dismissed by the Bank's critics as window-dressing), and adopted the policy of considering environmental factors in its economic assistance policy. McNamara acknowledged that finance institutions faced the problem of making sure that development assistance avoided environmental damage without slowing economic growth [17].

In 1972 the World Bank had published a handbook for those involved in development projects (including engineers, planners and finance institutions) [18]. It listed – point by point – the questions that should be raised during planning and appraisal. It was by no means perfect (covering industry, transport, utilities and energy, but barely touching on agriculture), and was also very general, making little allowance for the problems of specific communities. Yet it was the first major effort by a lending institution to establish criteria for evaluating the environmental impact of its investment projects [19].

The World Bank met early resistance to its new environmental concern from LDCs; many feared that building environmental protection into projects would add 25–50 percent to total project costs. These fears were placated by the Bank agreeing to cover any additional costs involved in meeting the necessary standards [20]. In the event, the Bank found that the additional costs were of the order of 0–3 percent. World Bank policy was that the environmental and health aspects of projects should be analysed at the formulation and design stages. An analysis of 1342 projects receiving World Bank loans between 1 July 1971 and 30 June 1978 found that 63 percent revealed no apparent or potential environmental problems. In 365 (27 percent of the total), those environmental problems that were identified were dealt with by Bank staff; in 110 (8 percent), the environmental problems appeared sufficiently serious to require special studies by consultants, and environmental safeguards were incorporated as a condition of lending. In the remaining 22 cases, other agencies had earlier determined the need for safeguards and appropriate action had been taken [21].

The second IIED study examined the environmental policies of six bilateral aid organisations (those of Canada, West Germany, The Netherlands, Sweden, the UK and the United States) [22]. It found that the confusion which had existed four years earlier over the meaning of "environment" had been resolved, and that the environment was not being seen as an additional subject for consideration but increasingly as a "new approach to development which gives greater weight to the sustainability of results and to the costs of destructive side effects of projects". However wide the acceptance of this view in principle though, it had still had "too little impact on the orientation and design of the projects or practical development policies of the agencies studied". An earlier study of the US Agency for International Development (USAID) had concluded that, despite the addition in 1977 of an Environment and Natural Resources sector to the Foreign Assistance Act, and the foundation of a number of USAID projects aimed at natural resource maintenance, USAID's efforts had lacked clear authority and had been "piecemeal and subject to tortuous justification" [23].

The IIED study of bilaterals concluded that environmental and resource objectives needed better definition in the context of aid policies as a whole; that urgent attention was needed to help LDCs study and address their own environmental problems; that environmental enhancement projects needed support comparable to that given to traditional development sectors; and that aid agency policy documents frequently lacked adequate attention to environmental factors. Four out of the six agencies had clearly defined focal points for environmental responsibility, but only one (that of the United States) systematically screened projects for their environmental impact [24]. There was consensus in the six agencies on the need to integrate a broad concept of "environment" into development thinking and planning, but "this rhetorical commitment, with exceptions, has not been quickly matched by specific action".

A separate study of the Canadian International Development Agency (CIDA) found "an informal and, at times, haphazard approach to environmental concerns" [25]. The study found that CIDA lacked a strong commitment to incorporating environmental concerns in regular policy planning, that there was no systematic assessment of the environmental consequences at the project proposal stage, and that inadequate monitoring and evaluation procedures meant that there was little feedback into CIDA on the environmental consequences of projects.

British aid policy was even less enlightened. In 1982 it was Overseas Development Administration policy to "take into account" the environmental implications of aid projects, and to bring the implications of these projects to the attention of recipient governments, but to give advice "strictly" on request; "it is for the governments of the developing countries themselves to decide what priority they wish to give environmental factors within their own development programmes. This is a political issue to be considered against the demands for economic and social development in any individual country" [26]. The policy of Commonwealth agencies involved in development was likewise to respond to requests for advice more often than to initiate ideas and programmes. Few, if any, Commonwealth activities acknowledged in any formal way the environmental dimension of development [27].

In September 1979, nine months after the publication of the first IIED study, representatives of the nine multilateral agencies examined met in Paris under the auspices of UNEP, the World Bank and the UN Development Programme (UNDP), and agreed a joint declaration (signed in New York in 1980) undertaking to pursue new policies in seven areas identified by the study, including the systematic examination of all development policies and projects to ensure that appropriate measures were proposed for compliance with the principles and recommendations of Stockholm. The declaration noted that economic development was essential to the alleviation of all major environmental problems, and acknowledged that aid agencies had a responsibility to ensure the sustainability of the economic development activities they financed [28].

The cumulative effects of ill-advised or badly planned development, and the role in this of development aid policies, were illustrated in a report published by the World Bank in 1984 on development in sub-Saharan Africa [29]. The report concluded that the region faced serious social and economic problems, with political instability, declining economic and agricultural output, growing malnutrition, and a deteriorating natural environment. The key causes, it argued, were population growth, declining returns from investment, and the effect of government and aid-donor policies on the efficiency of resource use.

While many aid agencies, encouraged by UNEP, had agreed in principle to undertake environmental impact assessments of aid projects, "this promise has yet to be translated into widespread action – and few privately financed projects receive proper advance environmental analysis" [30]. Nevertheless, UNEP believed that there had been a shift in emphasis from "an almost purely technical approach to a broader societal one, considering developmental goals from the point of view of values and ethics rather than purely from the point of view of quantitative economic growth, and the long-term rather than the short-term" [31]. This had apparently reached the point where some planners believed that real development could not be achieved by copying MDCs, where industrial growth had been exploitative, and so unsustainable [32].

Environmental policy in LDCs: Kenya and India

Just as MDCs reviewed their environmental policies in the late 1960s and early 1970s, so too did many LDCs. The number of less developed countries with environmental agencies grew from 11 in 1972 to 102 in 1980 [33]. But – as with MDCs – simply creating a new institution was not the same as creating an *effective* institution. The new LDC agencies not only faced many of the political and jurisdictional problems experienced by their counterparts in MDCs (notably a lack of authority), but had their own additional problems: the priority given to economic development at almost any cost, and the lack (with some exceptions) of a substantial middle class, an environmental movement, a firm institutional or legal framework, and a solid database.

Emil Salim, the Indonesian Minister for Population Affairs and the Environment, while agreeing with the need to protect his country's genetic wealth, pointed out in 1982 that Indonesia lacked "the precise knowledge of what constitutes our own natural wealth and how to protect it" [34]. UNEP noted that development of the legal framework (including regulatory agencies and procedures, backed up by trained personnel) for environmental action was uneven. Such laws as existed were often difficult to enforce or were poorly implemented, and few LDCs had explicit national environmental policies. While industrialised nations had some success in carrying out environmental inventories and implementing development plans, progress in poorer countries was variable. Concepts such as sustainable development were useful guides to development projects, but were not widely applied [35].

Kenya should, in theory, have fared better than most. It is the site of UNEP, it has hosted key environmental conferences, it has a relatively well developed NGO network, its tourist industry is based largely on its natural beauty, and it has enjoyed relative economic prosperity and political stability since independence in 1963. It has a limited arable land base, but enough productive land to feed (in theory at least) its rapidly growing population. It is also well endowed in other natural resources. Yet the indications in the 1980s were that it faced an "increasing, horrifying, long-term loss of natural resources for short-term returns" [36]. The losses resulted from overgrazing, the expansion of cultivation into marginal rainfall areas, deforestation, the uncontrolled expansion of new settlements, the destruction of upper catchment areas, and river siltation. Kenya's population growth rate of 4.2 percent is the fastest in the world, and shows little sign of slowing. If it continues, the national population will double every 18 years.

A 1980 study of environmental policy in Kenya concluded that Kenya had neither an environmental policy nor an integrated national land use policy [37]. This was despite major statements on environmental management by Presidents Kenyatta and Moi in turn, and general agreement among bureaucrats that such an environment policy was a priority. The Kenyan National Environment Secretariat (NES) concluded that plans for the introduction of an environmental impact assessment requirement would have no effect as long as there was no environment policy "and so long as its implementation will be vested in the very institutions which have exacerbated, if not precipitated, existing problems" [38]. In the 1979–83 Five-Year Plan, resource use policies were listed as the responsibility of the NES and the National Council for Science and Technology, yet neither was a policy-making body. Kenya in 1980 had 14 separate pieces of legislation relating to natural resources and resource management, but they were very rarely applied.

The 1980 study found – among other problems – an overlap and confusion of responsibilities (e.g. 26 institutions with an interest in water alone), the non-application of law, a conflict between members of parliament representing rural constituents facing land shortage and sectoral bodies supporting tougher and more comprehensive legislation, laws divorced from the social and economic reality of the situation they were supposed to police, an absence of organised monitoring and data gathering at the national level, and a National Environment Secretariat lacking policies, legislative authority, local representation and political power. The position was further complicated by inter-department rivalries: seven out of a total of 20 ministries had an interest in natural resource matters – the ministries of planning and national development, environment and natural resources, lands and settlement, water development, tourism and wildlife, agriculture and livestock development, and energy and regional development.

India's problems are similar, but obviously much bigger. It has an extensive body of environmental legislation dating back to the Shore Nuisance (Bombay and Kolaba) Act of 1853 [39]. A National Committee on Environmental Planning (NCEP) was set up in 1972 to act as an advisory body to the government (Indira Gandhi took an active personal interest in environmental issues). The limitations inherent in the power of an advisory body led in 1980 to the creation of a Department of the Environment (DOE), under the direct charge of the prime minister, to appraise development projects, monitor pollution, and regulate and conserve marine ecosystems and biosphere reserves.

The environmental appraisals have had some success, e.g. the inclusion of pollution abatement measures in a fertiliser plant near Bombay, and the amendment of plans to build a hydroelectric project inside a wildlife sanctuary in the state of Tamil Nadu [40]. The DOE has also identified potential biosphere reserves and made a nationwide survey of important wetlands, and the NCEP – before its closure – encouraged state governments to set up their own environmental boards. By 1985, 18 out of 22 states had their own environment departments, and there were more than 200 national and state laws relating to the environment [41].

But the failures outweigh the successes. Ramakrishna notes the degree of uncertainty about the legislative authority of central government to implement environmental statutes, enforcement problems, and the lack of a private right of action [42]. In a 1982 survey of 30 pieces of environmental law, the committee responsible for the creation of the DOE noted four basic flaws: (1) many promoted development and resource use for specific economic benefits without careful analysis of the potential environmental effects; (2) several state laws had potentially adverse environmental implications for neighbouring states; (3) many laws were clearly inadequate (e.g. the Insecticides Act of 1968 did not encourage a transition away from pesticides such as DDT which had been banned elsewhere, and lacked adequate provision for monitoring the incidence of pesticide residues); (4) the environment was such a new policy area that it was still widely ignored or overlooked within government departments [43]. The NCEP and DOE additionally had little credibility with other government departments. For a department with such potentially enormous responsibilities, the DOE in 1983–84 had just 237 staff and an annual budget of $16 million (200 million rupees) [44]. And despite the extensive body of pollution legislation, Indian industry remained either reluctant to control pollution or beyond the reach of the law; in 1985, the Minister of State for the Environment reported that there were about 4000 polluting industries in India, of which just 200 had installed effluent treatment plants [45].

Nowhere were the weaknesses in India's pollution control system more tragically or dramatically illustrated than in the escape of methyl-isocyanate (MIC) gas from a Union Carbide pesticide plant in Bhopal in December 1984. Estimates of the death toll vary from 1300 to 10 000; the figure most often quoted now is about 2500. UNICEF estimated that about 200 000 people in all were affected, of whom 75 percent were local slum-dwellers [46]. Three particular issues were underlined by the Bhopal accident. First, the inadequacy of regulations on pollution standards and chemical safety, and of the zoning system which allowed so many of India's poor to live so close to industrial plants; second, the inadequacy of the government's disaster response system ("the government's centralisation and lack of initiative", noted one Indian NGO, "so visible on ordinary days, caused it to literally collapse under stress" [47]); and third, the economic and political value system which allowed multi-national corporations to operate plants at standards of efficiency and safety below those they would have to meet in MDCs.

The sheer number of fatalities at Bhopal was unprecedented, but similar accidents had occurred before in India and elsewhere, and the probability of future incidents remains high. The attention drawn by Bhopal overshadowed another equally serious incident only the month before: the death of more than 500 people in the explosion of a liquefied petroleum gas store in Ixhuatepec, a shanty suburb of Mexico City. As many as 100 000 people – most of them migrants from rural areas – were settled in makeshift homes as close as 130 metres from the storage facility [48]. At fault in the accident were many of the same problems that underlay the Bhopal disaster.

Both Kenya and India have an active and vocal non-governmental environmental movement. Of the 60 Kenyan organisations active in tree-planting alone, the most prominent is the Green Belt Movement, set up by the National Council of Women of Kenya in 1977. Headed by Wangari Maathai, a former anatomy professor, the movement helps local communities establish tree plantations on open spaces, in school grounds and along roads [49]. By 1987, there were more than 1000 green belts, 20 000 "mini-green belts" on farmers fields, and 65 community tree nurseries. Another active group is the Kenya Energy NGOs Association (Kengo), which took part in the 1980s in a successful USAID-funded project to test and distribute cheaper and more efficient jikos (charcoal-burning stoves).

India boasts literally thousands of citizen groups, from local grassroots movements to broader national organisations. The power of grassroots movements is epitomised by the record of the Dasohli Gram Swarajya Mandal (DGSM) [50]. Formed in 1964 to encourage forest-based cottage industries in the northern state of Uttar Pradesh, DGSM quickly found that it had no rights or control over local forests, and that outside contractors were able to pay much less than the market value for local forest products. DGSM began a local public awareness campaign to draw the attention of local people to what was happening. Local resistance to the powers of outside contractors gradually became more militant, such that by 1973–74, local villagers (mainly women) were banding together to physically prevent the felling of trees. The resultant Chipko Andalan – or "movement to hug trees" – attracted worldwide attention and admiration for its non-violent Gandhianism, although more than a decade later its goal of changing state forestry policy in Uttar Pradesh remained unfulfilled.

Even more notice was later attracted by a similar movement in western Brazil. Local rubber tappers led by Chico Mendes refused to leave their homes to make way for cattle ranchers and settlers. After a 13-year struggle to block rain forest clearance, Mendes was murdered in December 1988, drawing new attention to threats to the Amazonian rain forest.

At the national level, India boasts one of the most energetic NGOs in the less developed world – the Centre for Science and Environment (CSE). Led by Anil Agarwal, CSE has published reports on the state of India's environment which have provided the most comprehensive and thorough assessments yet compiled of the environmental problems of an LDC (and, indeed, of any country) [51].

The World Conservation Strategy

Stockholm placed the environment firmly on the agenda of international relations. As the identification of transboundary problems (e.g. acid pollution) and problems common to several countries (e.g. soil erosion, pollution and deforestation) grew, so it became increasingly evident that much greater international cooperation was needed. Max Nicholson had written of the need for a world conservation programme as early as 1966, although the scheme he envisaged was limited to wildlife. He observed that limited resources and an insufficient information base were discouragements to a scheme at that time, but that by 1970 a world strategy could be a practical possibility: "such a programme might be of value in focussing world opinion on the scale, nature, and distribution of the main ascertainable conservation requirements. Presumably it would be for IUCN to take the initiative here, enlisting such help as might be required and appropriate" [52].

IUCN began considering a strategic approach to conservation at its General Assembly in New Delhi in 1969 [53]. Raymond Dasmann (author of the 1973 handbook on ecological guidelines) recalls that, at the time he joined IUCN in 1970 as a senior staff ecologist, there had been three changes in the Union: it had new leadership, a new organisational structure, and had been given a major grant from the Ford Foundation. Ford had suggested the need for more centralised control by IUCN headquarters over its activities. Dasmann noted the influence of a new intercommissional marine conservation programme at IUCN, which emphasised "planning, programming, strategy, and tactics" [54]. This approach now pervaded the work of all IUCN commissions and was, in Dasmann's view, "one impetus that led to the strategic approach to world conservation problems". A more significant development noted by Dasmann was the shift in emphasis at IUCN towards a concern for economic development; for example, conservation and development was the theme of the 1972 IUCN General Assembly in Banff, Canada.

Serious discussions on a strategic approach to conservation were begun at a meeting in 1975 between IUCN and UNEP, when UNEP asked IUCN to prepare a wildlife conservation strategy, designed solely to determine the priority actions needed to protect and save wild species. Over the next two years, Dasmann and Duncan Poore (acting directors-general in turn) worked on drafts of the strategy. UNEP appeared to have no clear idea of what form the strategy should take, so the initial design of the document was left largely to Dasmann and Poore [55]; its origins were very narrow, which Allen feels reflected, to an extent, IUCN's field of expertise. Lee Talbot (later IUCN director-general) recalls that "the first draft was essentially a wildlife textbook", but that each subsequent draft brought the previously opposing views of developers and conservationists closer together, and that the final draft was a consensus between the two points of view [56].

Until the late 1970s, IUCN conservation policy had been set every three years by the General Assembly and guided in the interim by the Executive Board. But IUCN lacked the benefit of a planned and integrated plan of action; its activities tended to be "a collection of projects, often individually valuable, but lacking the coherence and . . . impact of a planned programme" [57]. The first significant attempt to change this was the triennial strategy document for 1976–78, prepared by Duncan Poore. This outlined four main objectives for the Union: the conservation and protection of plant and animal species, representative ecosystems, and habitats, and the need to establish "a framework of wise use which ensures that the potential of renewable natural resources is maintained" [58]. IUCN should strike a balance between "working to a long-term, phased world conservation strategy" and reacting to short-term opportunities and urgent problems.

One of the guiding principles outlined in the document was that conservation programmes should be treated "as an integral part of the plans for social and economic development in the regions or nations concerned" [59]. Every effort should be made to involve local people in conservation projects, taking account of their needs, attitudes and knowledge. IUCN's priority was still clearly nature conservation, but there was evidence that it was becoming more interested in "ecodevelopment" (i.e. the development of a locality, taking fullest sustainable advantage of its physical, biological and cultural resources). This, noted Robert Allen in 1976, "appears to be the long-awaited reconciliation of conservation and development" in IUCN's programme [60].

IUCN announced that it was preparing a World Conservation Strategy (WCS) in October 1977. The final drafting was guided by Robert Allen (one of the authors of the *Blueprint for Survival*, and then IUCN head of publications) and David Munro IUCN's director-general ostensibly in consultation with UNEP, FAO and UNESCO, and with UNEP funding. The Strategy, said IUCN, would identify the main threats to species and ecosystems, and propose action and priorities. Although essentially a UNEP/

IUCN/WWF policy document, it would be available to other organisations, and would also be aimed at influencing governments, UN agencies and inter-governmental bodies. It would not be confined to threatened species or areas in need of special protection, but would also cover species and areas of economic value which were being misused, such as wild and semi-domesticated relatives of cultivated plant and animal species, or fisheries and their supporting coastal wetlands. It would provide "for the first time a global perspective on the many problems with which conservation is concerned" [61].

Early drafts were well received by IUCN General Assemblies, but omissions were noted, including a fuller, more focused discussion of the relationship between conservation and socio-economic factors, particularly population increase. A more thorough account was also needed of the development process, and more details were needed on conservation education, planning and legislation, pollution, toxic chemicals, soil and water conservation, and on the implementation of the Strategy: *how* the recommended action could be achieved rather than *what* action was necessary [62]. Many LDC delegates pointed out – as they had done before and since Stockholm – that they faced more pressing environmental concerns than the protection of nature, and that wildlife problems could not be treated in isolation.

The point was also made that IUCN had the opportunity to influence multilateral and bilateral aid policies, and should seize it. The Strategy did not pay enough attention to the potential for conservation-oriented development projects. IUCN should try to influence multilateral and bilateral aid agencies so their activities were in line with the WCS. IUCN resolved that the next version of the WCS, "while continuing to concentrate on conservation issues, shall place conservation firmly in its socio-economic context, with due reference to population and such other major influences as poverty, economic growth, the conservation of energy and raw materials, inappropriate technologies, and the satisfaction of basic human needs" [63]. This, IUCN noted, was a marked "departure from traditional conservation concerns" [64]. (Despite these hopes, the published Strategy – while including arguments about population, food and soil erosion – remained essentially a document on nature conservation.)

In February 1979, IUCN announced that the World Conservation Strategy would be launched in September that year, in an event designed to attract as much publicity as possible and achieve the greatest possible impact on policy-makers and the public [65]. The initial plan was that the WCS should be revised and updated every three years. In the event, the WCS was not itself updated, but was instead adapted through the formulation of national conservation strategies, the need for which was first realised as early as 1976 [66]. The final draft of the Strategy went before UNEP, FAO, UNESCO, WWF and the IUCN Council in August 1979 and was approved in October.

The simultaneous launch of the WCS in 40 or more countries in March 1980 confirmed the trend already evident of a reappraisal of policy at an organisational level within IUCN, and at a conceptual level in the conservation movement as a whole. As far as IUCN was concerned, it had been 25 years since its title had changed from "protection" to "conservation" of nature and natural resources, but until the launch of the WCS "there really was no broadly accepted platform reflecting this change, no reference base for reconciling the classical requirements of nature protection and those of sustainable economic progress" [67]. The definition of IUCN's goals had, in Talbot's opinion, been long overdue. The launch of the WCS gave substance to the reformulation of IUCN's agenda.

IUCN established two new ventures in the immediate wake of the Strategy. In April 1981, the Conservation for Development Centre was set up within IUCN to promote the integration of conservation in the planning and implementation of economic development. Its first tangible action on environmental impact assessment was a consultancy project to help the Natural Resources Board of Zimbabwe assess alternative energy development. In January 1982, IUCN established the Joint Environmental Service with IIED to help LDCs create or strengthen planning, education, NGOs and legal frameworks, thereby improving their ability to promote environmentally sound land-use planning and environmental impact assessment, mainly with LDC governments and international development agencies.

By the admission of its authors, the WCS was a compromise document. It not only represented a consensus of IUCN's members and the agencies involved in its drafting, but tried to set priorities for conservationists with different interests, and attempted to reach an accommodation between conservation and development. It also gave a generalised and simplified view of the problems and issues involved. The Strategy's aim was to "help advance the achievement of sustainable development through the conservation of living resources" [68]. It was needed, said its drafters, because of the rate at which resources were being destroyed or depleted, because of the rate at which demand was increasing, because corrective action would take time to implement and to show results, and because existing national and international conservation programmes were ill-organised and fragmented, exerting little influence over the development process. Conservation was defined as "the management of human use of the biosphere so that it may yield the greatest sustainable benefit to present generations while maintaining its potential to meet the needs and aspirations of future generations". This embraced "preservation, maintenance, sustainable utilization, restoration, and enhancement of the natural environment".

The specific objectives of conservation, as outlined by the WCS, were:

1) The maintenance of essential ecological processes and life-support systems such as soil, forests, agricultural systems and coastal and freshwater systems. This meant managing cropland, protecting watersheds and coastal fisheries, and controlling the discharge of pollutants.
2) The preservation of genetic diversity for breeding projects in agriculture, forestry and fisheries. This meant preventing the extinction of species, preserving as many varieties as possible of crop and forage plants, timber trees, animals for aquaculture, microbes and other domesticated organisms and their wild relatives, protecting the wild relatives of economically valuable and other useful species and their habitats, fitting the needs of ecosystems to the size, distribution and management of protected areas, and coordinating national and international protected area programmes.
3) Ensuring the sustainable use of species and ecosystems. This

meant ensuring use did not exceed the productive capacity of exploited species, reducing excessive yields to sustainable levels, reducing incidental take, maintaining the habitats of exploited species, regulating international trade in wild species, carefully allocating timber concessions and limiting firewood consumption, and regulating the stocking of grazing lands.

The Strategy opened by reiterating the view that conservation and development had long been seen as incompatible, and that conservationists had fostered this view by appearing to resist development. In fact, the Strategy argued, development that was sustainable and able to meet the needs of the world's rural poor in particular had to be based on sound conservation: "there is a close relationship between failure to achieve the objectives of conservation and failure to achieve the social and economic objectives of development – or, having achieved them, to sustain that achievement". Everything in the WCS was underwritten by the goal of sustainable development.

On a national level, the priorities included national conservation strategies, environmental planning, legislation and a review of organisation, training and research, public participation, education, and conservation-based rural development. National conservation strategies (NCSs) were promoted by IUCN as the best means by which individual countries could find their own way to sustainable development. Preparing an NCS would ideally be a cooperative venture in which government agencies, NGOs, private interests and the community would take part. In this way, IUCN hoped, "sectoral interests will better perceive their interrelationship with other sectors ... Indeed, unless those responsible for implementing the strategy have been involved in the process and are convinced of its message, the ultimate effect of the NCS will be severely limited" [69]. Furthermore, IUCN noted, an NCS could not and should not be produced according to pre-defined formulae – different countries had different needs. IUCN hoped that governments would take responsibility for preparing NCSs, since they would be responsible for implementation. The nation was not the only unit for a strategy – local provincial strategies or multi-country strategies were equally feasible.

The first three countries to complete national conservation strategies were South Africa, Spain and Britain; Britain's contribution was verbose and meandering, and did not augur well for the quality of national strategies in general. By 1987, 41 countries had acted or were thinking of action, but only five more – Australia, Madagascar, New Zealand, Vietnam and Zambia – had actually published an NCS [70]. Thus, seven years after the launch of the World Conservation Strategy, only eight countries (out of more than 160) had taken tangible action. There was clearly much more to be done before the WCS could be seen as a real breakthrough.

IUCN's own programme of technical assistance had been devoted almost entirely to LDCs, where it had only limited success, for several reasons. First, initial requests for help were normally made by natural resources or environment ministries rather than through central development planning authorities. Hence development aid agencies had found it difficult to provide financial support. The planning authorities were more inclined to deal with more conventional projects – such as energy, industry, agriculture or rural development – than to consider the logistics of requesting financial support for the development of a conservation strategy. Second, the achievement and maintenance of a long-term view on planning was hindered by frequent changes of government in LDCs. Third, the interests supporting rapid economic growth and returns were often powerful, better organised and more concentrated than those promoting the prevention of environmental degradation. Finally, the impact of MDC demands on the global resource base was considerable, so their trade policies had a major influence on the supply and demand of resources in LDCs.

The World Conservation Strategy was a useful step forward, but one that was ultimately incomplete. In some ways, it was behind the times, and too restricted to the more narrow traditional IUCN view of the natural world. By the late 1970s, it was already clear that environmental policy had to move well beyond the natural environment and into the sphere of the human environment; Stockholm had shown that only too clearly. The WCS was a useful and manageable first move; what the world would eventually need though was a more broad-ranging World Environment Strategy.

9

The Arrival of the Greens (1972–1990)

In March 1983, a new dimension was added to environmental politics in Western Europe with the arrival in the West German Bundestag of 27 members representing *Die Grünen* (the greens). Formed just three years before, the greens were the first new party to enter the Bundestag in 30 years, and seemed poised – at least initially – to displace the faltering Free Democrats as the third party in West German politics [1]. They took their seats in the Bundestag between the conservative Christian Democrats and the liberal-left Social Democrats, but in truth they were not easy to categorise in conventional political terms [2]. As Herbert Gruhl (one of their early leaders) put it, "we are neither left nor right; we are in front". As other greens put it, they were not so much a party as a movement, or even an anti-party. Although presenting an environmental platform, they also considered themselves the political voice of citizens' movements opposed to nuclear power and supporting peace, feminism and LDC issues.

By 1988, 15 West European countries had national green parties, 118 green representatives sat in nine national assemblies (Austria, Belgium, Finland, Italy, West Germany, Luxembourg, Portugal, Sweden and Switzerland), nine sat in the European Parliament, many hundreds more sat in regional, local and municipal assemblies, and comparisons were being made between the rise of socialism and the rise of the greens. There was talk of the arrival of an entirely new kind of political ideology, and of the creation of a new segment in the political spectrum.

The years since have seen green fortunes ebb and flow, with forecasts of the rapid demise of green politics apparently confounded by green victories in several West European legislatures, and the spread of the green movement to Eastern Europe. There have also been many assessments of green politics, offering a variety of social, economic and political explanations, but few have yet come to grips with its origins and nature, and none has yet been able to offer a satisfactory explanation of the circumstances surrounding the emergence of the green phenomenon. Whatever specific issues may have prompted the green movement, the foundations provided by the rise of the broader environmental movement cannot be ignored.

The rise of the greens

The origins of the West German greens have been variously ascribed to the effects of rapid post-war industrialisation on German society and the political values of the new German middle class, the emergence of local pressure groups known as *Bürgerinitiativen* (Citizens' Initiatives), a growing realisation among German environmentalists that environmental issues cut across traditional political ideologies, a deepening alienation between the Social Democrats and voters on the left, and even to being a tool of the communists (hence the water-melon analogy, suggesting that the greens were green on the outside but red in the middle) [3]. The German greens were given a further boost by an electoral system in which voters cast ballots both for individual candidates and party lists, and by a federal administrative system which allows voters to give smaller parties a chance without running the danger of seeing them win power at the national level. The emergence of the German greens was also fundamentally influenced by developments in the broader global environmental movement in the 1970s, by ideas contained in *The Limits to Growth* and in the work of such writers as Jim Lovelock, E F Schumacher, Murray Bookchin and Fritjof Capra [4] and, more specifically, in rising public concern about the implications of nuclear power [5].

Table 9.1 The rise of European green parties (by year of foundation)

Country	Party	Founded	First local seats won	First national seats won
Switzerland	Ecology Party/Green Party	1972	1973	1979
UK	Green Party	1973	1980	–
Belgium	Anders Gaan Leven (Agalev)	1976	1981	1981
	Parti Écologiste (Ecolo)	1980	1981	1981
Germany	Die Grünen	1980	1979	1983
Finland	Vihreat (The Greens)	1980	1980	1983
Italy	Liste Verdi (Green List)	1980	1985	1987
Sweden	Miljöpartiet (Environmental Party)	1981	1982	1988
Ireland	Green Party	1981	–	1989
Portugal	Os Verdes	1981	–	1983
France	Les Verts	1982	1977	–
Austria	United Greens of Austria (VGO)	1982	1984	1986
	Austrian Alternative List (ALO)	1982	1984	1986
Luxembourg	Alternative Lescht–Wiert Ich	1983	–	1984
Canada	Green Party	1983	–	–
Denmark	De Gronne	1983	1985	–
Switzerland	Fédération des Partis Écologistes de Suisse	1983	1983	1983
	Fédération Verte	1983	–	–
Luxembourg	Green Alternative	1983	1987	1984
The Netherlands	De Groenen	1983	–	–
Spain	Los Verdes	1984	–	–
Austria	Green Alternative	1986	–	1986
Poland	Green Party	1988	–	–
Greece	Alternative Ecologists	1989	–	1989
Czech Rep	Green Party	1989	–	1992
Moldova	Green Movement (Actiunya Verde)	1989	–	–

continued overleaf

Table 9.1 (*continued*)

Country	Party	Founded	First local seats won	First national seats won
Lithuania	Green Party	1989	–	1990
Slovenia	Slovene Greens	1989	–	1990
Romania	Ecological Movement	na	–	–
	Ecology Party	1989	–	1990
Bulgaria	Ecoglasnost	1990	–	1991
	Green Party	1990	–	1991
Albania	Green Party	1990	–	–
Slovakia	The Greens	na	–	–
Croatia	Green Action	na	–	–
Latvia	Green Party	1990	–	–
Estonia	Green Movement	1991	–	1992
Georgia	Green Party	na	–	–
Ukraine	na	na	–	–

na = information not available

Note. Finding accurate information on green parties is difficult; different sources often provide contradictory information, and several of the newer green parties have proved unstable and ephemeral. This table is based on comparing and combining information from a number of different sources, including the quarterly country reports published by the Economist Intelligence Unit, and the following: Mackie, T T and Craig, F W S, *Europe Votes 2* (Chichester: Parliamentary Research Services, 1985); Mackie, T T and Rose, Richard, *The International Almanac of Electoral History* (London: Macmillan, 1991) Parkin, Sara, *Green Parties: An International Guide* (London: Heretic Books, 1989); Mackie, T T, *Europe Votes 3* (Aldershot: Dartmouth Publishing, 1990); Rudig, Wolfgang (Ed) *Green Politics One 1990* (Carbondale, IL: Southern Illinois University Press, 1990)

Local green groups were founded in several parts of West Germany in 1977–78, but the first step towards the creation of a national party was taken in July 1978 with the foundation of *Grüne Aktion Zukunft* (GAZ) by Herbert Gruhl, a former Christian Democratic member of the Bundestag. Green parties contested state elections in 1978 and 1979, winning their first four seats in Bremen in October 1979. *Die Grünen* were formally established as a national political party at a meeting in Karlsruhe in January 1980. In addition to Gruhl, the party was also heavily influenced by Petra Kelly and Roland Vogt, members of the executive of the *Bundesverband der Bürgerinitiativen Umweltschutz* (Union of Citizens' Initiatives, or BBU). Kelly had been an administrator with the EU in Brussels during the 1970s, and resigned her membership of the Social Democratic Party in 1979 to join the greens. She won a Bundestag seat in 1983, and was replaced as leader in 1984 in the rotational system used by the greens.

Within two months of their formation, *Die Grünen* had won their first six state seats in Baden-Württemberg. They went on to win seats in Berlin, Lower Saxony, Hesse and Hamburg; in August 1983 the Greens precipitated a new election in Hesse by refusing to approve the 1983 budget, and although they lost two of their seats in the new election, they retained the balance of power. Along with the national breakthrough in the 1983 Bundestag elections, *Die Grünen* also took 49 state and city seats, and more than 320 community seats.

Die Grünen enjoyed more visibility and electoral successes than any other green party in the 1980s, but they were neither the first to contest a local or national election, nor even the first to win seats in a national legislature. Eleven years before, in March 1972, the United Tasmania Group was formed to contest elections in Tasmania on the single issue of preventing development of Lake Pedder. It won 7 percent of the vote, but no seats in the state parliament, and was finally wound up in 1977 [6]. In May 1972, the Values Party was founded in New Zealand, and in November became the first party in the world to contest national elections on a predominantly environmental platform. It won 1.98 percent of the vote (polling as high as 9 percent in some districts), but no seats [7]. Founded in May 1972 by journalist Tony Brunt and public relations executive Norman Smith, Values appealed mainly to young, well educated professionals. It was founded in the wake of growing concern in New Zealand about environmental issues, and a spreading undercurrent of anti-materialism among younger New Zealanders.

Despite leadership changes and internal problems, Values was sufficiently organised to contest every seat at the 1975 election, increasing its share of the vote to an impressive 5.2 percent, and taking third place in 29 of the 41 major city districts [8]. But members disagreed about its place in the political spectrum, and even about whether it should be a political party at all, rather than simply an interest group [9]. It managed only 2.5 percent of the vote in 1978, and although it contested elections in 1981 and 1984, its share of the vote collapsed, and it was finally disbanded. James notes that many party members considered Values less a potential governing party than a channel for influencing attitudes laterally and influencing public policy from below; by 1978 the novelty of the party's message had worn off, the larger parties had become more environmentally conscious, and Values may have suffered from a switch to the Labour Party by voters anxious to remove Prime Minister Robert Muldoon [10].

The first green party in Europe was the *Mouvement Populaire pour l'Environnement* (MPE), founded in 1972 in the Swiss canton of Neuchâtel. The party pursued a single issue – opposition to the construction of a new motorway along the shores of Lake Neuchâtel – and won nearly 18 percent of the vote and eight out of 41 seats in canton elections in May 1972. In October 1979, Daniel Brelaz became the first green candidate in the world to be elected to a national legislature [11]. The various local green parties in Switzerland finally formed a national federation in 1983, winning four national seats in that year's general election.

The first national green party in Europe was founded in Britain in February 1973 under the name People. Although it contested the two general elections of 1974, it first rose to national attention in 1979 as the Ecology Party, when it fielded 53 candidates and won an average 1.5 percent share of the vote in the districts it contested. It won its first local council seat in 1980, but although it contested the 1983 general election, failed to establish a strong following.

Renamed the Green Party in 1985, the party won new national prominence under the leadership first of Jonathan Porritt and then of Sara Parkin. Although its membership grew to 11 000, and it won more votes in the 1987 general election than either the Scottish or the Welsh Nationalists, it was unable to make a breakthrough at the national level. Smaller parties in Britain have long been handicapped by the mathematics of the first-past-the-post electoral system, which prevent parties from winning national seats unless they have large blocks of regional support. The effects of this system can be seen, for example, in the 1987 general election, when the Scottish Nationalists won 1.3 percent of the vote and three seats in parliament, while the Green Party (with their supporters more widely dispersed over the entire country) won 1.4 percent of the vote and no seats at all.

The effects of the British electoral system were again dramatically underlined in the 1989 European elections, when the greens surprised everyone (including themselves) by winning 2.29 million votes and nearly 15 percent of the British vote. This was the best result ever for any green party, and was more than twice the share anticipated by the greens themselves. Under a system of proportional representation, this would have entitled them to as many as 12 of Britain's 81 seats in the European Parliament; in the event, they again won no seats at all.

Rüdig and Lowe note four domestic factors which help account for the poor performance of the British greens: the absence of environmentally controversial development projects that would have stimulated radical ecology (the Germans had an active anti-nuclear power movement), the integration of such radicalism as there was into the realm of Labour Party politics, the accession by authorities to strong resistance against particular projects (thereby reducing the potential for local opposition), and the traditional preference among British environmental groups for changing the system from within [12].

The remarkable showing of the British greens in European elections can in turn be explained by the low level of interest in European elections among British voters (and a consequent inclination among voters to vote with their hearts rather than to follow their traditional inclinations), the proportionally greater turnout of more highly motivated green voters, and a reaction to the policies of the Conservative and Labour parties. Support for the greens subsequently collapsed, largely as a result of internal disputes within the party and a lack of strong leadership [13].

In France, an ecology movement born out of the 1968 student uprisings had first taken form in 1970. A local group in Alsace – *Écologie et Survie* – ran a candidate in National Assembly elections in 1973. In 1974, with the support of French ecology groups, Réné Dumont (a professor at the National Institute of Agronomy and a member of the Club of Rome) ran in the presidential election, winning 1.32 percent of the vote. In 1977, an electoral alliance of ecology groups was established, and fielded 200 candidates in the 1978 National Assembly elections under the banner *Écologie-78*, winning 2.1 percent of the first-round vote. In 1980, the *Mouvement d'Écologie Politique (MEP)* was established, and fielded Brice Lalonde (a 35-year-old journalist and veteran of the 1968 student uprisings) in the 1981 presidential election. Lalonde won a creditable 1.126 million votes (3.88 percent of the total), but MEP was unable to capitalise on this, and won only 1.08 percent of the vote at the National Assembly elections later that year. MEP was formally constituted as a political party in 1982, adopting the name *Les Verts-Parti Écologiste* (VPE). It won six percent of the vote and several dozen seats at 1983 municipal elections. In 1984, VPE merged with other green groups to form *Confédération Écologiste et Parti Écologiste*. Ecologists contested nearly a third of metropolitan districts in the 1986 National Assembly elections, winning 1.21 percent of the vote.

Elsewhere in Western Europe, the greens were more successful (see Table 9.2); two Belgian parties (the Walloon party *Ecolo* and the Flemish party *Agalev*) won national legislative seats in 1981, followed in 1983 by greens from Germany, Finland, Portugal and Switzerland, and thereafter by greens in Luxembourg (1984), Austria (1986), Italy (1987), Sweden (1988), and Greece and Ireland (1989). More recently, greens have made breakthroughs in Eastern Europe, winning seats in the national legislatures of Bulgaria, Romania, Slovakia, Slovenia and the three Baltic states. Motivated by the legacy of widespread environmental destruction perpetrated during the state socialist era, green politics in Eastern Europe has helped provide a focus for opponents to reformed communist parties, and in some cases has provided one of the few

Table 9.2 National elections contested, and seats won, by green parties, 1972–1990

	72	73	74	75	76	77	78	79	80	81	82	83	84	85	86	87	88	89	90
Austria											*	0	-	-	8	-	-	-	-
Belgium					*	0	0	-	-	9	-	-	-	15	-	17	-	-	-
Bulgaria																			*
Denmark												*	-	-	-	0	0	-	-
Finland									*	-	-	2	-	-	-	4	-	-	-
France							0	-	-	*0	-	-	-	-	0	-	0	-	-
Germany								*	0	-	-	27	-	-	-	42	-	-	-
Greece																		*1	1
Ireland									*	0	-	-	-	-	-	0	-	1	-
Italy									*	-	-	-	-	-	-	15	-	-	-
Latvia																			*
Lithuania																		*	2
Luxembourg								0	-	-	-	*	2	-	-	-	-	4	-
Moldova																		*	-
Netherlands												*	-	-	0	-	-	-	-
New Zealand	*0	-	-	0	-	-	0	-	-	0	-	-	0						
Poland																	*	-	-
Portugal										*	-	1	-	1	-	1	-	-	-
Romania																		*	21
Slovenia																		*	8
Spain													*	-	0	-	-	-	-
Sweden										*	0	-	-	0	-	-	20	-	-
Switzerland	*	-	-	-	-	-	-	1	-	-	-	4	-	-	-	9	-	-	-
UK	-	*	0	-	-	-	-	0	-	-	-	0	-	-	-	0	-	-	-

* year of formation of first major local or national party

Green parties have also been formed in Albania, Australia, Azerbaijan, Belarus, Canada, Croatia, the Czech Republic, Egypt, Estonia, Georgia, Slovakia, the Ukraine and the United States.

Sources: Mackie, T T and Rose, Richard, *The International Almanac of Electoral History* (London: Macmillan, 1991); Parkin, Sara, *Green Parties: An International Guide* (London: Heretic Books, 1989)

issues around which ethnically and religiously divided societies can unite. For example, the Moldovan Green Movement (Actiunya Verde) – founded in 1989 – is the only mass-based inter-ethnic party in the former Soviet republic, and could act as an important integrating force.

The nature of green politics

Popular conceptions of green politics as being concerned primarily with environmental issues do little justice to the breadth of green ideas. Green ideas were undoubtedly influenced by the growth in environmental awareness in MDCs in the 1960s and 1970s, but – as Porritt argues – while "a concern for the environment is an essential part of being green, it is . . . by no means the same thing as being green" [14].

The extent to which the words "green" and "environmental" have become synonymous reflects the extent to which green ideas have successfully infiltrated the broader base of traditional political ideas in most industrialised countries, and have been adopted by older, conventional parties. But green politics goes well beyond environmentalism, and proposes variations on the theme of re-ordering the entire basis upon which society is organised, and the creation of a new economic and political order in which humans can live in harmony with the planet. German greens, for example, are opposed to the consumer society and to unthinking growth. They envisage the transformation of society into decentralised and self-sufficient communities, with democratically organised econ-omic and administrative units (including the breakdown of large companies into smaller units). They favour a more egalitarian redistribution of wealth (higher taxes for higher income groups), greater rights for workers, the creation of a sustainable national economy, a 35-hour working week, support for human rights, support for gay and lesbian causes, unilateralism, an end to nuclear power, the sustainable use of natural resources, materials and energy conservation, and zero population growth.

Green philosophy traces its roots to developments in physics and ecology during the 20th century, and – more specifically – to the work of a number of scientists and philosophers writing in the 1960s and 1970s. One of the most influential contributions to green philosophy was the Gaia hypothesis outlined by Jim Lovelock, an independent British scientist who worked during the 1960s with the NASA space programme [15]. Lovelock argued that life on earth functions as a single organism which defines and maintains the conditions needed for its survival; "living organ-isms have always, and actively, kept their planet fit for life" [16]. Lovelock did not argue that all life on earth was threatened by human activities; he pointed out that the most pollutive and poisonous substances on earth were natural, and suggested that "the evidence for accepting that industrial activities either at their present level or in the immediate future may endanger the life of Gaia as a whole, is very weak indeed" [17]. While this reduced the usefulness of his argument to environmentalists, his portrayal of the nature of life on earth helped promote the idea of interdependence, and challenged humanity's self-appointed position at the centre of the natural system. His argument was a blow to the anthropocentrism which greens feel pervades conventional political ideologies.

The issue of the scale of society was addressed by the German-born British economist E F (Fritz) Schumacher (1911–1977). In his seminal work *Small is Beautiful*, Schumacher argued that economies, political units, societies and industry had become too big, and lost their human scale. He criticised "the idolatry of giantism", argued that inhuman scale both suffocated and debilitated human nature, and warned that "a way of life that bases itself on materialism, i.e., on permanent, limitless expansionism in a finite environment, cannot last long" [18]. He criticised overorganised systems as destructive both of the human spirit and of the environment, and attacked acquisitiveness, consumption, and humanity's desire to dominate rather than to understand. He supported the idea of restoring a human scale to institutions and processes, and of giving technology "a human face" (or a scale that was simple, controllable and non-violent).

Like all political ideologies, green politics is far from homogeneous, and is marked by many internal divisions, and disagreements over philosophy and structure. Dobson underlines the distinction between "ecologism" (which argues that care for the environment presupposes radical changes in human values, patterns of production and consumption, and relations with the environment) and "environmentalism" (which argues that environmental problems can be addressed without such fundamental changes) [19]. The beginnings of a distinction between the two can be traced to the Norwegian philosopher Arne Naess, who in 1972 used the term "deep ecology" [20] to differentiate between environmentalists concerned about the effects of pollution and other problems on humans (the "shallow" approach), and those promoting a deeper concern for ecological principles, and the need to move beyond the exploitative nature of industrial society towards a fuller understanding of the dynamics of the biosphere.

In their study of the German greens, Spretnak and Capra identify four philosophical strands: visionary/holistic greens (another label for deep ecologists), eco-greens (shallow ecologists focusing on environmental protection and sustainable development), peace movement greens (focusing on peace issues and disarmament), and radical-left greens (who overlapped with – and often entered green politics from – various communist groups) [21]. In addition, several European green parties have seen disagreements among their members over structure; while fundamentalists (or Fundis) have been critical of coalitions with other parties, favour decentralisation, and are doubtful about achieving change through conventional political institutions, realists (or Realos) believe in change through existing systems.

Greens argue that such problems as pollution, species extinction, famine and the overuse of natural resources demand more than amendments to existing political ideologies and economic philosophies. To a far greater extent than the broader environmental movement, the green movement intersects at various points with other movements aimed at reordering the basis of human society and its internal values and relationships: the peace movement, civil and human rights movements, feminism, development, and animal rights issues.

Several themes emerge from the green critique of society:

–   Greens argue that capitalism and socialism alike have failed to meet human needs. While capitalism preaches the ethic of growth, materialism, demand and ever higher levels of consumption, socialism preaches a similar obsession with growth and industrialisation, albeit to different ends. The green response has been to argue in favour of changes in the values, priorities and scale of societies, and to embrace sustainable growth.

–   Human society has lost its understanding of the interrelationships within the biosphere, no longer thinks holistically or ecologically, and instead thinks anthropocentrically. This is partly a consequence of industrialism, argue the greens, and of the distance that modern technology has placed between humans and nature. The necessary response, according to the greens, is to embrace deep ecology and to rediscover those connections and interrelationships, and for humans to see themselves once again as a part of the biosphere, and as dependent upon – rather than dominant over – the natural system.

– The obsession with maintaining global peace during the Cold War encouraged the major powers to develop weapons that had the potential to ensure the annihilation of the entire planet. Many greens argue that the response must include demilitarisation, non-nuclear defence strategies, disarmament and non-violence.

– The promotion of technological fixes to the demand for economic growth has led to worsening unemployment and inflation, and industrial society has brought about widespread spiritual decay and alienation. People feel increasingly cut off from their work, from each other and from their governments. Roszak argues that industrial economies have begun to "coagulate into a single, planet-wide society" dominated by "insensitive colossalism" [22]. The green response is the promotion of an emphasis on socially useful and personally rewarding work, human-scale technology, self-reliance, political decentralisation, and participatory democracy at every level of society. (Several green parties adopted the latter idea by instituting an ultimately confusing system of rotation among their leaders and elected members.)

– Human society has become inured to injustice, alienation and violence, and willing to tolerate the imposition of terrible suffering by one group upon another. Greens espouse a rejection of all exploitation and discrimination, recognition of fundamental human rights, and a renewed sense of social responsibility and "social ecology", arguing the need to restructure society in such a way as to promote social justice.

Explaining the greens

The environmental movement has never been homogeneous, has sprung from a variety of sources, and has pursued a variety of goals, often on the basis of very different motives and using very different methods. Sandbach, for example, identifies two different kinds of environmentalism: the ecological/scientific kind (which uses a scientific argument based on ecology and systems analysis), and the anti-establishment variety (concerned more with human alienation from society and nature, influenced by the New Left, anarchism and the counterculture) [23]. Cotgrove also identifies two kinds: traditional conservation (taking up in many ways the 19th century liberal revolt against economic individualism) and radical libertarianism (opposed to the present industrial system, and in favour of new lifestyles) [24]. To Cotgrove's classification, Porritt adds a third group: reformists (political centrists nervous of fundamental change) [25]. Porritt further argues that not all environmentalists are greens, and believes that most greens would fit into Cotgrove's second class.

To further complicate the picture, green values are often difficult to disaggregate from other indicators of social concern. Milbrath, for example, notes the close links between the environmental movement and the peace movement in most advanced industrial societies; in West Germany in the early 1980s, over half the population favoured both movements and more than 80 percent of environmentalists regarded themselves as strong supporters of the peace movement [26]. Rothacher notes that the platform of *Die Grünen* encompasses ecology, social concerns, grassroots democracy, and non-violence [27].

Environmentalists, especially the more radical among them, are not concerned simply with single-issue politics; they seek more wide-ranging and fundamental social changes [28]. Müller-Rommel believes the new green parties combined a mix of conservative and socialist tendencies, and drew their support from younger, better educated socialists and older liberals and conservatives. Both these groups shared favourable attitudes towards post-materialist values, and were concerned not only with environmental questions but with broader "quality of life" issues [29]. These new values, he argues, cannot be placed on a left/right axis, but must be placed on the new/old axis described by Barnes and Kaase et al. [30]. Hulsberg notes the heterogeneity of the green movement, and asks how this could have provided the basis for a stable party in Germany. He believes it is a reflection of a new attitude among the young, resulting from "the general social crisis and the unattractiveness of the traditional labour movement"; the new movement addressed itself to issues outside the domain of traditional parties [31].

Müller-Rommel identifies three categories of green parties in Western Europe: (1) small, pre-existing socialist parties which adopted environmental policies and changed (in the public perception) into ecology parties (e.g. The Netherlands); (2) liberal and agrarian parties which had traditionally emphasised environmental issues (e.g. the Swedish *Centrum* party, from which the *Miljöpartiet* emerged); and (3) new parties specifically set up to represent an environmentally conscious electorate (e.g., Sweden, Belgium, West Germany, Britain, France and Italy) [32]. The parties in this latter group, he argues, were set up in countries where social democratic parties with a large following inadequately reflected the concerns of environmentalists in their policy-making.

Perhaps the most basic explanation of the rise of green parties was the failure of older established parties to respond adequately to the demands of the environmental movement. The difficulties of defining and compartmentalising the environment as a policy issue have led to confusion and ineffectiveness, with the result that mainstream political parties only slowly (if at all) developed coherent and effective environmental policies. Despite the creation of new government agencies, and the expansion of their legislative authority, the environment was not to become a political issue of real concern until well into the 1970s.

The difficulties of tying down the origins of the greens are exemplified by the many different explanations offered for the rise of the German greens, whose emergence has been traced variously to the counterculture of the 1960s and the rebellion against material accumulation, characterised as the latest in a continuing cycle of German youth movements (a cycle which includes the Nazi youth movement, which was taught that nature was sacred), and associated with the "alternative" politics which arose from the student revolts of 1968 [33]. Other theorists suggest that the rise of the German greens was a cyclical protest phenomenon arising out of a mismatch between the supply of jobs and of qualified graduates, leading frustrated young people to support anti-establishment ideas [34]. The assumption with such arguments is that green political parties are destined to fade out once the rebellious younger generation becomes older and more satisfied with its economic situation.

Capra and Spretnak note the break-up of the Marxist/student movement after 1969 into a series of spontaneous movements. Some of these aligned themselves with the notion of a "march through institutions" espoused by Rudi Dutschke, i.e. entering social and political institutions in an attempt to change the system from within (the most extreme example being the Baader–Meinhof gang). Most Germans, however, were becoming apolitical and moderate, and materially comfortable enough to question challenges to the quality of life [35]. Jonathon Porritt ascribes the rise of *Die Grünen* to the passion of the West German anti-nuclear power movement, well established grassroots support, commitment to a peace movement not dominated by the left, and the federal parliamentary system (which allowed *Die Grünen* to break through in local elections before winning their Bundestag seats) [36].

One of the most widely quoted and discussed theories of the rise of green politics was the post-materialist thesis proposed by Ronald Inglehart in 1977. Inglehart argued that the values of Western publics had seen a shift from an emphasis on material values and physical security towards a greater concern for the quality of life. He noted the emergence of a new middle class that had been socialised under conditions of relative peace and security, and further argued that there had been an increase in the political skills of Western publics that had enabled them to play an increasingly active role in making specific political decisions. Inglehart argued that technological innovation, changes in occupational structures, economic growth, the expansion of higher education, the development of mass communication and the absence of total war among Western nations had combined to help bring change to individual and mass attitudes in the West. This had created new demands for participation in decision-making, and brought new "quality of life" issues into the public arena, among them a renewed concern for the environment [37].

Complementary arguments have been propounded in specific regard to the environment, with suggestions that the traditional yardstick by which the progress of industrial societies has been measured – economic growth – is no longer appropriate. Among others, Ophuls, Pirages, Rifkin and Robertson [38] argue that many of our dominant social beliefs, formed in times of abundance, have needed reassessment in the light of growing ecological scarcity. Pirages argues that environmental problems in industrial societies have their roots in the Dominant Social Paradigm, a set of beliefs and values that includes private property rights, faith in science and technology, individualism, economic growth, and the subjection of nature and exploitation of natural resources [39]. Pollution, energy shortages, and even inflation, economic recession and unemployment have been seen as challenges to the Dominant Social Paradigm [40].

According to these arguments, a reduced concern with immediate economic needs has given rise to greater concern for quality of life issues, leading to fears about the limits to growth and the implications of environmental mismanagement. These views have given rise in turn to a new world view more compatible with the realities of environmental limits. This view – which has all the hallmarks of an ideology – has been called the New Environmental Paradigm [41]. At its heart is a call for an entirely new kind of society. Lester Milbrath suggests that environmentalists constitute a vanguard, using education, persuasion and politics to try to lead people to their vision of a new, more sustainable society [42]. In this they are opposed by a rearguard (exemplified by Julian Simon and Herman Kahn [43]) which believes that modern industrial societies are working quite well, that there is no limit to human ingenuity, and that industrial society produces the most wealth and most equitable economic, social and political arrangements.

The essence of Inglehart's argument is that the basic principle underlying the value shift among Western publics is that people tend to be more concerned with immediate needs or threats than with those that seem remote or non-threatening. In other words, poor or hungry people will be too concerned with survival to be concerned about aesthetic satisfaction or the state of the environment. But an unprecedentedly large portion of Western populations have been raised under conditions of exceptional economic security, so that economic and physical security have a lower priority than they have had in the past [44], and this has given the Western middle classes more time to think about – and worry about – broader quality of life issues.

Inglehart believes that post-materialists give priority to such goals as a sense of community and the non-material quality of life, but live in societies that have traditionally emphasised economic gains above all, even at the expense of these non-material values. Hence they tend to be relatively favourable to social change. Inglehart notes the growing tendency of post-materialists to vote for the Left – not only for the old Left, but for the New Political Left. While the post-materialist share of the vote won by socialists and communists grew from 48 percent in 1970 to 53 percent in 1982–85, the share of the post-materialist vote for green parties over the same period rose from 13 percent to 22 percent. The post-materialist vote has thus become increasingly selective, going to parties with distinctive programmes tailored to post-material concerns [45]. At the same time, Inglehart perceives an increasing level of public interest and participation in national and international politics; mass publics are engaging increasingly in "elite-challenging" as opposed to "elite-directed" activities [46].

Certainly, there is much to suggest that the rise of the environmental movement in the 1960s was in part a reaction to the self-satisfied materialism of the 1950s, and that conditions of economic security have prevailed long enough in industrialised nations to afford people (and the young particularly) the time and the opportunity to turn their attention to qualitative issues such as the state of the environment, peace, racial and gender equality, and physical fitness and health. Such issues are addressed by the greens.

Class is an important factor in assessing the impact of the greens. Much of the literature on the environmental movement emphasises its clear middle-class basis. Repeated studies since the early 1970s have noted that the environmental movement has tended to draw most of its support from the middle and upper middle classes, from those with higher levels of education, from the young, and (in multi-racial societies) from whites [47]. Although the environmental movement in the United States of the 1960s drew much inspiration from the tactics and successes of the civil rights movement, there were few direct links between the two groups; indeed, by questioning the wisdom of economic growth, environmentalism seemed to pose a direct threat to the aspirations of the black working class.

The class analysis of environmentalism and the green movement would seem to fit in with Inglehart's thesis. He suggests that the evolution of advanced industrial society has produced new conflicts and new world views which have made the Marxist analysis of economic conflict less relevant. Economic factors tend to play a decisive role under conditions of economic scarcity, but as scarcity diminishes, other factors shape society to an increasing degree [48]. While most of the major political parties in Western countries tend to be aligned along a social class-based axis, support for new political movements and parties largely reflects the tension between materialist and post-materialist goals and values. The rise of post-materialist issues (such as environment-alism, the women's movement, unilateral disarmament, and opposition to nuclear power) tends to neutralise political polaris-ation based on social class, argues Inglehart, because part of the working class may side with the Right in order to reaffirm traditional materialist emphasis on economic growth, military security and domestic order. The Marxist argument of class-based polarisation is replaced by value-based polarisation [49].

Rudig and Lowe are not convinced by Inglehart; they question the interpretation of survey data and its interplay with post-material explanations, and suggest that an adequate analysis of the rise of the greens would have to go beyond the traditional study of voting behaviour [50]. They further observe that support for post-material values rose steeply in Britain and Germany, yet the British and German greens enjoyed very different fortunes. In Belgium, by contrast, where post-materialism has been declining, green parties are well established. They further argue that the development of green parties cannot be understood without consideration of the emergence of particular issues and protest movements, and the concrete circumstances of party formation [51].

Although this response is valid, it rests too much upon countering Inglehart's cross-national thesis by relating events in individual countries. There will always be exceptions to theories which attempt to be universal; by no means does Inglehart offer an explanation that is capable of withstanding all the tests of universal application. The British and German greens have experienced different fortunes, it is true, but this is perhaps less a function of internal weaknesses in the value-shift thesis than of peculiar national circumstances. The value shift has occurred in Britain, just as it has in other industrialised countries, but the nature of the electoral and party systems has prevented this change from helping the British green movement win seats in Parliament or in local government to the same degree as similar changes translated into national and local legislative seats for the German greens.

Similarly, why has there been no significant green party in the United States, despite the strength and impact of the American environmental movement? Again, this is probably less a function of weaknesses in the post-material argument than of the nature of the American political system. Some may argue that the United States went through a post-materialist phase in the 1960s and early 1970s, and then returned to a more materialist ethic under Reaganism; there is, for example, notably less public concern with human rights, feminism and LDC issues in the United States (even under the Clinton administration) than in Western Europe. Whatever the case, the considerable latitude evident in the policy platforms of the two major parties (the Republicans and the Democrats) has militated against the rise of new parties, if only because green issues could more easily infiltrate Republican or Democratic policies by virtue of the lack of party discipline (i.e. candidates and their policies are more important than parties and their policies). Causes for the lack of a significant green party in the United States must also be sought in the nature of the policy-making process, in which generally effective lobbying by often large and powerful environmental groups has combined with the traditional emphasis placed by many Americans on local and community politics to reduce the kinds of pressures and concerns that have led to the emergence of green parties in parliamentary systems.

How useful is the Inglehart thesis in explaining the rise of the greens? Intuitively, there would seem to be much in the notion of a value shift that would help explain the nature of support for green parties. In particular, Inglehart's suggestion that political polarisation has become less class-based and more value-based would seem to hold true for most West European nations. Post-materialists have grown up in years of relative economic and physical security, hence post-materialism is more prevalent among the post-war generation; this ties in with the relative youthfulness of green party supporters.

The growth of support for social movements is further indication of a shift towards concerns for quality of life issues. The link between material security and post-materialism is given further credence by the fact that although the first green parties emerged in the early 1970s, the period of greatest growth came only after 1979. Green parties might have ridden the crest of the wave of environmentalism in the 1970s, but it is conceivable that support for the greens was diverted in the period 1974–78 by two oil crises and an economic recession in most industrialised countries.

The relative success of green parties also bears a striking relationship to national wealth and the structure of economies. Of the 17 West European nations, those in which green parties have performed best in terms of seats or votes won (Austria, Belgium, Finland, Germany, Italy, Luxembourg, Sweden and Switzerland) rank among the wealthiest in terms of per capita GNP. The countries where green parties have performed worst (Ireland, Spain, Greece and Portugal) rank among the poorest in terms of per capita GNP. Green parties have also performed best in post-industrial societies where the bulk of GNP is generated by services. This would lend support to Inglehart's thesis, and to Eckersley's argument that the new educated middle class is the most likely to be aware of environmental problems and the least likely to shy away from remedial action, because of "its relative structural autonomy from the production process" [52].

Developing this argument, it might be concluded that greens have done best in those societies where a middle class has emerged that no longer directly experiences the industrial production process, has become focused on consumption rather than production, has the time and mobility to rediscover the pleasures of the country-side and to think about social problems, and has the education

Table 9.3   Green party results at European Parliament elections, 1979–1994

Country	1979 % vote	1979 seats	1984 % vote	1984 seats	1989 % vote	1989 seats	1994 % vote	1994 seats
Belgium	3.4	–	8.2	2	13.9	3	11.5	2
Denmark	–	–	–	–	–	–	–	–
France	4.4	–	3.4	–	10.6	8[a]	2.9	0
Germany	3.2	–	8.2	7	8.4	8	10.1	12
Greece	–	–	–	–	1.5	–	–	–
Ireland	–	–	0.5	–	3.7	–	7.9	2
Italy	–	–	–	–	7.5	7[b]	3.2	3
Luxembourg	–	–	6.1	–	11.3	–[c]	10.9	1
Netherlands	–	–	1.3	–	7.0	2[d]	3.7	1
Portugal	–	–	–	–	–	1[e]	–	–
Spain	–	–	–	–	2.8	1[f]	2.8	1
UK	0.1	–	0.5	–	14.9	–	3.2	0
Total seats		0		9		30		22

Note. Greece had its first elections in 1981, and Spain and Portugal in 1987

[a]   includes one independent
[b]   consists of three Green List MEPs, two Radical Party MEPs, and one MEP each from the Rainbow Greens and Proletarian Democracy
[c]   combined vote for Green List Ecological Initiative, Green Alternative and Green Alternative Alliance
[d]   in 1984, Dutch Greens ran as the Green Progressive Accord; in 1989, they ran as Rainbow, and their elected members included one MEP each from the Radical Political Party and the Communist Party
[e]   ran as a member of the United Democratic Coalition, whose four MEPs won 14.9% of the vote
[f]   share of vote earned by four competing Green parties; the "Green" MEP from Spain in fact represented the Basque Left (EE)

Source. 1979 and 1984 results from: Mackie, T T and Craig, F W S, *Europe Votes 2* (Chichester: Parliamentary Research Services, 1985); 1989 results from: Mackie, T T, *Europe Votes 3* (Aldershot: Dartmouth Publishing, 1990); 1994 results from *The Economist*, 18 June 1994

and world view that encourages a concern about phenomena (such as environmental degradation or social inequalities) that impinge upon the middle-class consumer lifestyle. How Inglehart's thesis fits with the rise of green parties in Eastern Europe is more uncertain, however, although it could be argued that heightened environmental awareness in the West has spilled over into the East, encouraging green parties to emerge as vocal critics of past economic policies.

10

The Global Environment

By the mid-1970s, few countries, if any, could claim to be unaffected either by environmental problems or by the rise of the environmental movement. Whether rich or poor, industrial or agrarian, authoritarian or democratic, socialist or capitalist, almost every society felt compelled to reassess its attitudes towards resource management and the condition of the human environment. Bolstered by improved data-gathering and analysis, awareness of national problems had grown to the point where it was now clear that there were many environmental problems that were either common to more than one country, or were transnational, regional or even global in their scope. Issues such as marine pollution, whaling, fisheries, desertification, acid rain, threats to the ozone layer, and carbon dioxide build-up could not be solved by individual states acting alone. Notice of this had been served by the nuclear fallout debate in the 1950s. The obvious response was greater international cooperation.

Stockholm had provided a compelling boost to internationalism. In a foreign policy address to the United States Congress in 1970, Richard Nixon had said: "We know that we must act as one world in restoring the world's environment, before pollution of the skies overwhelms every nation" [1]. In 1972, Falk observed that just because environmental problems manifested themselves most obviously at the domestic level, these were not "potentially the most serious for either the United States or for the world" [2]. In his Environmental Message to Congress in May 1977, Jimmy

Carter noted the growing understanding that environmental problems did not stop with national boundaries, and directed the CEQ and the State Department to study probable changes in global population, natural resources and the environment to the end of the century. Their findings were to serve as the basis for longer-term US planning policy. The resultant study – *The Global 2000 Report to the President* – was submitted in 1980.

Global 2000 and The Resourceful Earth

Global 2000 concluded that there was "the potential for global problems of alarming proportions by the year 2000", that changes in public policy were needed, and that, "given the urgency, scope, and complexity of the challenges before us, the efforts now underway around the world fall far short of what is needed. An era of unprecedented global cooperation and commitment is essential. The necessary changes go beyond the capability of any single nation" [3]. *Global 2000* – as its authors rightly noted – was not the first US government investigation into natural resource futures. Similar questions had been examined by Theodore Roosevelt's National Conservation Commission, Franklin D Roosevelt's National Resources Board, and Truman's Materials Policy Commission. What made *Global 2000* different was that it was the first attempt by any government anywhere to examine the interdependence of population, resources and environment from a longer-term global perspective. Cleveland feels that the real importance of *Global 2000* lay not in the discovery and extrapolation of known trends in familiar categories, but in the fact that a single national government had pulled projections on a variety of issues into "a package that compels, or at least strongly encourages, a comprehensive view" [4].

Although it did not set out to make predictions, the outlining of projections in the future tense made *Global 2000* sound very much like a predictive document [5]. It warned that if "present trends continue, the world in 2000 will be more crowded, more polluted, less stable ecologically, and more vulnerable to disruption than the world we live in now. Serious stresses involving population, resources, and environment are clearly visible ahead. Despite greater material output, the world's people will be poorer in many ways than they are today" [6].

Specifically, the report concluded that by the year 2000:

1) world population would increase by a half, the greatest growth being in less developed countries;
2) the gap between the richest and the poorest – measured in terms of per capita GNP, and the consumption of food, energy and minerals – would widen;
3) there would be fewer resources available – notably land, water and petroleum;
4) important life-supporting ecosystems – such as forests, the atmosphere, soil and wildlife species – would be reduced;
5) prices of many of the most vital resources would increase;
6) the world would be more vulnerable to natural disaster and to disruptions from human causes.

While *Global 2000* outlined the problems, possible solutions were listed in a subsequent document, *Global Future: Time to Act* [7]. Three reasons were given for why the United States should take an interest in global resource impoverishment and environmental degradation: the moral question of poverty and misery for the world's poorest people; the "future generations" argument; and self-interest, viz. the threat to US political and economic security. Broadly speaking, *Global Future* recommended increased financial and scientific assistance from the United States for international programmes, together – in some cases – with setting a good example at home, e.g. by using its agricultural land sustainably, and working towards ensuring that 20 percent of US energy be derived from renewable resources by the year 2000.

If there was one clear lesson to be learned from the *Global 2000* exercise, the authors of *Global Future* noted, it was that the United States government lacked the capacity to anticipate and respond effectively to global issues. Hence, among other things, changes in governmental institutions were needed. The authors recommended the creation of a new government centre to coordinate data-gathering and modelling to support long-term global policy analysis, a new office in the White House devoted solely to long-term global issues, an inter-agency coordinating committee, and assignment of these tasks to the CEQ. By then, however, the

Reagan administration had come into office, and chose to ignore *Global 2000*.

The report also had its detractors outside the Reagan administration. In the tradition of the earlier critics of the prophets of doom came the New Pollyannas, led by Professor Julian Simon, an economist at the University of Illinois and then of Maryland, and Herman Kahn of the Hudson Institute (then based in New York). In 1981, Simon argued that while there had been regular warnings of deteriorating natural resources and growing human needs, the trends in both areas were in fact *positive*; the authors of *Global 2000* offered no persuasive evidence to support their case, and the facts, as he read them, pointed in quite the opposite direction [8].

Kahn and Schneider argued that the generally positive response to *Global 2000* served to reinforce the prevailing pessimism of society. They were concerned at the effects on social morale of reports like *Global 2000*, which, they felt, were inspired by the "prejudices, guilt feelings, and class interests . . . of the affluent, the elite, and the privileged". They regarded *Global Future* as more restrained and reasonable, "perhaps because it appears to reflect the thinking of bureaucrats more than the predispositions of professional environmentalists" [9].

In 1983, Simon and Kahn collaborated on *The Resourceful Earth* [10], intended not so much to evaluate or critique *Global 2000* as to provide an alternative view. In their commentary, they questioned all the major findings of *Global 2000* and argued, like Maddox before them (see Chapter 4), that far more credit should be given to human ingenuity in solving problems. This was a valid point, but – here and elsewhere – Simon, Kahn and Schneider revealed a perception of the world that was otherwise parochial and limited, and often based on a selective use of data.

For example, *Global 2000* had argued that income disparities between the wealthiest and poorest nations were projected to widen. Kahn and Schneider proclaimed that "only by consulting a statistical table in *Global 2000* can the reader learn that GNP per capita is projected to rise from $382 for the LDCs in 1975 to $587 in 2000, an increase of 50 per cent in two decades" [11]. This was true enough. Yet that same table [12] shows that GNP per capita over the same period in MDCs was projected to rise by *96 percent*, and that while per capita GNP in MDCs in 1975 was over 11 times greater than that in LDCs, by the year 2000 it would be more than 14 times greater. This clearly supports the conclusion of *Global 2000*.

Simon and Kahn, for their part, suggested that "the world's people" had increasingly higher incomes, better housing, mobility, better roads and more vehicles. If "the world's people" were defined as those North Americans, West Europeans and Japanese with jobs, this was true. It was, however, patently not true in many LDCs. Simon and Kahn also argued that income in poorer countries was rising at a percentage rate as great or greater than in richer countries. Yet a very poor country would find it difficult *not* to increase its income proportionately faster than a very rich country, if only because it started from a much narrower base. Although the projected growth rate in LDCs in 1975–85 was 5 percent (compared to 3.9 percent in MDCs), there was a considerable difference between the projected per capita GNP for LDCs and MDCs – respectively $1841 and $7150.

Agreements on the global environment

One measure of the newly perceived importance of multi-national responses to environmental issues was the growth in the number of international treaties and agreements in the post-Stockholm decade. Almost as many new international environmental agreements were reached in those ten years as had been reached in the previous 60 years (see Table 10.1). A 1984 UNEP register [13] lists 108 agreements, of which 58 date from the period 1971–83. The more comprehensive list compiled in 1985 by Burhenne [14] includes 257 multilateral treaties, 200 (77 percent) of which were signed after 1960, and 108 of those (42 percent of the total) after 1970. This proliferation was a function of four main factors: (1) the work of the new national environmental agencies and the growing body of national laws, (2) the availability of better – and more compelling – data, (3) the influence of greater public awareness, and (4) the trend towards greater international co-operation on a wide variety of issues.

Table 10.1 International conventions, protocols, treaties and amendments relating to the environment: 1911–1990

Subject	Year signed							
	1911–20	21–30	31–40	41–50	51–60	61–70	71–80	81–90
Pollution (including marine)	–	–	–	–	1	5	19	15
Marine/fisheries	–	–	–	3	8	4	10	7
Nature/natural resources	1	1	2	1	–	1	3	–
Toxic substances (including radiation)	–	–	–	–	3	4	2	–
Animals	–	–	–	1	1	1	6	–
Regional development	–	–	–	–	1	2	4	–
Insect pests	–	–	–	–	–	4	–	–
Plants	–	–	–	–	4	–	–	–
Ecosystems	–	–	–	–	–	–	2	–
Birds	–	–	–	–	1	1	–	–
Environment	–	–	–	–	–	–	1	–
TOTAL	1	1	2	5	19	22	47	22

Sources: Lyster, Simon, International Wildlife Law (Cambridge: Grotius Publications, 1985); United Nations Environment Programme, Register of International Treaties and Other Agreements in the Field of the Environment UNEP/GC/INFO/11 (Nairobi: UNEP, May 1984); Tolba, Mostafa et al., The World Environment 1972–92 (London: Chapman and Hall, 1992)

But the quality of the new laws and agreements did not always match the quantity. The success of any agreement must be measured by the level of actual compliance by signatories. This in turn is a function of the efficiency of enforcement, which is a function of the financial and personnel resources available, which is a function of political will. On this basis, international treaties with an environmental dimension vary in their efficacy from the Partial Test Ban Treaty (total compliance) to the Convention on International Trade in Endangered Species (CITES) (steady progress, with the benefit of a secretariat and reasonably strong funding) to the Wetlands Convention (little progress, few legally binding obligations and no secretariat).

Most international treaties – especially multilateral agreements – are undermined by three major weaknesses. First, there is the problem of enforcement. Although international treaties are by definition firm and binding rules of law, compliance cannot be enforced in the same sense as domestic law [15]. In many cases, the appeal is made less to the letter of law than to morality and "playing the game" – signatories are influenced as much as anything by the opprobrium of attracting the criticism of other members if they do not adhere to the spirit of an agreement. Early European conventions, the Western Hemisphere Convention and the 1968 African Convention all became "sleeping conventions" because none had established adequate systems of enforcement or administration [16].

If negotiations fail to resolve a dispute, states have recourse to international arbitration or – more rarely – to the International Court of Justice. On the whole, the best means of ensuring compliance is through non-judicial mechanisms, e.g. regular meetings of the parties to a convention (which remind them of the provisions of the treaty), the establishment of administrative bodies to oversee the treaty, and regular reporting requirements. Lyster notes also the influence of NGOs in improving compliance with treaties: by attending meetings of signatories, NGOs not only provide technical expertise, but can police the implementation of conventions and publicise contraventions or discrepancies [17].

The second weakness of international treaties is structural: as the goals of treaties have become more complex, so their contents have become less precise, and their effectiveness less predictable [18]. Haigh cites the example of the convention on long-range trans-boundary air pollution (see below). A comparison of the text of the convention with that on which it was modelled – a Nordic Council convention – reveals that the greater number and variety of contracting parties produced a convention that was less precise, less constraining, and less likely to be effectively enforced than its progenitor [19].

Finally, once an agreement has been ratified, there is the problem of transforming its principles into national law, and then of actually implementing national law. Because treaties and conventions are often no more than agreements in principle, influenced (and even weakened) by the need to accommodate the different priorities of signatory nations, there is often a great difference between what is agreed during negotiations and what is subsequently found to be acceptable to national legislatures [20]. A treaty such as CITES, for example, depends for its implementation on domestic law, which in turn depends on the effectiveness of government agencies, which is almost universally limited (see Chapters 7 and 8).

The bartering that precedes an international agreement often results in a text so general and non-specific that every state can interpret it differently, producing different national legislation and different results [21]. The Stockholm Declaration provides some examples. Principle 3 observes that "the capacity of the earth to produce vital renewable resources must be maintained and, *wherever practicable*, restored or improved" (my emphasis); Principle 16 notes the need to apply demographic policies *"which are deemed appropriate* by the governments concerned"; Principle 21 notes that states have, in accordance with the principles of international law, "the sovereign right to exploit their own resources pursuant to their own environmental policies".

Some of the effects of these weaknesses are illustrated by the mixed record of international treaties on wildlife and the natural environment. Between 1900 and 1980, 18 such treaties were agreed, ten of them between 1968 and 1980 (see Table 10.2). The four agreements generally regarded as most important were those on wetlands, the world natural and cultural heritage, international

Table 10.2   Multilateral international wildlife treaties

Year signed	Name of convention
1900	Convention for the Preservation of Wild Animals, Birds and Fish in Africa
1902	Convention for the Protection of Birds Useful to Agriculture
1911	Treaty for the Preservation and Protection of Fur Seals
1933	Convention Relative to the Preservation of Fauna and Flora in their Natural State (London Convention)
1940	Convention on Nature Protection and Wildlife Preservation in the Western Hemisphere
1946	International Convention for the Regulation of Whaling
1950	International Convention for the Protection of Birds
1957	Interim Convention on the Conservation of North Pacific Fur Seals
1968	African Convention on the Conservation of Nature and Natural Resources
1970	Benelux Convention on the Hunting and Protection of Birds
1971	Convention on Wetlands of International Importance Especially as Waterfowl Habitat (Ramsar Convention)
1972	Convention for the Conservation of Antarctic Seals
1972	Convention Concerning the Protection of the World Cultural and Natural Heritage
1973	Convention on International Trade in Endangered Species of Wild Fauna and Flora (CITES)
1973	Agreement on the Conservation of Polar Bears
1979	Convention on the Conservation of Migratory Species of Wild Animals (Bonn Convention)
1979	Convention on the Conservation of European Wildlife and Natural Habitats (Berne Convention)
1980	Convention on the Conservation of Antarctic Marine Living Resources
1992	United Nations Convention on Biological Diversity

trade in endangered species, and migratory species, all signed between 1971 and 1979 [22].

The Wetlands Convention was the first treaty to aim for truly worldwide participation, and the first to concern itself exclusively with habitat [23]. Designed to protect a global chain of wetlands used by waterfowl in their annual migrations, it was signed in February 1971 and came into force in December 1975. Unlike earlier conventions touching on habitat, which emphasised the setting aside of exclusive protected areas, the convention emphasised sustainable use; the only restriction it placed on the use of wetlands was that their ecological character should not be harmed. Maltby notes that the convention was a first step towards placing international obligations on the land management decisions of sovereign states [24]. It has helped prevent development in listed wetlands of international importance, e.g. plans to dam Britain's River Ouse in 1976 were changed when it was pointed out that the Ouse Washes were listed under the convention [25]. But it has also had too few legally binding obligations on its parties (Lyster notes that requiring parties to "promote the conservation of listed sites" does not legally oblige them to ensure that listed wetlands are actually protected [26]). Parties have been reluctant to list more than one or a few sites, and there have been too few non-European parties (and particularly too few from tropical regions) [27]. It has also lacked adequate finance and a secretariat.

The World Heritage Convention, which is administered by UNESCO and came into force in December 1975, is aimed at protecting natural and cultural sites of global significance. The convention is limited by its selectivity; listed sites must be considered to be both of national and universal value. But listing gives sites a prestige value that provides poorer parties with the prospect of receiving financial and technical assistance for the protection of sites [28]. (In 1985 the future of the convention was cast into doubt by the withdrawal of the United States and Britain from UNESCO; the United States had been contributing 25 percent of the annual budget of the World Heritage Fund.)

The convention on trade in endangered species (CITES), which was signed in March 1973 and came into force in July 1975, aims to regulate or prevent trade in a specified list of endangered or threatened wild animal and plant species. By 1992, more than 100 states were party to CITES, which had the benefit of a full-time paid secretariat, initially funded by UNEP but subsequently by CITES parties. Most of the major wildlife trading nations had signed CITES within a decade of its being opened for signature. The fourth major convention – the Migratory Species Convention, or Bonn Convention – was a direct product of the Stockholm conference. It was signed in Bonn in June 1979, but came into force only in November 1983, by which time it was clear that to be effective it needed a large number of signatories. It also faced financial and administrative restraints. By 1991, only 34 states had signed; the United States and Canada were not among them.

Regional organisations: The environment in Western Europe

When it comes to enforcing international agreements, regional or inter-governmental organisations have two clear advantages: they can exert direct moral, if not legal, pressure on national governments, and they provide administrative continuity (the OAS and the Western Hemisphere Convention being one notable exception). Western Europe has a plethora of IGOs and INGOs, many of which have addressed environmental issues. Air pollution, for example, has been addressed by the Nordic Council, the specialised UN agencies, the UN Economic Commission for Europe, the OECD and even NATO. Declaring its intention in 1970 to change from pursuing economic growth for its own sake to pursuing qualitative growth, the OECD set up an Environment Committee to collect information to be fed into OECD policy- and decision-making.

The Europeans have managed to agree on shared problems – particularly ocean, river and air pollution – more quickly than has been the case almost anywhere else in the world. The first major body in Europe – and the first broadly based international body anywhere [29] – to take an interest in the environment was the Council of Europe (founded in 1949). In 1963, the Council set up the European Committee for Conservation of Nature and Natural Resources (CDSN) to draw up a plan of action on the management of Europe's natural resources. In the same year, following the success of National Nature Week in Britain, the Council declared 1970 European Conservation Year (ECY) with the aim of promoting a communal European sense of the extent and value of Europe's natural resources, of the character of humanity's destructive abilities, and of the need for sound long-term management. ECY promoted public awareness and influenced political opinion in the period prior to Stockholm, and spawned a series of European ministerial conferences on the environment (Vienna 1973, Brussels 1976, Bern 1979, Athens 1982). ECY also provided a focus for the debate on population, pollution and growth, accidentally drawing into the environmental debate a wider and more conservative audience [30].

But ECY also had its critics. "All talk and little action – that's the state of play in European Conservation Year", noted Britain's then opposition environment spokesman Christopher Chataway [31]. "Already the cynics are calling it European Conversation Year" noted Robert Allen in *The Ecologist*. While conceding that ECY had "put new heart into the conservationists, bringing them in from the wilderness they so earnestly strive to protect", Allen argued that at the close of the year most politicians had side-stepped its deeper implications, and that had the British government taken it more seriously there would already have been some constructive political action [32].

In 1967, the Council of Europe established a European Information Centre for Nature Conservation within CDSN to promote awareness of the environment. Later, a project to create a network of representative European nature reserves led to the drawing up of the Convention on the Conservation of European Wildlife and Natural Habitats (the Berne Convention), which was opened for signature in 1979 and came into force in 1982. The Council also promoted architectural conservation, town planning, regional planning, and pollution control (e.g. the 1968 Water Charter and the 1972 Soil Charter).

Because of its unique powers to pass laws that are binding on its member states, the European Union (EU) is the regional body with the greatest potential for taking effective action on the European environment. When Britain entered the Union (then European Community) in 1973, there were those who feared that it might have undesirable environmental implications; Brian Johnson suggested that Britain's traditionally steady but slow economic growth had left it with an essentially green and pleasant land despite the rigours of the Industrial Revolution (Britain in fact had less forest cover than any EU state but Ireland, and had been losing wildlife and habitat steadily since the Second World War); the doctrine of economic growth espoused by Europe would create as many problems for Britain as it solved, he argued, and Britain's total environmental prospects might be "bargained away in political-economic package deals like the federation of Europe" [33].

For all its teething problems (notably those resulting from misplaced agricultural policies), the EU has achieved positive action on the environment. This began in October 1972, when a meeting of EU heads of state and government concluded that economic development had resulted in inequalities in living conditions within the Union, that the ecological basis of this development was threatened, that economic expansion was not an end in itself, and that more attention should be paid to social goals such as the quality of life. So they declared themselves in support of a European environmental policy. Since then, there has been a steadily growing body of EU directives, regulations and decisions on water, air and noise pollution, waste, chemicals, wildlife and the countryside. Further boosts to EU activity came with the 1987 Single European Act and the 1993 Treaty on European Union, which made environmental quality a legitimate interest of the EU, and forced greater EU attention to the environment in the interests of harmonising national standards.

Most EU laws have been agreed unanimously and with only temporary blockages, notes Haigh, and without reaching the point of near immobility which tends to afflict many other areas of EU policy. Indeed, he argues, environmental policy "can now be counted as one of the quiet success stories" of the EU, and is being seen to be increasingly important as acid deposition, vehicle emissions, and the movement of hazardous wastes across frontiers show that national measures are not enough [34]. The effect of EU membership on Britain has been significant; Haigh argues that it is harder to point to changes in British domestic environmental policy resulting from Stockholm than to changes resulting from membership of the EU [35]. EU directives on air pollution have introduced the concept of air quality standards to Britain [36], and some of the confusion in the division of domestic responsibilities between local, regional and national authorities in Britain has been bypassed by the transference of certain powers to the EU (e.g. on setting the lead content of petrol).

EU environment policy is determined largely by the trans-national nature of many European environmental problems. It is aimed, says the EU, at bringing economic expansion "into the service of man" through environmental protection and natural resource management. The Union uses the polluter pays principle, has proposed the introduction of US-style environmental impact assessments, and is developing an ecological mapping project. The First Action Programme (1973–77) concentrated on control of pollution and nuisances, while the Second Action Programme (1977–81) was based on the principle of combining environmental considerations with economic policies [37].

The Third Action Programme (1982–86) included proposals for a common EU position on global environmental issues: "The Community will continue to speak in various international organisations with a single voice, using to advantage the influence it has acquired in other areas of international co-operation . . . More specifically it will use this influence to ensure that plans drawn up at the international level . . . are actually implemented" [38]. The Programme went on to note the importance of environmental protection as an integral part of development policy. EU action programmes are not binding on member states, and there is no guarantee that words will become actions [39]; nonetheless, further programmes were launched in 1987 and 1993, and EU membership grew to 15 in January 1995, widening the reach of its environmental policies.

EU activities on the environment have owed much to the role of NGOs. A key cooperative channel is the European Environmental Bureau (EEB), set up in 1974 as a response to the assumption of environmental responsibilities by the EU [40]. The EEB provides environmental groups with a direct channel of access to the EU. The European Commission (the primary EU bureaucracy) regards the Bureau as a source of advice and information, and provides it with funding (which to some extent forces the EEB to moderate its stand on EU policy rather than to be openly confrontational). Its status under Belgian law means it must avoid overt political stances, has limited powers of sanction against disputed policies, and must reach a compromise between the differing tactics of its member organisations and the different national political styles of lobbying [41].

Single-issue agreements: Acid rain and the LRTAP Convention

No matter how much agreement there may be between two or more countries on an issue, there are some problems that cannot be solved with anything short of regional or even global agreement. Nowhere is this more clearly illustrated than in the question of air pollution, historically treated as a local issue, but ultimately addressed by most industrialised states only because of growing international pressure.

In an attempt to control local air pollution in Britain and other industrial countries in the 1950s, tall smokestacks were built at many power stations and factories. London happily lost its yellow smog (about which George Gershwin had written so eloquently), but only at the cost of dumping the pollution further afield. Sulphur dioxide (SO_2) and nitrogen oxides (NO_x) given off by the burning of fossil fuels had long been implicated in the acidification of soils and surface waters. Now, as research confirmed the long-range effects of this pollution, acid rain became one of the most serious of all international environmental issues, straining relations between governments (e.g. the United States and Canada, Britain and Norway), dividing countries into polluters and polluted, and testing political will to protect the environment.

Acid pollution is often described as a modern problem, but links between industrial emissions and the health of people and plants were noticed in England as early as the 17th century by John Evelyn and John Graunt [42]. They also noticed that some of the pollution was drifting across to France, and suggested even then that taller chimneys be used to disperse the pollution. The process of acid pollution was first fully spelt out by the British chemist Robert Angus Smith, who noted the correlation between coal-burning and acid pollution in and around Manchester in the mid-19th century. He published his findings in 1872 in *Air and Rain: the Beginnings of a Chemical Climatology* [43]. He was the first to use the term "acid rain", and to describe the connection between the burning of coal, wind direction, corrosion and acid damage to vegetation. In 1881, a Norwegian scientist attributed "dirty snow-fall" in Norway to either a large town or an industrial district in Britain.

By 1942, research on acid precipitation had spread to Austria, the United States, Canada, Sweden, Italy and Ireland [44]. In 1948, on Swedish instigation, systematic monitoring of precipitation on a Europe-wide basis was begun. In the 1960s, Svante Oden – a soil scientist at the Agricultural College, near Uppsala, Sweden –

demonstrated a link between industrial emissions and environmental damage (largely to fish and lakes). He argued that
precipitation over Scandinavia was becoming more acidic, and
that large quantities of the sulphur compounds that caused the
acidification came from British and central European industrial
emissions. It now appeared conceivable that pollutants could
travel 1000 km (600 miles) or more. In April 1972, the OECD
launched a four-year study into the causes, transport and effects
of sulphur emissions. The results, published in 1977 [45], provided
further evidence of the causes of acid pollution, and confirmed
that airborne pollutants could be and were being transported
across frontiers, and were measurably affecting precipitation in
other countries. In five of the 11 participating countries (Finland,
Norway, Sweden, Austria and Switzerland), more than half the
total deposition of sulphur was estimated to come from foreign
sources. The OECD project also revealed that the problems were
not confined to Western Europe, but involved all European
countries north of the Alps.

In 1975, Sweden and Norway began promoting the idea of a
convention on long-range trans-boundary air pollution to be
signed by all European states, the United States and Canada [46].
The UN Economic Commission for Europe (ECE) was chosen as
the best forum for discussion, mainly because it included East and
West European states. Sweden and Norway wanted a strong
convention that would halt increases in SO_2 emissions (the
"standstill" clause), together with a clause that specified SO_2
abatement by fixed percentage levels of up to 50 percent (the
"rollback" clause). Britain and West Germany objected to legally
binding controls, the former because it questioned whether
Scandinavian acidification was caused by British pollution, the
latter because it was reluctant to be policed by the ECE [47].

West Germany eventually accepted a compromise convention
consisting of general obligations on the signatories to at least limit
– and preferably reduce – air pollution, including long-range
trans-boundary air pollution. This was to be done with the use of
the "best available technology that is economically feasible" in
new and retrofitted plants. These terms – "best available technology" and "economically feasible" – were subsequently given
wide and loose interpretation [48]. Britain too finally accepted the

convention, because it believed that its plans for increased reliance on nuclear power would bring a net reduction in emissions, so it could meet the terms of the convention without changing its existing energy or pollution control policies [49]. The Nordic plans for goals, timetables, abatement requirements and enforcement provisions were dropped.

The Convention on Long-Range Transboundary Air Pollution (the LRTAP Convention) was signed in Geneva in November 1979 by 33 countries (including Britain, the United States, West and East Germany, and France), and entered into force in March 1983. It has since been criticised for its lack of real power, yet it was the first time that the countries of East and West Europe and North America had joined in the signing of an environmental agreement. It also had the positive effect of strengthening the European data gathering systems.

To keep up the momentum, Sweden now invited all the signatories to the Convention to the Conference on the Acidification of the Environment, held in Stockholm in June 1982 (the tenth anniversary of the 1972 conference). A scientific and technical meeting scrutinised all the evidence on the causes, transport and effects of trans-boundary air pollutants, and concluded that human-made sulphur and nitrogen compounds were primarily responsible for acid deposition; a decrease in emissions over a large industrialised region would lead to an "approximately proportionate" decrease in acid deposition; the technology was commercially available that could radically reduce emissions of air pollutants; and the fact that improved technologies may emerge in the future did not justify waiting and delaying the use of existing technology.

A ministerial meeting adopted these conclusions, agreed that acidification problems were serious, and concluded that even if total deposition rose no further, damage to soil and water would continue to increase unless prompt action was taken within the framework of the Convention. West Germany took the opportunity to announce a complete reversal of its previously lukewarm policy on acid pollution; it announced that it would try to halve its SO_2 emissions in ten years and would raise the question of the international environment at the next world economic summit.

The volte-face was ascribed to the growing momentum of *Die Grünen* and the first confirmed reports of widespread West German forest damage [50].

The 1982 Stockholm conference also sped up the process of ratifying the LRTAP Convention; within a few months, all the European Union states had ratified. But it still had little substance, and the Nordic countries were still dissatisfied with the lack of real political action. Keeping up the pressure, they now proposed a mutual 30 percent reduction of SO_2 emissions in the ten years 1983–93, calculated from emission levels in 1980. In March 1984, representatives from ten countries met in Ottawa to sign a five-point declaration undertaking to reduce the emissions that led to acid pollution. The minimum was the 30 percent SO_2 reduction proposed by the Scandinavians – hence the agreement was dubbed the "30 Percent Club". By April 1985, 21 countries had joined the Club.

A second international conference (the Multilateral Conference on the Environment) was held in Munich in June 1984, with the partial aim of encouraging more countries to join the 30 Percent Club. In July 1985, a protocol was agreed to the LRTAP Convention committing its signatories to a 30 percent cut in annual national sulphur emissions or trans-boundary fluxes by 1993 at the latest, based on 1980 levels. The 21 members of the 30 Percent Club immediately signed, but Britain and the United States again deferred. Their original accession to the LRTAP Convention had now become almost meaningless.

Britain finally changed its mind in 1988; worsening relations with Norway, combined with growing scientific certainty about the links between cause and effect, altered the policy climate. The final push came from the EU and the passage of a 1988 directive on large combustion plants; in June 1988, the Thatcher administration approved the terms of the directive, committing Britain to a 60 percent reduction in SO_2 by 2003, and a 30 percent reduction in NO_x by 1998. The United States – increasingly isolated, and faced with growing criticism from Canada – followed suit under the Bush administration in 1990, passing amendments to the 1970 Clean Air Act. All the major industrialised nations had now agreed to take action to stop acid pollution.

The negotiations that brought these changes had four major characteristics. First, the level of government interest and action was often in direct proportion to the degree of domestic damage identified. The Scandinavian countries and Canada – where most of the damage had been confirmed – were the most vocal; the West Germans changed policy only when faced with proof of substantial forest damage within their own borders; Britain only agreed to action when a 1987 Europe-wide forest survey revealed that it had the highest percentage of damaged forests in Europe. Second, governments were often concerned less with whether to act to curb emissions than with the costs involved, and who should pay. Britain and the United States argued that too little was known about the causes and effects of acid pollution to justify the expense of controls; Britain argued that it had anyway reduced SO_2 emissions by 42 percent between 1970 and 1985 simply by using lower sulphur coals, using energy more efficiently, and "industrial restructuring"; Poland – another laggard – argued that for economic reasons there was very little chance of it being able to reduce its emissions [51].

Third, there was a marked lack of governmental interest in taking action on matters that did not have immediate national benefits. The only costs seriously considered by governments were those involved in reducing emissions. Theoretical estimates of the cost of damage to crops, forests, lakes, fisheries, health and buildings carried little weight in political decisions. Finally, individual states only agreed to act when international pressures became too hard to ignore; the weight of scientific evidence, worsening relations with neighbouring states, and the demands of international law ultimately combined to make it hard to avoid taking action.

Protecting the global commons: The ozone layer

If agreement on shared resources or problems of trans-boundary air pollution seemed elusive during the 1980s, agreement on the much more nebulous concept of "the global commons" seemed out of the question – unless there was compelling evidence that national governments could not deny. Use of the oceans and the atmosphere was widely regarded as a free-for-all, the former as a medium of transport and a source of fish and minerals, and both as a useful dumping ground for effluents. However, improved data-gathering in the post-Stockholm decade began to reveal new threats to the quality of the atmosphere. Monitoring carried out since 1957 at the Mauna Loa observatory in Hawaii had already revealed a rise in the concentration of atmospheric carbon dioxide (CO_2), from 315 ppm in 1957 to 335 ppm in 1980, or 6 percent in 23 years [52]. The burning of fossil fuels was identified as the main source, but research in the late 1970s suggested that deforestation and the removal of vegetation were also partly responsible [53]; more CO_2 was stored in the earth's biomass than was held in the atmosphere. There were fears that the rise in CO_2 could lead to major climatic changes – including the so-called greenhouse effect – with profound social, economic and political implications.

Similar fears were raised by the prospect that emissions of chlorofluorocarbons (CFCs), chlorinated compounds, carbon dioxide and nitrogen oxides could react with stratospheric ozone, depleting the ozone layer and increasing the level of harmful ultra-violet radiation reaching the surface of the earth. The effect of CFCs (compounds used in aerosol propellants, refrigeration, foam-blowing and industrial solvents) was outlined by two University of California scientists – Mario Molina and F S Rowland – in 1974 [54]. They warned that CFC use was on the rise, and that ozone concentrations could be reduced by 20 percent. (Subsequent estimates by UNEP and by the National Academy of Sciences and the National Research Council in the US put the figure at 10 percent, 16.5 percent and 3–5 percent respectively [55], which says much about the difficulty of interpreting data and identifying trends.) The United States, Canada and Sweden almost immediately banned the non-essential use of CFC propellants in sprays. The apparent result was a decrease in global CFC production between 1974 and 1979 of between 13 percent and 17 percent [56].

Concerted UN action on ozone began with the launch in 1977 of the World Plan of Action on the Ozone Layer. Led by the World Meteorological Organisation, the aim of the Plan was to increase the number of monitoring stations. The meeting also set up a Co-ordinating Committee on the Ozone Layer (CCOL), which collected information about ongoing and planned research, publishing short annual summaries in the *Ozone Layer Bulletin*. By 1982, about 20 countries had taken action to control CFC emissions [57]. A study of six of those countries (including Britain and the US) suggested that public attitudes, the presence of a strong regulatory agency, and the limited influence of CFC production on the national economy were key factors [58].

In 1981, a working group of legal and technical experts had begun work on a global ozone layer convention, following the pattern of UNEP's Regional Seas Programme. In March 1985, the Global Convention on the Protection of the Ozone Layer was signed in Vienna by 28 countries. The adoption of protocols on control strategies was prevented by a disagreement between the EU and Japan, and the "Toronto Group" of countries (the US, Canada, Finland, Norway and Sweden); the former proposed a limit on production *capacity* (allowing a 30 percent growth in production), while the latter wanted more immediate and substantial reductions in aerosol use and a ceiling on per capita usage [59].

The issue was given new urgency with the discovery in 1985 by British scientists of a thinning (or a "hole") in the Antarctic ozone layer [60]. The hole was roughly the size of the continental United States, and appeared to be growing. Whether it was caused by CFCs, solar radiation or polar meteorological conditions was unclear. Whether it was a phenomenon unique to the Antarctic or a warning of future changes in global ozone was also uncertain [61]. The scientists had noticed a dramatic drop in ozone levels ten years before, but the change had been so marked and abnormal that it had been put down to computer or human error [62].

In February 1987, representatives of the major industrialised nations met in Vienna in an attempt to reach agreement on a freeze on CFC production levels, and a gradual phasing out thereafter. By April, agreement had been reached in principle following a shift by the EU away from a longer timetable for the freeze and reduction. Final agreement was reached in September 1987 at a meeting in Montreal, when 56 countries drew up an agreement to freeze consumption of the five most common types of CFC in 1990 at 1986 levels, followed by reductions of up to 50 percent by the year 2000. To prevent non-signatories being given a competitive edge, the protocol included trade provisions allowing signatory countries to ban CFC-related imports from countries refusing to sign [63]. By 1991, about 70 countries – representing about 90 percent of global CFC production and consumption – had signed the Vienna Convention.

The need for scientific certainty

Inconsistent and incomplete scientific data have been repeatedly quoted by governments and industries opposed to action on environmental questions. The ozone issue showed how quickly governments could in fact agree on addressing a problem before the long-term effects were fully understood and agreed; the Vienna Convention was the first environmental agreement based on prevention rather than cure. Yet it also emphasised the problems of collecting and interpreting data on the atmosphere. Atmospheric conditions vary so much by time and place, and the combinations of factors (natural or human-made) involved in atmospheric changes can be so complex, that pin-pointing cause and effect can be very difficult. Over time, fluctuations increase, making it difficult to know whether changes are part of a new trend or a longer-term oscillation. Added problems arise from the lack of long time series, the effects of local factors on recording stations, and the relative lack of stations over the oceans [64].

For UNEP, the application of the Stockholm Plan of Action had always demanded improved monitoring, data-gathering techniques and information exchange. Concerted attempts to improve the quality of data had begun with the International Biological Programme (see Chapter 3). This closed in 1974, and the initiative passed to the UNESCO Man and the Biosphere (MAB) programme. A product of the Biosphere Conference, MAB was designed as an inter-governmental and inter-disciplinary research programme based on 14 themes, from human interaction with ecosystems to the role of urban areas as ecological systems [65]. MAB had a small secretariat within UNESCO, but operated in real terms through a network of 102 national committees (made up mainly of scientists from universities or national research institutions), and representatives of relevant public and private bodies. The programme had four main aims:

1) to identify and assess changes in the biosphere resulting from human activities (and the effects of those changes on humans);
2) to study the interrelationships between natural ecosystems and socio-economic processes;
3) to develop ways of measuring quantitative and qualitative changes in the environment in order to establish scientific criteria for the rational management of natural resources and the establishment of standards of environmental quality;
4) to encourage greater global coherence in environmental research [66].

The coordination and effectiveness of environmental research was helped by advances in computerised data storage and retrieval. The data collected were more precise and accurate, and many earlier assumptions based on inadequate information were undermined. For example, the rates of tropical rain forest loss assumed in the early 1970s were shown to have been exaggerated. For all its deficiencies (see chapter 6), the UNEP Earthwatch programme had contributed to this progress. The MAB research and information exchange network had meanwhile helped provide a better understanding of the links between cause and effect in environmental problems at local, national and international levels alike. It was now more clearly understood, for example (even if it was hardly a recent discovery), that the removal of forest cover on a hillside could lead to soil erosion, which could lead to siltation in rivers tens or hundreds of kilometres downstream. The impact on food chains of environmental changes was better understood and appreciated, as were the mechanics of phenomena such as acid pollution.

In 1979, the World Meteorological Organisation, in conjunction with a number of UN specialised agencies, including UNEP and FAO, launched the World Climate Programme with the goal of determining the extent of human influence on the climate. Different components of the programme would work to improve the availability and reliability of climatic data and promote consideration of climatic factors in development planning. By

1981, a network of monitoring stations in 71 countries had been set up in cooperation with UNEP to monitor, for example, CO_2 and contaminants in precipitation. Climatic variability is a natural phenomenon, and while climatic extremes are no evidence of climatic change, it seemed to many in the 1970s and 1980s that such extremes were becoming more common: severe droughts, low rainfall, high rainfall, heatwaves, "the hottest summer for 50 years", "the driest/mildest winter this century", and so on.

By 1986, greater consensus was emerging on the question of global climatic change. New and more sophisticated computer models suggested that the climate was not only growing warmer, but was doing so faster than scientists had predicted [67]. There was talk of a build-up of CO_2 trapping more of the earth's heat in the atmosphere, leading to a greenhouse effect that could increase global temperatures by 3.5–4.2°C by the mid-21st century [68] and raise global sea levels by 20–40 cm [69]. Scientists recommended that regional studies be carried out on the impact of and possible policy responses to such changes, and warned that ozone depletion and climatic changes could no longer be considered unrelated issues [70]. This led to heated political debates that have yet to be resolved in the form of clear policy decisions.

Meanwhile, the data on other problems remained incomplete or unreliable. Wildlife conservation provides an example. Without a complete inventory of the world's species, it is difficult to know which are endangered, to what extent they are endangered, and why they are endangered. Only about 1.6 million species have been classified and named; estimates of the actual total range from 5 to 30 million [71]. It is increasingly accepted that except in the cases of the rarest species, where captive breeding may be essential, wildlife can only be effectively protected in its natural habitat. Yet that habitat is being constantly changed and exploited. Given the rate of habitat destruction and the limited range of many species, it is conceivable that species extinction is a daily event. As recently as the 1960s, national parks were regarded as an effective method of protecting wildlife; by the late 1970s it was clear that few national parks in LDCs could continue to exist without more obvious economic benefits to local communities. Natural areas could not last "as fortress islands in seas of hungry people", notes Eckholm [72]. "Where large numbers lack a means to make a decent living, some are sure to invade national parks to grow food and cut wood . . . Nature reserves cannot be successfully managed in isolation from local society. They must be planned within the context of broader regional development".

One area of particular concern was the narrowing of the genetic base of many of the world's crops and livestock, making them more vulnerable to pests, diseases and changes in soils and climate. The destruction of wetlands and tropical moist forests, and the pollution of coastal waters, posed critical threats to wild genetic resources. In 1974 the International Board for Plant Genetic Resources (IBPGR) was set up in Rome to coordinate and encourage the collection, preservation and exchange of plant genetic material. It made field collections of genetic material, and rethought the best means for conserving genetic resources. The register of sites for *in situ* conservation was incomplete, and protection was not always adequate; hence *ex situ* germplasm collections were considered necessary. Much more progress was made in *ex situ* conservation; the IBPGR promoted base collections covering more than 20 of the world's most important crops, including wheat, rice, maize and barley [73]. In 1975, only eight institutions had the facilities for long-term seed storage; by 1983, the number had risen to 33 [74].

In 1982, UNEP warned that "the number of environmental parameters for which global trends can be stated quantitatively can be counted on one hand" [75]. Holdgate et al. observed that while there were relatively complete data on food production, fisheries, population growth and industrial development, there was little reliable information on marine pollution and the status of inland waters, and conflicting evidence on rates of tropical deforestation. They concluded that the world community had not yet achieved one of the major goals of the Stockholm conference: "the compilation, through a global programme of monitoring, research and evaluation, of an authoritative picture of the state of the world environment" [76].

Furthermore, while the new data which *had* been collected were more accurate, they had the unfortunate effect of casting doubt on many earlier environmental assessments; Holdgate et al. note that "these advances hampered comparisons that might have revealed changes in the world environment between 1970 and 1980 because they cast doubt on so much of the earlier information" [77]. Nonetheless, there were few who could now deny the global scope of many environmental problems. In a 1982 report, the OECD concluded that "a major implication of economic and ecological interdependence is that, as it inevitably increases, the ability of governments to deal unilaterally with problems on a national scale will diminish" [78]. There would always be local or national problems demanding appropriate responses, but bilateral and regional responses had been proved to be workable if well planned. At the end of the day, the problems of the global environment demanded workable responses. Another global summit was needed.

11

Rio and Beyond

The debate over achieving a balance between environmental management and economic development continued to build during the 1980s, and it became increasingly obvious that much more thought needed to be given to the means of achieving such a balance. Rich and poor nations continued to have very different perceptions about the relative place of the environment on the policy agenda, and about the relative priorities of short-term growth and long-term planning. The tension between the two sides of the debate dated back to the very beginnings of the environmental movement, and had grown steadily through the decades since. Stockholm had focused an unprecedented level of attention on the environment/development issue, but problems continued to grow, and it became increasingly obvious that there was much more that needed to be done.

Brundtland paves the way

In September 1983, 34 years after UNSCCUR and 11 years after Stockholm, the UN General Assembly passed a resolution calling for the creation of a new independent commission charged with addressing the question of the relationship between environment and development, and with listing "innovative, concrete and realistic" proposals to deal with the question. The World Commission on Environment and Development held its first meeting in Geneva in October 1984, chaired by Gro Harlem Brundtland, the former prime minister of Norway. The Commission had 23 members – 12 from LDCs, seven from Western MDCs (among them Maurice Strong), and four from the communist bloc.

An unprecedented growth in pressures on the global environment had made grave predictions about the future commonplace, the Commission noted; a more prosperous, just and secure future demanded policies aimed at sustaining the ecological basis of development, and at changing the nature of cooperation between governments, business, science and people. Avoiding a reiteration of problems and trends, the Commission selected eight key issues (including energy, industry, food security, human settlements, and international economic relations) and examined them from the perspective of the year 2000. Between March 1985 and February 1987, it sponsored more than 75 studies and reports, and held meetings or public hearings in ten countries, garnering the views of an impressive selection of individuals and organisations. In 1987, the report of the Commission was published as *Our Common Future* [1].

The report concluded that environment and development were inextricable, and that policy responses were handicapped by the fact that existing institutions tended to be independent, fragmented, too narrowly focused, and too concerned with addressing effects rather than causes, and so tended to address issues such as acid pollution as discrete policy problems. The goals of these agencies were too often focused on increasing investment, employment, food, energy, and other economic and social goods rather than on sustaining the environmental resource capital on which these goals depended [2]. National frontiers had become so porous that the distinctions between local, national and international issues had become blurred; domestic policies increasingly had effects well beyond national frontiers (e.g. acid pollution again). Greater international cooperation was needed, but international agencies – notably the UN system – were under siege at the time they were most needed.

Furthermore, the Commission concluded, environmental policy was too often accorded a secondary status; environmental agencies often learned of new initiatives in economic, trade or energy policy (with possible consequences for resources) long after the effective decisions had been taken. It was time that "the ecological dimensions of policy [were] considered at the same time as the economic, trade, energy, agricultural, industrial, and other dimensions – on the same agendas and in the same national and international institutions" [3]. The Commission had several specific recommendations:

- national environmental protection agencies needed urgent strengthening, particularly in LDCs;
- UNEP's work needed to be reinforced and extended (notably through increased funding);
- monitoring and assessment needed better focus and co-ordination;
- policy-makers needed to work more closely with NGOs and industry;
- law and international conventions needed strengthening and better implementation;
- the UN should work towards a universal declaration and later a convention on environmental protection and sustainable development.

In the Brundtland Commission's critique of conventional environmental management and in its global view, Redclift sees the most radical departure yet from previous approaches to sustainable development. Yet, even before the final publication of the report, he felt it unlikely that MDCs or LDCs would act on the measures recommended by Brundtland; they could not do so "without involving themselves in very radical structural reform, not only of methodologies for costing forest losses or soil erosion, but of the international economic system itself" [4]. Whether this process of reform had begun, or whether it could make headway against conventional political and economic attitudes to natural resources, struck at the very heart of the goals and philosophies of the environmental movement.

The Rio summit

The findings of the Brundtland Commission added to those of the World Conservation Strategy and UNEP's own conclusions to increase the pressure for a new summit to follow up on

Stockholm. The special session of the UNEP Governing Council held in 1982 to review progress in the decade since Stockholm had concluded that much more long-term planning was needed. The Brundtland Commission had argued the need to understand the links between environment and development, and argued that environmental protection should not be seen as an obstacle to growth so much as an integral and supportive element in that growth. It recommended that an international conference be convened to review progress and decide on future action.

In December 1989, the UN General Assembly passed a resolution agreeing to call the conference, which Brazil subsequently offered to host. The decision to hold it in an LDC obviously had enormous political significance and symbolism. The United Nations Conference on Environment and Development (UNCED) drew representatives from 178 countries to Rio de Janeiro during two weeks in June 1992, becoming the largest international conference ever held. It was criticised and even dismissed by many environmentalists as an exercise in public relations by national governments and international agencies, and once the media hype had died down, it was obvious that there was once again going to be a gap between word and deed. Nevertheless, Rio added further substance to the debate over global environmental issues.

Sustainable development was always going to be the major theme of UNCED, but events in the late 1980s made sure that other, more specific, problems also went to the top of the conference agenda. Notable among these were the growing concerns about global warming and threats to the ozone layer, and continuing concerns about species extinction and threats to biodiversity. Preparatory meetings for UNCED were held in Nairobi (August 1990), Geneva (March 1991) and New York (March 1992), during which a draft agenda was produced, the active participation of NGOs at Rio agreed, and much of the text of the Rio Declaration and Agenda 21 agreed [5].

Governments were invited to draw up and submit national reports on their policies and their hopes for UNCED. Although many failed to meet the deadline, almost every state in the world had prepared a report by the end of 1992. Several conferences were also held involving UN agencies, national governments and

NGOs to discuss sustainable development issues, many of which produced conclusions that fed into UNCED.

The outcomes of Rio can be summarised in five key agreements.

1) The *Framework Convention on Climate Change*. Although this was a legally binding convention, it was focused less around specific action than around providing an international framework and a set of principles that would guide future action. Negotiations on the convention began in early 1991 under the direct auspices of the UN General Assembly, and the convention was signed at Rio by 153 states and the European Union.

One of the key problems underlying the debate about global warming was the lack of scientific consensus on the existence (let alone the causes) of the problem. The major significance of the Rio convention was that it established the principle that climate change was a serious problem that needed "precautionary measures" that could not await the resolution of questions about scientific certainty. It also emphasised the role of MDCs in the production of greenhouse gases. MDCs agreed to take steps to cut greenhouse gas emissions to 1990 levels by the year 2000, and agreed to meet regularly and to submit reports on their plans and policies.

Discussions were driven in part by concerns among some LDCs that the greenhouse debate was a conspiracy by MDCs to retard their development, so agreement was reached that MDCs should take the lead on action, and compensate LDCs for any additional costs they incurred. This would be done through the Global Environmental Facility, a body to be run on an interim basis by UNEP, UNDP and the World Bank. (In essence, the LDCs said they would do nothing unless MDCs paid.)

The wording of the convention was so ambiguous that it was open once again to widely differing interpretation, and no hard commitments were made. Signatories, for example, agreed to take action subject to the measures being "cost effective", and the convention emphasised the need for continued research, and re-evaluation of action in the light of new findings. The best that can be said about the convention was that it reflected growing political concern for the issue of global warming, and brought the economic and political conflicts over the issue into the open. It forced governments to at least discuss the issue, but did nothing to ensure that anything would actually be done.

2) The *Convention on Biological Diversity*. Negotiated under the auspices of UNEP, this convention was aimed at preserving global biological diversity through the protection of species and ecosystems. Since most of the threats were being experienced in LDCs, and most biotechnology was based in MDCs, discussions were again based around attempts to reach a compromise between the needs of the two sides.

The convention was widely criticised as representing the absolute minimum that governments could get away with, and for including far too many of the opt-out phrases reminiscent of so many international agreements. Much like the climate change convention, the best that can be said is that the biological diversity convention was a step in the right direction. It was signed at Rio by 155 states and the European Union. The United States refused to sign, President Bush arguing that it posed a threat to the US biotechnology industry and to American jobs.

3) *Agenda 21*. This was an action plan for sustainable development, integrating the goals of environmental protection and economic development, and based on local community and free market principles. Agenda 21 ensured that the concept of sustainable development became a permanent principle of the UN. The Rio conference secretariat estimated that about $125 billion per year would be needed to implement Agenda 21, a sum that was so unlikely to be forthcoming that the huge gap between words and deeds was emphasised once again. A recommendation was made for the creation of a UN Commission on Sustainable Development to oversee the implementation of Agenda 21. The Commission was established in late 1992, and consists of ministerial representatives from 53 states who meet in plenary session once a year for two to three weeks to review progress and set annual goals. It is due to complete a five-year review in 1997 in time for a special session of the UN.

4) The *Rio Declaration on Environment and Development*. This consisted of 27 principles guiding action on environment and development, and building on the Stockholm Declaration of 1972.

The preparatory debates over the declaration saw LDCs empha-sising development and global equity, while MDCs emphasised environmental concerns [6]. Among the more contentious of the principles was the third, which affirmed the "right to develop-ment", a clause intended to assure LDCs that their basic devel-opment plans would not be slowed or compromised. The United States issued a disclaimer, rejecting such a right on the grounds that it might be used to override other rights (such as civil rights).

5) The *Forest Principles*. These were all that remained from controversial attempts to draw up a global forest convention in 1990–91. They emphasise the sovereign right of individual states to exploit forest resources, but within general principles of forest protection and management.

Rio perplexed many inside and outside the environmental movement. It drew unparalleled levels of public attention to the problems of the environment, and represented another major step along the road to a workable resolution of the tensions between environmental management and economic development. It also drew lines in the sand regarding the basic principles on which governments would approach environmental management. It brought national governments yet closer together in agreeing the underlying goals of their environmental policies. At the same time, though, it suffered most of the weaknesses common to all big international gatherings – and since Rio was that much bigger, involved so many states, and had such a complex and all-encompassing brief, those weaknesses were magnified. Its major weakness lay in the extent to which its outcomes were diluted by the need to reach consensus among the dozens of participating states. Given the size of its task, though, it is difficult to see how it could have produced anything more than diluted compromise statements. Despite the criticisms it attracted from many environmentalists, it stood as a clear benchmark of just how far the environmental debate had come in 20 years.

Into the 21st century

"The report of my death", once observed a robust Mark Twain, "was an exaggeration." He might have been speaking for the environmental movement. With a persistent and misguided regularity, environmentalism has been declared dead, dying or defunct since almost before it was born. As early as 1954, Grant McConnell lamented that the United States would never again see the like of the Progressive Conservation movement [7]. In 1972, Anthony Downs warned that most social issues eventually enter a stage of prolonged limbo (although he conceded that environmental issues might retain their interest longer) [8]. In 1975, James Bowman perceived a gradual decline of intense interest in the environment [9]. In 1980, Francis Sandbach, quoting opinion polls and diminishing newspaper inches, saw no reason to disagree with Bowman [10].

Against this background, the views of Clay Schoenfeld were in a notable minority. Far from being a passing fad, he argued in 1972, the environmental movement (in the United States at least) seemed destined to be a permanent fixture [11], for several reasons. First, environmental degradation was a high-visibility problem that millions could see, smell, taste and hear. Second, environmentalism was not a wholly new movement; it had a long-established and solid infrastructure from which to operate and expand. Third, the diversity inherent in the movement boded well for its survival. Fourth, affluence gave more people the opportunity to make hard choices. Finally, the movement had a good deal of internal integrity in that it was part of a coherent, fundamental shift in values.

Certainly there were opinion polls in the 1970s that seemed to indicate declining support for the environmental movement. There have been as many since that indicate exactly the opposite [12]. They are all missing the point. The robustness and significance of a social movement cannot always be measured in opinion polls, because too many look at the environmental movement from a perspective limited in historical, geographical and ideological terms.

For those Europeans or Americans who lived through the emotional heyday of mass environmentalism in the 1960s and 1970s, the relative sobriety of the late 1970s and 1980s – distracted as they were by economic recessions, energy crises, and returning affluence and ideological conservatism – must have seemed anticlimactic. The environmentalism of the streets declined, it is true; but the broader movement did not. Rather, it was transformed. During the 1960s, it was fixed in the arena of mass protest and citizen action; by the 1980s, it had scaled (and in some places breached) the citadel of public policy. During the 1960s, activists demanded changes in policy-making, planning goals, and economic and social values; by the late 1970s, their demands were slowly being met.

Qualitatively, the actions of governments and the efficacy of law often have left much to be desired, but there is no denying the advent of the environment as a public policy issue. In manifestos, platforms and campaign speeches, energy and the environment regularly take their place alongside statements on economic and foreign policy, welfare, education, crime, health, agriculture and other more "traditional" policy areas. By the late 1980s, it was regularly argued that the greens were on the wane because their environmental policies were being adopted by the older, larger parties. This is a debatable contention in itself, but it clearly showed that the environment was becoming increasingly nonpartisan.

As the 21st century approaches, and as the nature of the environment continues to broaden and change, it is difficult to know whether to be optimistic or pessimistic about the future. In the credit column, there has been a notable change of attitude.

- At the most fundamental level, the lifestyle of the Western middle classes is changing, and green consumerism is on the rise: people are driving more fuel-efficient cars, recycling, conserving energy at home, reducing the size of their families, and supporting environmental groups and their aims. Environmental awareness is taken increasingly for granted.
- There are more examples of corporate responsibility, notably through the growing use of environmental impact assessments. The record is still far from perfect, and the roots of such change may not always be as honourable as they appear (social responsibility does not yet always exceed the profit motive), but the trend is hopeful.
- Citizen and grassroots movements in MDCs and LDCs alike are building impressive records of achievement. In Britain, the

National Trust alone has ensured the protection in perpetuity of thousands of acres of countryside. In Kenya, the Green Belt Movement has helped turn tree-planting into a national crusade. In Mexico, Malaysia and India, citizens' movements play a growing role in planning decisions. In the United States, environmental groups have proved effective lobbyists, and have repeatedly made the environment an issue in national, state and local politics. Bill Clinton and Al Gore responded by making the environment a key element of their 1992 election campaign, but disappointed the environmental lobby by doing little to tighten environmental regulation in the first two years of their administration.

- Although still far from perfect, the number of national government agencies and institutions dealing with the environment has grown, their work supported by a growing body of local, national and international law. Environmental policy-making – while still bound too often by the confines of ideology and incomplete data – is improving. Green parties have had mixed fortunes, but older established parties have given more thought to the environment as a policy area.

The environment has traditionally fallen more easily into the constituency of moderate/liberal political ideology, but 1988 saw signs of a new interest among anti-regulation conservatives. During the 1988 US presidential campaign, for example, George Bush made it clear that he was not going to rely on free market mechanisms to resolve environmental problems, unlike his predecessor Ronald Reagan.

Even more surprisingly, Margaret Thatcher – after years of ardent opposition to government regulation (especially on environmental questions) and growing pressure from environmentalists and members of her own party – apparently underwent an abrupt conversion to environmentalism. In October 1988, she suddenly declared that protecting the balance of nature was one of "the great challenges" of the late 20th century, and called for emergency action to safeguard the ozone layer, curb acid pollution, and avoid global climatic warming. The announcement took many environmentalists by surprise; it seemed to some that the Conservatives were launching an attempt to claim the environment as the natural preserve of the Right.

- The data are still far from complete, but much more is known about the state of the environment and about the kind of protection it needs. Environmental research is more coordinated and effective; IBP, MAB, Earthwatch and GEMS have brought a better understanding of the interconnectedness of cause and effect in environmental problems. The new data have revealed more clearly the geographical scope of environmental problems.
- Whether green parties continue to exist in their present form, or wither away as their policies are adopted by the older parties, the advent of green politics has already shaken our assumptions about the old left/right axis in politics. Many greens argue that an entirely new political philosophy is needed to respond adequately to the needs of environmentalism, and that conservatism, liberalism and socialism in all their existing hues are too "unecological". Jonathon Porritt argues that green politics "challenges the integrity of [existing] ideologies, questions the philosophy that underlies them, and fundamentally disputes today's accepted notions of rationality" [13].
- Environmentalism has moved beyond the despair of the prophets of doom and has entered a more mature and measured phase in which the accumulated knowledge of the past two centuries, and particularly of the past two decades, is increasingly being put to effective use. Planners in MDCs and LDCs have begun to agree in seeing many environmental problems as being as much global as local concerns. The nature and scope of the work of international agencies is evidence in itself of a broader and more rational view of environmental issues and problems.

Yet despite such progress, there are problems on the debit side of the balance sheet which cannot be ignored. Although there is more certainty about the threats to the environment, there is perhaps less certainty about the prospects for addressing those threats.

- Despite the creation of new environmental agencies and the passage of new legislation in MDCs, the political will to implement the spirit – let alone the letter – of environmental protection, has been patchy. The ratio of words to action is weighted too heavily towards the former, and while public understanding of environmental imperatives was increased since Stockholm, and new institutions have evolved, many of the social, economic and technological causes of environmental problems have continued unchecked [14].

- The break-up of the Soviet Union began to reveal the extent of environmental devastation in much of Eastern Europe and the former USSR, a problem long suspected by Western environmentalists. The extent to which the upheavals of the post-Soviet transition will interfere with attempts to address environmental problems in Eastern Europe and the former Soviet republics remains to be seen.

- The litany of problems afflicting LDCs meanwhile grows with worrying persistence. Incidents such as Bhopal and Ixhuatepec not only cast a shadow over planning and development priorities, but – as most of their victims were shanty-dwellers – also underline the dire social and economic problems of LDC cities, where economic inequality is creating a growing underclass, and where population growth frequently outpaces the provision of housing, clean water and sanitation.

  The rapid and dramatic growth of countries such as Brazil, Argentina, China, Malaysia and Thailand will bring new wealth to poorer states, and underpin political stability, but it also raises the prospect of the same kind of severe environmental problems as Western Europe and the United States saw during the early phase of their industrialisation.

  Sub-Saharan Africa gives the greatest cause for concern. Spiralling population growth, widespread soil erosion, falling food production, political instability, bureaucratic incompetence, and economic corruption and mismanagement have all too often combined to produce a sub-continent in crisis. If current trends continue, the region is promised continuing human and environmental catastrophe.

- Overarching almost everything has been the emergence first of problems affecting many different parts of the planet (acid pollution, toxic wastes, nuclear contamination, deforestation, and the killing of wildlife), and then of problems affecting the planet as a whole. Agreement on dealing with the threats to the ozone layer was reached remarkably quickly; more serious now, though, is the greenhouse effect. With the increased use of coal, oil and natural gas, the concentration of carbon dioxide (CO_2) in the earth's atmosphere has risen steadily since the industrial revolution. Acting like a greenhouse, this CO_2 has been trapping solar radiation in the earth's atmosphere.

Warnings of a global warming were made as early as 1970. Then, they sounded very much like science fiction, with seemingly fantastic suggestions that a warmer climate would lead to changes in crop production patterns, the melting of the polar ice caps, and a rise in global sea levels, inundating many coastal areas. By the late 1980s, those warnings had begun to seem much more real as records for extreme weather began to be broken over much of the northern hemisphere. Whether this really was part of the greenhouse effect, or simply the latest cyclical extreme in continental weather patterns, it provided many with a taste of the possible consequences of global warming. But the level of doubt was enough to give governments the excuse they needed to limit their responses.

In 1982, UNEP published *The World Environment 1972–1982* as an audit of "the first ten years in which mankind [had] consciously and co-operatively attempted the rational management" of the earth. In his foreword, UNEP Executive Director Mostafa Tolba noted that "preventive rather than curative actions have been gaining momentum and wide acceptance" and that the importance of international cooperation had been brought into focus. But, he warned, "ten years after Stockholm it is clear that we still have a very imperfect knowledge of the state of the major components of our environment and of the interacting mechanisms", and he emphasised the need for long-term planning: "the problems which overwhelm us today are precisely those which, through a similar [lack of foresight], we failed to solve decades ago" [15].

UNEP repeated the exercise in 1992 with *The World Environment 1972–1992*. Tolba noted the paradox between growing public concern and media interest in the environment, and a faltering political response. There had been isolated achievements, he noted, but progress had slowed, and the gap between commitment and action persisted [16].

At the global level, finding out and understanding what is needed in the management of resources is much easier than actually implementing multi-national management programmes. Science provides an understanding of the mechanics of environmental problems, but the causes and solutions are ultimately a question of human behaviour. In the final analysis, the environment is a political issue. Whether or not solutions are effectively applied will continue to depend upon politics and policy, upon the attitudes of leaders, parties, industry and the public, and upon a complex cross-referencing and cooperative system involving international agencies, national environmental agencies, NGOs, and a series of often non-binding international conventions and agreements.

Whatever the short-term prognosis, however, the longer-term changes in attitude have been heartening for the environmental movement. Bowman sees environmentalism as the last stage in a process that has taken humans "from fearing, to understanding, to using, to abusing, and now, to worrying about the physical and biological world" around them [17]. There has been a marked trend away from the notion of environment as divorced from humanity and towards a new focus on the human costs of environmental deterioration and mismanagement. It is no longer simply a question of what we are doing to the environment, but of what the despoliation of the environment is doing to us. Environmentalists argue that we can no longer take the environment for granted. It is already too late to save many species and habitats, and more will undoubtedly suffer through ill-advised development. Pollution has been curbed or reduced in some parts of the world, but it is worsening in others. Forests and fertile land are being lost in some parts, and restored in others. Sooner or later, a workable balance must be achieved. However long this takes, the rise of the global environmental movement has made sure that the relationship between humans and their environment will never be quite the same again.

References

Introduction

1. Earthscan, *Cropland or Wasteland: The Problems and Promises of Irrigation* (London: Earthscan, 1984), 22–23.
2. Darby, H C, "The Clearing of the Woodland in Europe", in Thomas, William L, *Man's Role in Changing the Face of the Earth* (Chicago: University of Chicago Press, 1956), 185.
3. Hughes, J Donald, *Ecology in Ancient Civilizations* (Albuquerque: University of New Mexico Press, 1975), 97.
4. Earthscan, reference 1, 23.
5. Deevey, E S, Don S Rice, Prudence M Rice, H H Vaughan, Mark Brenner, and M S Flannery, "Mayan Urbanism: Impact on a Tropical Karst Environment", in *Science* 206: 4416, 19 October 1979, 298–306.
6. Darby, reference 2, 187.
7. Evelyn, John, *Fumifugium: or the Inconvenience of the Aer and Smoake of London Dissipated*, reproduced in Lodge, James P, *The Smoake of London: Two Prophecies* (New York: Maxwell Reprint Company, 1969), 14–16.
8. See especially Nicholson, Max, *The Environmental Revolution* (London: Hodder and Stoughton, 1970); Nicholson, Max, *The New Environmental Age* (Cambridge: Cambridge University Press, 1987); Caldwell, Lynton K, *In Defense of Earth: International Protection of the Biosphere* (Bloomington: Indiana University Press, 1972); Caldwell, Lynton K, *International Environmental Policy: Emergence and Dimensions* (Durham, North Carolina: Duke University Press, 1984).
9. *New Republic* 1 March 1970, 8–9.
10. Petulla, Joseph M, *American Environmentalism: Values, Tactics, Priorities* (College Station, Texas: Texas A & M University Press, 1980).

Chapter 1

1. Thomas, Keith, *Man and the Natural World: Changing Attitudes in England 1500–1800* (Harmondsworth: Penguin, 1983).
2. Gilpin, William, *Observations on the Highlands of Scotland* (Richmond, Surrey: Richmond Publishing, 1973), 112.
3. Wordsworth, William, *A Guide Through the District of the Lakes* (Bloomington, Indiana: Indiana University Press, 1952), 127.
4. Worster, Donald, *Nature's Economy* (San Francisco: Sierra Club Books, 1977), 179.
5. Lowe, Philip and Jane Goyder, *Environmental Groups in Politics* (London: George Allen & Unwin, 1983), 19.
6. Lowe, Philip, "Values and Institutions in the History of British Nature Conservation", in Warren, Andrew and F B Goldsmith, *Conservation in Perspective* (Chichester: Wiley, 1983), 333.
7. Sheail, John, *Nature in Trust* (London: Blackie, 1976), 9.
8. Allen, David Elliston, *The Naturalist in Britain* (Harmondsworth: Penguin, 1978), 197–198.
9. Lowe, reference 6, 331.
10. Sheail, reference 7, 12.
11. *Ibid.*, 13.
12. Ashby, Eric and Mary Anderson, *The Politics of Clean Air* (Oxford: Clarendon Press, 1981), 7.
13. Smith, Robert Angus, *Air and Rain: The Beginnings of a Chemical Climatology* (London: Longmans, Green & Co, 1872).
14. Sheail, reference 7, 60.
15. *Ibid.*, 63.
16. MacEwen, Ann and Malcolm, *National Parks: Conservation or Cosmetics?* (London: George Allen & Unwin, 1982), 5.
17. Lovett, H Verney, "The Development of the Services 1858–1918", in *The Cambridge History of India Vol VI* (Cambridge: Cambridge University Press, 1932), 364.
18. Quoted in Bolton, Guy, *Spoils and Spoilers* (Sydney: George Allen & Unwin, 1981), 37.
19. *Ibid.*, 15.
20. Stokes, Captain John Lort, to Sir Francis Beaufort, 31 January 1849 (Hydrography Office, Taunton), quoted by Bolton, reference 18, 55.
21. Mosley, J G, "Towards a History of Conservation in Australia", in Rapoport, Amos (Ed), *Australia as Human Setting* (Sydney: Angus and Robertson, 1972), 147.
22. Grove, Richard, "Incipient Conservationism in the Cape Colony and the Emergence of Colonial Environmental Policies in Southern Africa", unpublished paper presented to conference: *The Scramble for Resources: Conservation Policies in Africa, 1884–1984*, Cambridge, April 1985.
23. *Ibid.*

24. Pringle, John, *The Conservationists and the Killers* (Cape Town: Books of Africa, 1982), 11, 44.
25. Tabler, Eric C, *The Far Interior* (Cape Town: A A Balkema, 1955).
26. *Ibid.*, 51–52.
27. Huth, Hans, *Nature and the American: Three Centuries of Changing Attitudes* (Berkeley: University of California Press, 1957), 9.
28. Nash, Roderick, *Wilderness and the American Mind* (New Haven, Connecticut: Yale University Press, 1973).
29. Worster, reference 4, 67.
30. Nash, reference 28, 96–97.
31. Worster, reference 4, 71.
32. Marsh, George Perkins, *Man and Nature* (Cambridge, Massachusetts: Harvard University Press, 1965), 36.
33. Udall, Stewart L, *The Quiet Crisis* (New York: Holt, Rinehart & Winston, 1963), 94.
34. Huth, reference 27, 148.
35. Catlin, George, *North American Indians* (Philadelphia: Leary, Stuart & Co, 1913), 294–295.
36. Thoreau, Henry David, *The Maine Woods* (New York: W W Norton, 1950), 321.
37. Nash, reference 28, 102.
38. Roper, Laura Wood, *FLO: A biography of Frederick Law Olmsted* (Baltimore: Johns Hopkins University Press, 1973), 283.
39. Nash, Roderick, "The American Invention of National Parks", in *American Quarterly* 22: 3, Fall 1970, 726–735.
40. Nash, reference 28, 108.
41. *Ibid.*, 118–119.
42. Runte, Alfred, *National Parks: The American Experience* (Lincoln, Nebraska: University of Nebraska Press, 1979), 7–9, 11–18.
43. Nash, reference 28, 132.
44. Rusk, Ralph L (Ed), *The Letters of Ralph Waldo Emerson Vol 6* (New York: Columbia University Press, 1939), 155.
45. Pinkett, Harold T, *Gifford Pinchot: Private and Public Forester* (Urbana, Illinois: University of Illinois Press, 1970), 9.
46. *Ibid.*, 10–11.
47. Pinchot, Gifford, *The Fight for Conservation* (New York: Doubleday Page & Co, 1910), 40–52.
48. Worster, reference 4, 267–268.
49. Hays, Samuel P, *Conservation and the Gospel of Efficiency* (Cambridge, Massachusetts: Harvard University Press, 1959), 271–276.
50. Jones, Maldwyn A, *The Limits of Liberty* (New York: Oxford University Press, 1983), 369.
51. Fox, Stephen, *John Muir and his Legacy: The American Conservation Movement* (Boston: Little Brown & Co, 1981), 128.
52. Roosevelt, Theodore, *An Autobiography* (New York: Macmillan, 1913), 402.
53. Hays, reference 49, 8, 108–109.

54. Penick, James, *Progressive Politics and Conservation* (Chicago: University of Chicago Press, 1968), 9.
55. Report of the National Conservation Commission, Senate Doc. 676, 60th Congress, 2nd Session, p. 1, quoted in McGeary, Martin N, *Gifford Pinchot: Forester-Politician* (Princeton, New Jersey: Princeton University Press, 1960), 100.
56. McGeary, Martin N, *Gifford Pinchot: Forester-Politician* (Princeton, New Jersey: Princeton University Press, 1960), 100.
57. Boardman, Robert, *International Organization and the Conservation of Nature* (Bloomington, Indiana: Indiana University Press, 1981), 28.
58. *Ibid.*
59. Fitter, Richard S R, *The Penitent Butchers* (London: Collins, 1978), 13.
60. *Ibid.*, 7–8.
61. Fitter, reference 59, 8.
62. In Schillings, Carl G, *With Flashlight and Rifle* (London: Hutchinson, 1905), xv.
63. Schillings, Carl G, *In Wildest Africa* (London: Harper & Brothers, 1907), 111.
64. Tjader, Richard, *The Big Game of Africa* (New York: D Appleton & Co, 1910), 299–303.
65. Cranworth, Lord, *Profit and Sport in British East Africa* (London: Macmillan, 1919), 391.
66. *Ibid.*, 208.
67. Sleeman, James, *From Rifle to Camera: The Reformation of a Big Game Hunter* (London: Jarrolds, 1947), 192–193.
68. Boardman, reference 57, 146.
69. Worster, reference 4, 269.
70. Leopold, Aldo, *Game Management* (New York: Scribner's, 1933), 21.
71. Leopold, Aldo, *Sand County Almanac* (New York: Oxford University Press, 1949), 204, 214.
72. *Ibid.*, viii.
73. Fox, reference 51, 199.
74. Worster, reference 4, 222.
75. *Ibid.*, 226.
76. Great Plains Committee, *The Future of the Great Plains* (Washington DC: US Government Printing Office, 1936).
77. Anderson, David, "Depression, Dust Bowl, Demography, and Drought: The Colonial State and Soil Conservation in East Africa During the 1930s", in *African Affairs* 83: 332, July 1984, 321–343.

Chapter 2

1. Boardman, Robert, *International Organization and the Conservation of Nature* (Bloomington, Indiana: Indiana University Press, 1981), 29.
2. Lowe, Philip and Jane Goyder, *Environmental Groups in Politics* (London: George Allen & Unwin, 1983), 165.

3. Boardman, reference 1, 31.
4. Lyster, Simon, *International Wildlife Law* (Cambridge: Grotius Publications, 1985), 110–111.
5. Nixon, Edgar B (Ed), *Franklin D Roosevelt and Conservation 1911–1945 Vol 2* (New York: Franklin D Roosevelt Library, 1957), 599.
6. *Ibid.*, 607.
7. Nixon, reference 5, 627.
8. *Ibid.*, 635.
9. Nixon, reference 5, 644–647.
10. McGeary, Martin N, *Gifford Pinchot: Forester-Politician* (Princeton, New Jersey: Princeton University Press, 1960), 426.
11. UNSCCUR Memorandum from Chairman to members of NRC Co on UNESCO, pp. 8–9, quoted in Boardman, reference 1, 39.
12. United Nations, *United Nations Yearbook 1946–47* (New York: Department of Public Information, United Nations, 1947), 694.
13. *Ibid.*, 492.
14. Hambidge, Gove, *The Story of FAO* (New York: Van Nostrand, 1955), 14.
15. *Ibid.*
16. United Nations, reference 12, 694.
17. Russell, Sir John, "World Population and World Food Supplies", Presidential Address to the British Association for the Advancement of Science, in *Advancement of Science* 6: 23, October 1949, 173–183.
18. Boyd Orr, John, *The White Man's Dilemma: Food and the Future* (London: George Allen & Unwin, 1953), 71.
19. Chase, Stuart, *Rich Land, Poor Land* (New York: McGraw-Hill, 1936).
20. Sears, Paul B, *Deserts on the March* (Norman, Oklahoma: University of Oklahoma Press, 1937).
21. Bennett, Hugh H, *Soil Conservation* (New York: McGraw-Hill, 1939); Whyte, R O and G V Jacks, *Vanishing Lands* (New York: Doubleday, 1939).
22. Pearson, Frank and Floyd Harper, *The World's Hunger* (Ithaca, New York: Cornell University Press, 1945).
23. Osborn, Fairfield, *Our Plundered Planet* (Boston: Little Brown & Co, 1948), 201.
24. Osborn, Fairfield, *The Limits of the Earth* (Boston: Little Brown & Co, 1953), 6.
25. Fox, Stephen, *John Muir and His Legacy: The American Conservation Movement* (Boston: Little Brown & Co, 1981), 307.
26. Vogt, William, *Road to Survival* (New York: William Sloane & Associates, 1948), 34–37.
27. *Ibid.*, 284–288.
28. Buttikofer, Johann, *Report on the Conference for the International Protection of Nature* (Basle: Swiss League for the Protection of Nature, 1946), 34.
29. *Ibid.*, 35.
30. Buttikofer, reference 28, 39.

31. Nicholson, Max, Personal communication, Sept/Nov 1981.
32. Adrian, E D, "Activities of UNESCO in the Natural Sciences during 1948", in *Advancement of Science* 6: 22, July 1949, 90–104.
33. Huxley, Sir Julian, *Memories II* (New York: Harper & Row, 1973), 50–51.
34. Buttikofer, Johann, *Proceedings of the International Conference for the Protection of Nature* (Basle: Swiss League for the Protection of Nature, 1947), 12.
35. *Ibid.*, 152.
36. Buttikofer, reference 34, 160.
37. Nicholson, reference 31.
38. IUCN, *IUCN Yearbook 1973* (Morges: IUCN, 1974), 20.
39. Huxley, reference 33, 127.
40. Dixey, F, "Conservation and Utilization of World Resources: United Nations Conference", in *Nature* 164: 4176, 12 November 1949, 813–815.
41. Nicholson, Max, *The Environmental Revolution* (London: Hodder & Stoughton, 1972), 196.
42. UNESCO, *Proceedings and Papers of the International Technical Conference on the Protection of Nature*, August 1949 (Paris/Brussels: UNESCO, 1950), 181.
43. Nicholson, Max, *The First World Conservation Lecture* (London: World Wildlife Fund, 1981).
44. IUPN, *Proceedings and Reports of the 2nd Session of the IUPN General Assembly*, 1950 (Morges: IUPN, 1951), 71.
45. Nicholson, reference 31.
46. IUCN, reference 38, 19.
47. Harroy, Jean-Paul, "A Pioneer's Reward", in *IUCN Bulletin* 14: 4–6 1983, 35–43.
48. Nicholson, reference 31.
49. Beltran, Enrique, "A Forgotten Chapter in IUCN's History", in *IUCN Bulletin* 14: 10–12, 1983, 108–109.
50. UNESCO, reference 42, 183.
51. Boardman, reference 1, 60.
52. Nicholson, reference 31.
53. Allen, Robert, How to Save the World (London: Kogan Page, 1980), 96.
54. Coolidge, Harold J, "The Growth and Development of International Interest in Safeguarding Endangered Species", in *Proceedings XV International Congress of Zoology*, London, 16–23 July 1958, 58.
55. Nicholson, reference 41, 201.
56. Nicholson, reference 43.
57. IUCN, reference 38, 44.
58. Nicholson, reference 43.
59. Coolidge, Harold, Profile in *The Environmentalist* 1: 1, 1981, 65–74.
60. *Ibid.*
61. Coolidge, reference 59.

62. World Wildlife Fund, *The Ark Under Way: 2nd Report of the World Wildlife Fund 1965–1967* (Morges: WWF, 1967), 49.
63. World Wildlife Fund, *World Wildlife Fund Yearbook 1969* (Morges: WWF, 1969), 16.
64. *Ibid.*, 167.
65. World Wildlife Fund, reference 62, 212.
66. *IUPN Bulletin* II: 6, 1953, 2.
67. *Proceedings of the 5th IUCN General Assembly*, Edinburgh, 1956 (Morges: IUCN, 1956), 22.
68. Watterson, Gerald (Ed), *Report of the Pan-African Symposium on the Conservation of Nature and Natural Resources in Modern African States, September 1961* (Morges: IUCN, 1963), 61.
69. *IUCN Bulletin* No 1, August 1961, 1.
70. *IUCN Bulletin* No 2, December 1961, 7.
71. Hillaby, John, "Conservation in Africa: A Crucial Conference", in *New Scientist* 11: 250, 31 August 1961, 536–538.
72. Watterson, reference 68, 19.
73. *Ibid.*, 49.
74. *IUCN Bulletin* No 4, July/September 1962, 2.
75. *IUCN Bulletin* No 6, January/March 1963, 7.
76. *IUCN Bulletin* No 8, July/September 1963, 1.
77. *IUCN Bulletin* No 9, October/December 1963, 3.
78. Train, Russell E, "A World Heritage Trust", in World Wildlife Fund, reference 62, 36.
79. Boardman, reference 1, 151.
80. World Wildlife Fund, *World Wildlife Fund Yearbook 1968* (Morges: WWF, 1968), 46–47.
81. IUCN, reference 38, 47.
82. *Ibid.*

Chapter 3

1. Fox, Stephen, *John Muir and His Legacy: The American Conservation Movement* (Boston: Little, Brown & Co, 1981), 292.
2. *Time* 4 January 1971, 21–22.
3. *Life* 30 January 1970, 23.
4. Morrison, Denton E, Kenneth E Hornback and W Keith Warner, "The Environmental Movement: Some Preliminary Observations and Predictions", in Burch, William R, Neil H Cheek and Lee Taylor, *Social Behavior, Natural Resources and the Environment* (New York: Harper & Row, 1972), 261–262.
5. Nash, Roderick, *Wilderness and the American Mind* (New Haven, Connecticut: Yale University Press, 1973), 251–252.
6. Means, Richard L, "The New Conservation", in *Natural History* 78: 7, August–September 1969, 16–25.

7. Cotgrove, Stephen, *Catastrophe or Cornucopia* (Chichester: Wiley, 1982), 5.
8. Sandbach, Francis, *Environment, Ideology and Policy* (Oxford: Basil Blackwell, 1980), 21–22.
9. Maddox, John, *The Doomsday Syndrome* (London: Macmillan, 1972), 135.
10. Quoted in Pursell, Carroll (Ed), *From Conservation to Ecology: The Development of Environmental Concern* (New York: Thomas Y Crowell Co, 1973), 4.
11. Lowe, Philip, Jane Clifford and Sarah Buchanan, "The Mass Movement of the Decade", in *Vole* January 1980, 26–28.
12. Lowe, Philip and Jane Goyder, *Environmental Groups in Politics* (London: George Allen & Unwin, 1983), 25.
13. O'Riordan, Timothy, *Environmentalism* (London: Pion Ltd, 1981), 37.
14. Cotgrove, reference 7, 74–100.
15. Raushenbush, Stephen, "Conservation in 1952", in *The Annals of the American Academy of Political and Social Science* 281, May 1952, 1–9.
16. Leuchtenburg, William E, *A Troubled Feast: American Society Since 1945* (Boston: Little Brown & Co, 1979), 37–38.
17. Galbraith, John Kenneth, *The Affluent Society* (Boston: Houghton Mifflin, 1958).
18. Downs, Anthony, "Up and Down With Ecology – The 'Issue–Attention' Cycle", in *The Public Interest* 28, 1972, 38–50.
19. Voss, Earl H, *Nuclear Ambush: The Test-Ban Trap* (Chicago: Henry Regnery Company, 1963), 33.
20. Baines, Graham, "Nuclear Games in the South Pacific", in *The Ecologist* 1: 18, December 1971, 9–11.
21. American Society for the Advancement of Science, *Report of the Air Conservation Commission* (Washington DC: ASAS, 1965).
22. Ward, Barbara and René Dubos, *Only One Earth* (Harmondsworth: Penguin, 1972), 297; Commoner, Barry, *The Closing Circle: Nature, Man and Technology* (New York: Knopf, 1971), 56.
23. Maddox, reference 9, 13.
24. Voss, reference 19, 33.
25. Commoner, reference 22, 50.
26. *Ibid.*, 49.
27. Voss, reference 19, 37.
28. Prins, Gwyn (Ed), *Defended to Death: A Study of the Nuclear Arms Race* (Harmondsworth: Penguin, 1983), 75.
29. Lepper, Mary Milling, *Foreign Policy Formulation: A Case Study of the Nuclear Test Ban Treaty of 1963* (Columbus, Ohio: Charles E Merrill, 1971), 51.
30. Commoner, reference 22, 53.
31. American Institute of Public Opinion, December 1961, quoted in Terchek, Ronald J, *The Making of the Test Ban Treaty* (The Hague: Martinus Nijhoff, 1970), 116.

32. American Institue of Public Opinion, April 1955 and December 1961, quoted in Terchek, reference 31, 116.
33. Harris Survey, 16 September 1963, quoted in Terchek, reference 31, 121.
34. Terchek, reference 31, 119–120; Schlesinger, Arthur M, *A Thousand Days: John F. Kennedy in the White House* (Boston: Houghton Mifflin, 1965), 460, 895; Seaborg, Glenn T, *Kennedy, Khrushchev and the Test Ban* (Berkeley: University of California Press, 1981), 31–32.
35. Terchek, reference 31, 149–150.
36. *Ibid.*, 149, 169.
37. Lepper, reference 29, 40.
38. Jacobson, Harold Karan and Eric Stein, *Diplomats, Scientists and Politicians: The United States and the Nuclear Test Ban Negotiations* (Ann Arbor: University of Michigan Press, 1966), 382.
39. Commoner, reference 22, 57–58.
40. Dupuy, Trevor N and Gay M Hammerman, *A Documentary History of Arms Control and Disarmament* (New York: R R Bowker Co, 1973), 525.
41. Terchek, reference 31, 200.
42. Shea, Kevin P, "A Celebration of Silent Spring", in *Environment* 15: 1, January–February 1973, 4–5.
43. Schnaiberg, Allen, "Politics, Participation and Pollution: The 'Environmental Movement'", in Walton, John and Donald E Carns (Eds), *Cities in Change: Studies in the Urban Condition* (Boston: Allen and Bacon Inc, 1977), 466.
44. Graham, Frank, *Since Silent Spring* (Boston: Houghton Mifflin, 1970), 17.
45. Carson, Rachel, *Silent Spring* (Boston: Houghton Mifflin, 1962), 8.
46. *Ibid.*, 13.
47. Brooks, Paul, *The House of Life: Rachel Carson at Work* (Boston: Houghton Mifflin, 1972), 230–231.
48. *Ibid.*
49. Brooks, reference 47, 294.
50. Claus, George and Karen Bolander, *Ecological Sanity* (New York: David McKay Co, 1977), 10.
51. Brooks, reference 47, 308.
52. Fox, reference 1, 292.
53. *Ibid.*, 298.
54. Ashby, Eric and Mary Anderson, *The Politics of Clean Air* (Oxford: Clarendon Press, 1981), 104.
55. Herbert, Roy, "The Day the Reactor Caught Fire", in *New Scientist* October 14 1982, 84–87; Hall, Tony, *Nuclear Politics* (Harmondsworth: Penguin, 1986), 57–63.
56. Johnson, Stanley, *The Politics of Environment: The British Experience* (London: Tom Stacey, 1973), 82.
57. Gundlach, Erich R, "Oil Tanker Disasters", in *Environment* 19: 9, December 1977, 16–27.

58. Johnson, reference 56, 84.
59. Lowe, Philip, "Science and Government: The Case of Pollution", in *Public Administration*, Autumn 1975, 287–298.
60. Foster, M, M Neushul and R Zingmark, "The Santa Barbara Oil Spill, Part 2: Initial Effects on Intertidal and Kelp Bed Organisms", in *Environmental Pollution* 2: 2, October 1971, 115–134.
61. Council on Environmental Quality, *Environmental Quality 1979* (Washington DC: US Government Printing Office, 1979), 10–11.
62. Molotch, Harvey and Marilyn Lester, "Accidental News: The Great American Oil Spill as Local Occurrence and National Event", in *American Journal of Sociology* 81: 2, September 1975, 235–260.
63. *Ibid.*
64. Council on Environmental Quality, *Environmental Quality 1970* (Washington DC: US Government Printing Office, 1970), 38.
65. *Ibid.*
66. Council on Environmental Quality, *The Global 2000 Report to the President* (Harmondsworth: Penguin, 1982), 318.
67. Huddle, Norie and Michael Reich, "The Octopus that Eats its Own Legs", in *The Ecologist* 3: 8, August 1973, 292–295.
68. Fox, reference 1, 302.
69. Waddington, C H, in Worthington, E Barton (Ed), *The Evolution of IBP* (Cambridge: Cambridge University Press, 1975), 11.
70. *Ibid.*, 8–10.
71. Worthington, reference 69, 126.
72. *Ibid.*, 60, 137.
73. Holdgate, Martin, Mohammed Kassas and Gilbert White, *The World Environment 1972–82* (Dublin: Tycooly Publishing, 1982), 230.
74. Bourliere, Francois, in Worthington, reference 69, 138–139.
75. Taylor, Richard and Colin Pritchard, *The Protest Makers: The British Nuclear Disarmament Movement of 1958–1965 Twenty Years On* (Oxford: Pergamon, 1980), 3.
76. *Ibid.*, 45–46.
77. Schnaiberg, reference 43, 465.
78. See for example Fox, reference 1, 345–346, 355–357; Harry, Joseph, Richard Gale and John Hendee, "Conservation: An Upper-Middle Class Social Movement", in *Journal of Leisure Research* 1, Summer 1969, 246–254; Devall, William B, "Conservation: An Upper-Middle Class Social Movement: A Replication", in *Journal of Leisure Research* 2, Spring 1970, 123–126; Cotgrove, Stephen and Andrew Duff, "Environmentalism, Middle-Class Radicalism and Politics", in *Sociological Review* 28, 1980, 333–351; Lowe and Goyder, reference 12, 27–31.
79. Zinger, Clem L, Richard Dalsemer and Helen Magargle, *Environmental Volunteers in America* (Washington DC: EPA, 1973), 20–21.
80. Ridgeway, James, *The Politics of Ecology* (New York: E P Dutton and Co, 1970), 204.

81. Skolnick, Jerome H, *The Politics of Protest: A Task Force Report Submitted to the National Commission on the Causes and Prevention of Violence* (New York: Simon and Schuster, 1969), xx.
82. *Ibid.*, 79.
83. Cox Commission, *Crisis at Columbia: Report of the Fact-Finding Commission Appointed to Investigate the Disturbances at Columbia University in April and May 1968* (New York: Vintage Books, 1968), 4.
84. Skolnick, reference 81, 79–81.
85. Lipset, Seymour Martin, "Student Activism", in *Current Affairs Bulletin* 42: 4, 15 July 1968, 52–58.
86. Searle, John, *The Campus War* (Harmondsworth: Pelican, 1972), 14–17.
87. Nash, reference 5, 252–253.
88. Cotgrove, reference 7, 12.
89. Reich, Charles, *The Greening of America* (New York: Random House, 1970).
90. Nash, reference 5, 257–258.
91. Fox, reference 1, 325.
92. Bowman, James S, "The Environmental Movement: An Assessment of Ecological Politics", in *Environmental Affairs* 5: 4, 1976, 649–667.
93. *Ibid.*
94. Means, reference 6.
95. Schnaiberg, reference 43, 466.
96. Downs, reference 18.
97. Enzensberger, Hans Magnus, "A Critique of Political Ecology", in *New Left Review 84*, March–April 1974, 3–31.
98. Hardin, Charles M, "Observations on Environmental Politics", in Nagel, Stuart S (Ed), *Environmental Politics* (London: Praeger, 1974), 182.
99. Golub, Robert and Jo Townsend, "Malthus, Multinationals and the Club of Rome", in *Social Studies of Science* 7, 1977, 201–222.
100. Fox, reference 1, 315.
101. *Time*, 2 February 1970, 56.
102. *New Republic*, 7 March 1970, 9, and 31 October 1970, 5.
103. Udall, Stewart L, *The Quiet Crisis* (New York: Holt, Rinehart and Winston, 1963), viii.
104. Davis, Kenneth S, *The Politics of Honor: A Biography of Adlai E. Stevenson* (New York: G P Putnam's Sons, 1967), 500.
105. Boulding, Kenneth E, "The Economics of Coming Spaceship Earth", in Jarrett, Henry (Ed), *Environmental Quality in a Growing Economy* (Baltimore: Johns Hopkins University Press, 1966), 9.
106. Clarke, Arthur C, *The Promise of Space* (New York: Harper and Row, 1968), 149.

Chapter 4

1. Petty, Sir William, *Mankind and Political Arithmetic* (New York: The Mershon Co, no date).
2. Malthus, Thomas, in Appleman, Philip (Ed), *An Essay on the Principle of Population* (New York: W W Norton, 1976).
3. Brower, David, quoted in *Newsweek*, 3 October 1966, 108.
4. Appleman, Philip, *The Silent Explosion* (Boston: Beacon Press, 1965).
5. Ehrlich, Paul R, in *Playboy* 17: 8, August 1970, 56.
6. Ehrlich, Paul R, *The Population Bomb* (New York: Ballantine Books, 1968), xii.
7. Commoner, Barry, *The Closing Circle: Nature, Man and Technology* (New York: Knopf, 1971), 140–177.
8. Holden, Constance, "Ehrlich versus Commoner: An Environmental Fallout", in *Science* 177: 4045, 21 July 1972, 245–247.
9. *Ibid.*
10. Commoner, reference 7, 128–133.
11. Ehrlich, Paul R and John P Holdren, "The Closing Circle", in *Environment* 14: 3, April 1972, 24–39.
12. Commoner, Barry, "The Closing Circle", in *Environment* 14: 3, April 1972, 23–52.
13. Pole, Nicholas, "An Interview with Paul Ehrlich", in *The Ecologist* 3: 1, January 1973, 18–24.
14. Ehrlich, Paul R and Anne H Ehrlich, *The End of Affluence* (New York: Ballantine Books, 1974).
15. Pole, reference 13.
16. Ehrlich, reference 5.
17. Pole, reference 13.
18. Ehrlich, reference 6, 26.
19. Ehrlich, Paul R and Richard L Harriman, *How to be a Survivor: A Plan to Save Spaceship Earth* (New York: Ballantine Books, 1971), author's note.
20. Pole, reference 13.
21. Hardin, Garrett, "The Tragedy of the Commons", in *Science* 162: 3859, 13 December 1968, 1243–1248.
22. See, for example, Olson, Mancur, *The Logic of Collective Action* (Cambridge, Massachusetts: Harvard University Press, 1965).
23. Hardin, reference 21.
24. For further discussion, see Sandbach, Francis, "The Rise and Fall of the *Limits to Growth* Debate", in *Social Studies of Science* 8: 4, November 1978, 495–520.
25. Ordway, Samuel H, *Resources and the American Dream* (New York, Ronald Press Co, 1953).
26. Hecox, Walter E, "Limits to Growth Revisited: Has the World Modelling Debate Made Any Progress?", in *Environmental Affairs* 5: 1, Winter 1976, 65–96.

27. *Ibid.*
28. Peccei, Aurelio, *The Chasm Ahead* (London: Macmillan, 1969).
29. Schwartz, S I and T C Foin, "A Critical Review of the Social System Models of Jay Forrester", in *Human Ecology* 1: 2, September 1972, 161–173.
30. Meadows, Donella H, Dennis L Meadows, Jorgen Randers and William W Behrens III, *The Limits to Growth* (New York: New American Library, 1972), xi.
31. Study of Critical Environmental Problems, *Man's Impact on the Global Environment: Assessment and Recommendations for Action* (Cambridge, Massachusetts: MIT Press, 1970), 5.
32. *Ibid.*, 253.
33. Forrester, Jay W, "Counterintuitive Behavior of Social Systems", in *Technology Review* 73: 3, January 1971, 53–68.
34. Forrester, Jay W, *World Dynamics* (Cambridge, Massachusetts: Wright-Allen Press, 1971).
35. Meadows et al., reference 30, 29.
36. *Ibid.*, 159.
37. Meadows et al., reference 30, 194–198.
38. *Ibid.*, 189.
39. Hardin, reference 21.
40. Meadows et al., reference 30, 195.
41. *The Ecologist, Blueprint for Survival* (Harmondsworth: Penguin, 1972).
42. *Ibid.*, 9.
43. Schumacher, E F, *Small is Beautiful: Economics as if People Mattered* (London: Abacus, 1974).
44. Ehrlich, Paul R and Anne H Ehrlich, *Population, Resources, Environment* (San Francisco: W H Freeman and Co, 1970), 1.
45. Ward, Barbara and René Dubos, *Only One Earth* (Harmondsworth: Penguin, 1972), 25.
46. Inglis, Barclay, "Concorde: The Case Against Supersonic Transport", in Barr, John (Ed), *The Environmental Handbook* (London: Ballantine/Pan, 1971), 180.
47. *Life* 30 January 1970, 22.
48. Brown, Lester (Ed), *State of the World 1984* (New York: W W Norton, 1984), 188.
49. Ehrlich, Paul R, in update of *The Population Bomb* (New York: Ballantine Books, 1978), 203.
50. Sills, David L, "The Environmental Movement and its Critics", in *Human Ecology* 3: 1, 1975, 1–41.
51. Kaysen, C, "The Computer That Printed Out W*O*L*F*", in *Foreign Affairs* 50: 4, 1972, 660–668.
52. O'Riordan, Timothy, *Environmentalism* (London: Pion Ltd, 1981), 59.
53. Allen, Robert, "European Con Year", in *The Ecologist* 1: 6, December 1970, 4–7.

54. See National Caucus of Labor Committees, *Blueprint for Extinction* (New York: NCLC, 1972).
55. Martin, A, *The Last Generation: The End of Survival?* (London: Fontana, 1975); Maddox, John, *The Doomsday Syndrome* (London: Macmillan, 1972).
56. Council on Environmental Quality, *The Global 2000 Report to the President* (Harmondsworth, Penguin, 1982), 607.
57. Cole, H S D, Christopher Freeman, Marie Jahoda and K L R Pavitt, *Thinking About the Future: A Critique of the Limits to Growth* (London: Chatto & Windus, for Sussex University Press, 1973).
58. Peccei, Aurelio, *The Human Quality* (Oxford: Pergamon, 1977), 85.
59. Cole et al., reference 57, 5–13.
60. *Ibid.*, 12.
61. Sandbach, Francis, *Environment: Ideology and Policy* (Oxford: Basil Blackwell, 1980), 205.
62. O'Riordan, reference 52, 60–72.
63. Meadows et al., reference 30, 191.
64. Pehrson, E W, "The Mineral Position in the United States and the Outlook for the Future", in *Mining and Metallurgy Journal* 26, 1945, 204–214.
65. See Sandbach, reference 24, 205, for many examples.
66. For discussion of the strengths and weaknesses of the model, see Hecox, reference 26.
67. McCormick, John, *Acid Earth: The Global Threat of Acid Pollution* (London: Earthscan, 1989).
68. Council on Environmental Quality, reference 56, 608.
69. Hecox, reference 26.
70. Mesarovic, Mihaljo and Eduard Pestel, *Mankind at the Turning Point* (New York: Dutton, 1974).
71. Maddox, John, *The Doomsday Syndrome* (London: Macmillan, 1972), vii.
72. Grayson, Melvin J and Thomas R Shepard Jr, *The Disaster Lobby: Prophets of Ecological Doom and Other Absurdities* (Chicago: Follett Publishing Co, 1973), 21–43.
73. Beckmann, Petr, *Eco-hysterics and the Technophobes* (Boulder, Colorado: Golem Press, 1973), 8–9, 206–212.
74. "Aurum", "British Architects and the Environment", in *Bulletin of the Atomic Scientists* 28: 3, March 1972, 42.
75. Killian, Lewis M, "Social Movements", in Faris, Robert E L (Ed), *Handbook of Modern Sociology* (Chicago: Rand McNally, 1964), 450.
76. *Newsweek*, 4 May 1970, 27.
77. Bagge, Carl E, "Radicalism Perils Supply of Minerals", Speech quoted in *Salt Lake City Tribune*, 29 June 1971, 6.
78. Albrecht, Stan L, "Environmental Social Movements and Counter-Movements: An Overview and an Illustration", in *Journal of Voluntary Action Research* 1, October 1972, 2–11.
79. Allen, reference 53.

80. Maddox, reference 71, 236–237.
81. Luten, Daniel B, quoted in *The Boston Globe*, 12 May 1985, A21.
82. Meadows et al., reference 30, 198.
83. Marx, Karl, *The Poverty of Philosophy* (New York: International Publishers, 1963), 195.

Chapter 5

1. UN Economic and Social Council, Annexes, Agenda Item 12 (Doc E/4466/Add.1) at 2 (New York: ECOSOC, 1968).
2. Boardman, Robert, *International Organization and the Conservation of Nature* (Bloomington: Indiana University Press, 1981), 82.
3. UNESCO, *Use and Conservation of the Biosphere* (Proceedings of the Biosphere Conference) (Paris: UNESCO, 1970), foreword.
4. *Ibid.*, 210.
5. UNESCO, *Backgrounder: The MAB Programme* (Paris: UNESCO, 1982), 2.
6. Doud, Alden L, "International Environmental Developments: Perceptions of Developing and Developed Countries", in *Natural Resources Journal* 12, October 1972, 520–529.
7. United Nations, Resolution 2398 (XXIII) of the General Assembly, 3 December 1968.
8. United Nations, *Yearbook of the United Nations 1970* (New York: Office of Public Information, United Nations, 1970), 449.
9. United Nations Environment Programme, *Review of the Areas of Environment and Development and Environmental Management* UNEP Report No 3, Nairobi, 1978, 6.
10. United Nations, Report of the Secretary-General to the Third Session of the Preparatory Committee, UN Doc A/CONF.48/PC.11, (New York: United Nations, 1971).
11. Rodgers, K, "With the Developing Countries at Founex", in *Uniterra* 1, 1982.
12. Holdgate, Martin, Mohammed Kassas and Gilbert White, *The World Environment 1972–1982* (Dublin: Tycooly Publishing, 1982), 7.
13. Strong, Maurice F, "The International Community and the Environment", in *Environmental Conservation* 4: 3, Autumn 1977, 165–172.
14. United Nations, reference 10.
15. Johnson, Brian, "The Bureaucrat and the Biosphere", in *The Ecologist* 2: 6, June 1972, 30–36.
16. United Nations, reference 10.
17. United Nations, *The UN System and the Human Environment* Gen. Ass. Doc A/CONF.48/12, 17 December 1971, 71.
18. *Ibid.*, 5.
19. United Nations, reference 17, 72.

20. Landsberg, Hans H, "Reflections on the Stockholm Conference", Washington DC, August 1972 (unpublished).
21. *Ibid.*
22. United States Department of State, *Stockholm and Beyond* Department of State Publication 8657, (Washington DC, 1972), 129.
23. Johnson, Brian, reference 15.
24. National Academy of Sciences, *International Arrangements of International Environmental Co-operation* (Washington DC: NAS, 1972), 4.
25. Sohn, Louis B, "The Stockholm Declaration on the Human Environment", in *The Harvard International Law Journal* 14: 3, Summer 1974, 423–515.
26. Landsberg, reference 20.
27. *Ibid.*
28. Landsberg, reference 20.
29. Ward, Barbara, Interview with Jon Tinker 1981 (unpublished).
30. Ward, Barbara and René Dubos, *Only One Earth* (Harmondsworth: Penguin, 1972).
31. International Institute for Environmental Affairs, Minutes of the fifth meeting of the International Institute for Environmental Affairs Board of Directors, Paris, February 1972 (unpublished).
32. Wilson, Thomas W, Draft Plan for the International Institute for Environmental Affairs, 21 September 1970 (unpublished).
33. *Ibid.*
34. Wilson, Thomas W, Proposal to Establish an International Center for Environmental Affairs, 26 June 1970 (unpublished).
35. IIEA, reference 31.
36. United Nations, *Yearbook of the United Nations 1972* (New York: Office of Public Information, United Nations, 1972), 319.
37. Ward and Dubos, reference 30, 24.
38. Talbot, Lee M, "A Remarkable Melding of Contrasts and Conflicts", in *Uniterra* 1, 1982.
39. Holdgate, Martin, "Beyond the Ideals and the Vision", in *Uniterra* 1, 1982.
40. Ward, Barbara, Speech to the UN Conference on the Human Environment, June 1972 (unpublished).
41. Eckholm, Erik, *Down to Earth* (New York: W W Norton, 1982), xi.
42. International Union for Conservation of Nature and Natural Resources, *IUCN Yearbook 1971* (Morges: IUCN, 1972), 14.
43. Budowski, Gerardo, "A Certain Pre-Event Anxiety", in *Uniterra* 1, 1982.
44. International Union for Conservation of Nature and Natural Resources, *IUCN Yearbook 1972* (Morges: IUCN, 1973), 20.
45. Johnson, Keith, "A Second Copernican Revolution", in *Uniterra* 1, 1982.
46. Aaronson, Terri, "World Priorities", in *Environment* 14: 6, July/August 1972, 4–13.

47. Landsberg, reference 20.
48. Aaronson, reference 46.
49. *Ibid.*
50. Reported in *Stockholm Conference Eco*, 14 June 1972, 1.
51. Aaronson, reference 46.
52. Haley, Mary Jean (Ed), *Open Options: A Guide to Stockholm's Alternative Environmental Conferences* (Stockholm, 29 May 1972), 3.
53. Landsberg, reference 20.
54. Talbot, reference 38.
55. Sandbrook, Richard, "NGOs and the UNEP Council – Governments No Longer Listen", in *IUCN Bulletin* 11: 6, June 1980, 65.
56. United Nations Environment Programme, *Review of Major Achievements in the Implementation of the Action Plan for the Human Environment* UNEP Doc. Na.82-0006-1142C, Nairobi, 26 January 1982, 46.
57. Lowe, Philip and Jane Goyder, *Environmental Groups in Politics* (London: George Allen & Unwin, 1983), 163.
58. European Environmental Bureau, *Reports 1975/1976* (Brussels: EEB, 1976), 163.
59. Lowe and Goyder, reference 57, 165.
60. Holdgate, reference 39.
61. Ward, reference 29.
62. In Eckholm, reference 41, xi-xii.
63. Talbot, reference 38.
64. Holdgate et al., reference 12, 7.
65. Ward, reference 29.
66. United Nations, *Yearbook of the United Nations 1972* (New York: Office of Public Information, United Nations, 1972), 320–321.
67. Landsberg, reference 20.
68. Sandbrook, Richard, "The UK's Overseas Environmental Policy", in *The Conservation and Development Programme for the UK: A Response to the World Conservation Strategy* (London: Kogan Page, 1983), 390.
69. In Eckholm, reference 41, xii.

Chapter 6

1. United Nations, Resolution 2997 (XXVII) of the General Assembly, 15 December 1972.
2. United Nations, Resolution 3004 (XXVII) of the General Assembly, December 1972.
3. Hardy, Michael, "The United Nations Environment Program", in *Natural Resources Journal* 13, April 1973, 235–255.
4. United Nations, reference 1.
5. Sandbrook, Richard, "The UK's Overseas Environmental Policy", in *The Conservation and Development Programme for the UK: A Response to the World Conservation Strategy* (London: Kogan Page, 1983), 391.

6. Clarke, Robin and Lloyd Timberlake, *Stockholm Plus Ten* (London: Earthscan, 1982), 50.
7. Sandbrook, reference 5, 390.
8. *Ibid.*, 391.
9. United Nations Environment Programme, *The Environment in 1982: Retrospect and Prospect* Paper prepared for the Session of a Special Character, UNEP Doc UNEP/GC (SSC)/2, Nairobi, 29 January 1982, 22; Sandbrook, reference 5, 391.
10. Sandbrook, reference 5, 392.
11. United Nations Environment Programme, *Earthwatch: An In-depth Review* UNEP Report No 1, Nairobi, 1981.
12. *Ibid.*, 76.
13. United Nations Environment Programme, *Review of Major Achievements in the Implementation of the Action Plan for the Human Environment* UNEP Doc. Na.82–0006–1142C, Nairobi, 26 January 1982, 58.
14. Sandbrook, reference 5, 388.
15. Porter, Gareth and Janet Welsh Brown, *Global Environmental Politics* (Boulder, Colorado: Westview Press, 1991), 48.
16. United Nations Environment Programme, *1989 Annual Report of the Executive Director* (Nairobi: UNEP, 1990), 197.
17. United Nations Environment Programme, Report on the Present State of UNEP, prepared by the Permanent Representatives of the European Community Countries, 1980 (unpublished).
18. *Ibid.*
19. United Nations Environment Programme, reference 13, 61.
20. Clarke and Timberlake, reference 6, 48.
21. Porter and Brown, reference 15, 50.
22. Holdgate, Martin, "UNEP: Some Personal Thoughts", in *Mazingira*, March 1984, 17–20.
23. Clarke and Timberlake, reference 6, 48.
24. *Ibid.*, 52.
25. Clarke and Timberlake, reference 6, 56.
26. United Nations Environment Programme, reference 9, 20.
27. *Ibid.*, 21; Clarke and Timberlake, reference 6, 47.
28. Holdgate, reference 22.
29. *Ibid.*
30. Holdgate, reference 22.
31. Clarke and Timberlake, reference 6, 49.
32. United Nations Environment Programme, *Report of the Environment Co-ordination Board on its Sixth Session, New York, 20–21 October 1976* UNEP/GC/89 (Nairobi: UNEP, 1976), 1–2.
33. United Nations Environment Programme, *Memoranda of Understanding Between the UN Environment Programme and Other Organisations of the United Nations System, 19 December 1977* UNEP/GC/INFO/6 (Nairobi: UNEP, 1977).
34. Clarke and Timberlake, reference 6, 70.

35. United Nations Environment Programme, reference 9, 74.
36. Earthscan, *The Polluted Seas* (London: Earthscan, 1978), 12.
37. Clarke and Timberlake, reference 6, 43.
38. United Nations Environment Programme, *Achievements and Planned Development of UNEP's Regional Seas Programme and Comparable Programmes Sponsored by Other Bodies* UNEP Regional Seas Reports and Studies No 1 (Nairobi: UNEP, 1982).
39. Hulm, Peter, "The Regional Seas Program: What Fate for UNEP's Crown Jewels?", in *Ambio* 12: 1, 1983, 2–13.
40. Clarke and Timberlake, reference 6, 43.
41. Grainger, Alan, *Desertification* (London: Earthscan, 1982), 5.
42. *Ibid.*, 8.
43. Timberlake, Lloyd, *Africa in Crisis* (London: Earthscan, 1985), 61.
44. Sen, Amartya, *Poverty and Famines* (Oxford: Clarendon Press, 1981).
45. Timberlake, reference 43.
46. Twose, Nigel, *Why the Poor Suffer Most: Drought and the Sahel* (Oxford: Oxfam, 1984), 4.
47. Murdoch, William W, *The Poverty of Nations: The Political Economy of Hunger and Population* (Baltimore: Johns Hopkins University Press, 1980), 293.
48. *Ibid.*, 298.
49. Grainger, reference 41, 19.
50. Tolba, Mostafa K, "Desertification is Stoppable" (Speech delivered to UNEP Governing Council, Nairobi, May 1984).
51. *Ibid.*
52. Grainger, reference 41, 88.
53. United Nations Environment Programme, *General Assessment of Progress in the Implementation of the Plan of Action to Combat Desertification 1978–1984* UNEP/GC.12/9 (Nairobi: UNEP, 1984), 32.
54. Grainger, reference 41, 88.
55. United Nations Environment Programme, reference 53, 32.
56. Grainger, reference 41, 51.
57. United Nations Environment Programme, reference 53, 33.
58. *Ibid.*
59. Timberlake, Lloyd, "Alone in the Wastelands" Earthscan Feature (London: Earthscan, May 1984).
60. Grainger, reference 41, 53.
61. International Institute for Environment and Development, *Report on the African Emergency Relief Operation 1984–1986* (Draft) (London: IIED, 1986), 213, 221.
62. World Bank, *Toward Sustained Development in Sub-Saharan Africa* (Washington DC: World Bank, 1984), 4.
63. Timberlake, reference 43, 7.
64. United Nations Environment Programme, reference 9, 22.
65. United Nations Environment Programme, reference 16, 2.
66. United Nations Environment Programme, reference 13, 68–69.
67. Clarke and Timberlake, reference 6, 50.

Chapter 7

1. Organisation for Economic Cooperation and Development, *The State of the Environment in OECD Member Countries* (Paris: OECD, 1979).
2. Council on Environmental Quality, *Environmental Quality 1971* (Washington DC: US Government Printing Office, 1971), 28.
3. World Environment Center, *The World Environment Handbook* (New York: WEC, 1983).
4. In *Environment and Health* (Washington DC: Congressional Quarterly, 1981), 130–131.
5. McCormick, John, *British Politics and the Environment* (London: Earthscan, 1991).
6. World Resources Institute/International Institute for Environment and Development, *World Resources 1986* (New York: Basic Books, 1986), 191.
7. Organisation for Economic Cooperation and Development, *The State of the Environment 1985* (Paris: OECD, 1985), 241.
8. WRI/IIED, reference 6, 192.
9. Barker, A, "Local Amenity Societies, A Survey and Outline Report", in Civic Trust, *The Local Amenity Movement* (London: Civic Trust, 1976).
10. Gregory, Roy, *The Price of Amenity* (London: Macmillan, 1971), 38.
11. Tinker, Jon, "Britain's Environment: Nanny Knows Best", in *New Scientist* 53: 786, 9 March 1972, 530.
12. Scarrow, Howard A, "The Impact of British Domestic Air Pollution Legislation", in *British Journal of Political Science* 2: 3, July 1972, 261–282.
13. Johnson, Stanley, *The Politics of Environment: The British Experience* (London: Tom Stacey, 1973), 172–173.
14. Royal Commission on Environmental Pollution, *Second Annual Report* (London: Her Majesty's Printing Office, Cmnd 4894, 1972).
15. Enloe, Cynthia, *The Politics of Pollution in Comparative Perspective* (New York: David McKay, 1975), 273.
16. Johnson, reference 13, 98–99.
17. *White Paper on the Reorganisation of Central Government* (London: Her Majesty's Printing Office, Cmnd 4506, October 1970).
18. Bennett, Graham, "Pollution Control in England and Wales: A Review", in *Environmental Policy and Law* 5: 2, 12 April 1979, 93–99.
19. Pollard, E, M D Hooper and N W Moore, *Hedges* (London: Collins, 1974), 42.
20. Pye-Smith, Charlie and Chris Rose, *Crisis and Conservation: Conflict in the British Countryside* (Harmondsworth: Penguin, 1984), 83.
21. Shoard, Marion, *The Theft of the Countryside* (London: Temple Smith, 1980), 99.

22. Lowe, Philip and Jane Goyder, *Environmental Groups in Politics* (London: George Allen and Unwin, 1983), 75.
23. Barker, reference 9, 3.
24. McCormick, reference 5, 152.
25. Council on Environmental Quality, *Environmental Quality 1970* (Washington DC: US Government Printing Office, 1970), vii.
26. Dunenberg, R V, *Understanding American Politics* (London: Fontana, 1984), 99–100.
27. Rosenbaum, Walter A, *Environmental Politics and Policy* (Washington DC: CQ Press, 1985), 52–54.
28. Wandesforde-Smith, Geoffrey, "National Policy for the Environment: Politics and the Concept of Stewardship", in Cooley, Richard and Geoffrey Wandesforde-Smith (Eds), *Congress and the Environment* (Seattle: University of Washington Press, 1970), 210.
29. Davies, J Clarence and Barbara S Davies, *The Politics of Pollution* (Indianapolis: Pegasus, 1975), 108.
30. *Ibid.*
31. See annual Council on Environmental Quality reports.
32. Council on Environmental Quality, *The Global 2000 Report to the President: Entering the Twenty-First Century* (Harmondsworth: Penguin, 1982), 695.
33. Davies and Davies, reference 29, 117.
34. Quarles, John, *Cleaning Up America* (Boston: Houghton Mifflin, 1976), 19–20.
35. Rosenbaum, reference 27, 51.
36. Rosenbaum, Walter A, "The Clenched Fist and the Open Hand: Into the 1990s at EPA", in Vig, Norman J and Michael E Kraft (Eds), *Environmental Policy in the 1990s* 2nd edition (Washington DC: CQ Press, 1994), 126.
37. Council on Environmental Quality, *Environmental Quality 1979* (Washington DC: US Government Printing Office, 1979), 177.
38. *Ibid.*, 181.
39. Vig, Norman J and Michael E Kraft, "Environmental Policy from the Seventies to the Eighties", in Vig, Norman J and Michael E Kraft (Eds), *Environmental Policy in the 1980s: Reagan's New Agenda* (Washington DC: CQ Press, 1984), 4.
40. Culhane, Paul J, "Sagebrush Rebels in Office: Jim Watt's Land and Water Politics", in Vig and Kraft, reference 39, 294.
41. Rosenbaum, reference 27, 54.
42. Conservation Foundation, *State of the Environment 1982* (Washington DC: Conservation Foundation, 1982), 387–392.
43. Rosenbaum, reference 27, 73–74.
44. Council on Environmental Quality, *Environmental Quality 1980* (Washington DC: US Government Printing Office, 1980), 418–419.
45. *Ibid.*, 421–422.
46. Fox, Stephen, *John Muir and His Legacy: The American Conservation Movement* (Boston: Little Brown & Co., 1981), 316.

47. Wild, Peter, *Pioneer Conservationists of Western America* (Missoula, Montana: Mountain Press, 1979), 157.
48. Cotgrove, Stephen and Andrew Duff, "Environmentalism, Middle-Class Radicalism and Politics", in *Sociological Review* 32, 1980, 92–110.
49. Brower, David, Personal communication, December 1984; Burke, Tom, "Friends of the Earth and the Conservation of Resources", in Willetts, Peter, *Pressure Groups in the Global System* (London: Frances Pinter, 1982), 106.
50. Burke, reference 49, 107.
51. Friends of the Earth, Newsletter, in *The Ecologist* 1: 18, December 1971, 33.
52. Morgan, Robin and Brian Whitaker, *Rainbow Warrior* (London: Arrow Books, 1986), 115–116.
53. *Ibid.*, 120–121.
54. Flavin, Christopher, *Nuclear Power: The Market Test* (Washington DC: Worldwatch Instituute, December 1983), 6–7.
55. Patterson, Walter, *Nuclear Power* (Harmondsworth: Penguin, 1983), 120–122.
56. *Ibid.*, 132–133.
57. Hall, Tony, *Nuclear Politics* (Harmondsworth: Penguin, 1986), 135.
58. Patterson, reference 55, 154.
59. Council on Environmental Quality, *Environmental Quality 1979* (Washington DC: US Government Printing Office, 1979), 361.
60. Patterson, reference 55, 162–163.

Chapter 8

1. Watterson, Gerald (Ed), *Report of the Pan-African Symposium on the Conservation of Nature and Natural Resources in Modern African States, September 1961* (Morges: IUCN, 1963), 19.
2. *Ibid.*, 61.
3. National Parks Service, *First World Conference on National Parks* (Washington DC: Department of the Interior, 1962), 381.
4. *IUCN Bulletin* No 6, January/March 1963.
5. International Institute for Environment and Development, *IIED Annual Report 1981–1982* (London: IIED, 1982), 7.
6. United Nations Environment Programme, *Report of the Governing Council of the United Nations Environment Programme, Fourth Session, 30 March–14 April 1976* (Nairobi: UNEP, 1976).
7. United Nations Environment Programme *Report of the Governing Council of the United Nations Environment Programme, Fifth Session, 9–25 May 1977* (Nairobi: UNEP, 1977).
8. UNEP, reference 6.
9. UNEP–UNCTAD, *Report of the Expert Group on the Impact of*

Resource Management Problems and Policies in Developed Countries on International Trade and Development Strategies April 1974.

10. Spero, Joan Edelman, *The Politics of International Economic Relations* (New York: St Martin's Press, 1985), 293–342.
11. Corea, Gamani and Maurice Strong, Letter to Barbara Ward, 18 July 1974.
12. Eckholm, Erik, *Down to Earth* (New York: W W Norton, 1982), 15.
13. Chenery, Hollis, Montek S Ahluwalia, C L G Bell, John H Duloy and Richard Jolly, *Redistribution With Growth* (Oxford: Oxford University Press, 1974).
14. Dasmann, Raymond F, J P Milton and P H Freeman, *Ecological Principles for Economic Development* (Chichester: John Wiley, 1973).
15. Stein, Robert E and Brian Johnson, *Banking on the Biosphere?* (Lexington, Massachusetts: Lexington Books, 1979); Johnson, Brian and Robert O Blake, *The Environment and Bilateral Development Aid* (London: IIED, 1980).
16. Stein, Robert and Brian Johnson, *Banking on the Biosphere?* (Lexington, Massachusetts: Lexington Books, 1979), 11, 22.
17. World Bank, *Environment and Development* (Washington DC: World Bank, 1979), 3.
18. World Bank, *Environmental, Health and Human Ecologic Considerations in Economic Development Projects* (Washington DC: World Bank, 1972).
19. "World Bank Group Committed to Protecting Environment of Underdeveloped Countries", in *Environment Reporter* 8: 16, August 1977, 19.
20. Stein and Johnson, reference 16, 12.
21. World Bank, reference 17, 9.
22. Johnson, Brian and Robert O Blake, *The Environment and Bilateral Development Aid* (London: IIED, 1980), iii.
23. Stoel, Thomas B, S Jacob Scherr and Diana C Crowley, *Environment, Natural Resources and Development: The Role of the US Agency for International Development* (Washington DC: Natural Resources Defense Council, 1978), 30.
24. Johnson and Blake, reference 22, v.
25. Ehrhart, R, A Hanson, C Sanger and B Wood, *Canadian Aid and the Environment* (Halifax, Nova Scotia: Dalhousie University, 1981), 59.
26. Sandbrook, Richard, "The UK's Overseas Environmental Policy", in *The Conservation and Development Programme for the UK: A Response to the World Conservation Strategy* (London: Kogan Page, 1983), 381.
27. *Ibid.*, 396.
28. *Declaration of Environment Policies and Procedures Relating to Economic Development*, reproduced in Sandbrook, reference 26, 383.
29. World Bank, *Toward Sustained Development in Sub-Saharan Africa* (Washington DC: World Bank, 1984).
30. Eckholm, reference 12, 9.
31. United Nations Environment Programme, *A Review of the Major*

Achievements in the Implementation of the Stockholm Action Plan on the Human Environment UNEP Doc. Na. 81–4960 (Nairobi: UNEP, 1981), 67.

32. Clarke, Robin and Lloyd Timberlake, *Stockholm Plus Ten* (London: Earthscan, 1982), 61.
33. Center for International Environment Information, "Government Agencies with Environmental Responsibilities in Developing Countries", in *World Environment Report* 6: 9, April 1980.
34. Salim, Emil, *Conservation and Development* The Second World Conservation Lecture (London: World Wildlife Fund, 1982).
35. UNEP, reference 31, 69.
36. Baker, Randall and David Kinyanjui, *Recommendations on the Institutional Framework for Environmental Management in Kenya* School of Development Studies, University of East Anglia, Occcasional Paper No 9, November 1980, 3.
37. *Ibid.*, 7.
38. National Environment Secretariat, quoted in Baker and Kinyanjui, reference 36, 7.
39. Ramakrishna, Kilaparti, "The Emergence of Environmental Law in the Developing Countries: A Case Study of India", in *Ecology Law Quarterly* 12: 4, 1985, 907–935.
40. Centre for Science and Environment, *The State of India's Environment 1982* (New Delhi: CSE, 1982), 84, 178.
41. Centre for Science and Environment, *The State of India's Environment 1984–85* (New Delhi: CSE, 1985), 327, 343.
42. Ramakrishna, reference 39.
43. CSE, reference 40, 180–181.
44. CSE, reference 41, 327.
45. *Ibid.*, 348.
46. CSE, reference 41, 206–226.
47. *Ibid.*, 206–226.
48. Pearce, Fred, "After Bhopal, who remembered Ixhuatepec?", in *New Scientist*, 18 July 1985, 22–23.
49. Harrison, Paul, *The Greening of Africa* (Harmondsworth: Penguin, 1987), 187–188.
50. CSE, reference 41, 338–339.
51. *Ibid.*, 330.
52. Nicholson, Max, "Requirements for a World Conservation Programme", International Biological Programme, 1966 (unpublished).
53. Poore, Duncan, Personal communication, April 1986; Talbot, Lee M, "The World Conservation Strategy", in Thibodeau, F R and H H Field (Eds), *Sustaining Tomorrow* (Hanover: University Press of New England, 1985), 14.
54. Dasmann, Raymond, "An Introduction to World Conservation", in Thibodeau, F R and H H Field (Eds), *Sustaining Tomorrow* (Hanover: University Press of New England, 1985), 17, 19.

55. *Ibid.*; Allen, Robert, Personal communication, April 1984.
56. Talbot, Lee M, "The World Conservation Strategy", in Thibodeau, F R and H H Field (Eds), *Sustaining Tomorrow* (Hanover: University Press of New England, 1985), 14.
57. International Union for Conservation of Nature, *IUCN Yearbook 75– 76* (Morges: IUCN, 1976), 2.
58. *Ibid.*, 3.
59. IUCN, reference 57, 3.
60. Allen, Robert, "Ecodevelopment: A long-awaited concept", in *IUCN Bulletin* 7: 5, May 1976, 30.
61. "IUCN Prepares World Strategy", in *IUCN Bulletin* 8: 10, October 1977, 59.
62. "The Strategy Gets a Warm Welcome", in *IUCN Bulletin* 9: 10/11, October/November 1978, 64.
63. IUCN, "Resolutions of the 14th Session of the General Assembly of IUCN", in *IUCN Bulletin* 9: 10/11, October/November 1978.
64. IUCN Bulletin, reference 62.
65. "Strategy Launched in September", in *IUCN Bulletin* 10: 2, February 1979, 15.
66. Poore, Duncan, Personal Communication, April 1986.
67. IUCN, *Achievements 1978–81* Report of the Director-General (Gland: IUCN, 1981).
68. *World Conservation Strategy* (Gland: IUCN/UNEP/WWF, 1980), iv.
69. IUCN, *National Conservation Strategies: A Framework for Sustainable Development* (Gland: CDC/IUCN, 1984), 3.
70. World Resources Institute/International Institute for Environment and Development, *World Resources 1987* (New York: Basic Books, 1987), 248, 344–345.

Chapter 9

1. Kolinsky, Eva, "The Greens in Germany: Prospects of a Small Party", in *Parliamentary Affairs* 37: 4, Autumn 1984, 434–447.
2. Capra, Fritjof, and Charlene Spretnak, *Green Politics* (London: Hutchinson, 1984), 3.
3. Parkin, Sara, *Green Parties: An International Guide* (London: Heretic Books, 1989), 113–115.
4. Spretnak, Charlene and Fritjof Capra, *Green Politics: The Global Promise* (London: Paladin Books, 1985), 13.
5. Frankland, E Gene and Donald Schoonmaker, *Between Protest and Power: The Green Party in Germany* (Boulder, Colorado: Westview Press, 1992), 34.
6. Rainbow, Stephen L, "Why did New Zealand and Tasmania Spawn the World's First Green Parties?", in *Environmental Politics* 1: 3, Autumn 1992, 321–346.
7. Brunt, Tony, "In Search of Values", in Edwards, Brian (Ed), *Right*

Out – *Labour Victory '72: The Inside Story* (Wellington: A H & A W
Reed Ltd, 1973), 79.

8. James, Colin C, "Social Credit and the Values Party", in Penniman,
Howard R, *New Zealand at the Polls: The General Election of 1978*
(Washington DC: American Enterprise Institute for Public Policy
Research, 1980), 164.

9. Levine, Stephen, *The New Zealand Political System: Politics in a Small
Society* (Sydney: George Allen & Unwin, 1979), 82.

10. James, reference 8, 166; Levine, reference 9, 81.

11. Church, Clive H, "The Development of the Swiss Green Party", in
Environmental Politics 1: 2, Summer 1992, 252–282.

12. Rüdig, Wolfgang and Philip Lowe, "The Withered 'Greening' of
British Politics: A Study of the Ecology Party", in *Political Studies* 34:
2, June 1986, 262–284.

13. Evans, Gavin, "Hard Times for the British Green Party", in
Environmental Politics 2: 2, Summer 1993, 327–333.

14. Porritt, Jonathon, *Seeing Green* (Oxford: Basil Blackwell, 1984), 5.

15. Lovelock, Jim, *Gaia: A New Look at Life on Earth* (Oxford: Oxford
University Press, 1979).

16. Lovelock, Jim, "Gaia: The world as living organism", in *New
Scientist*, 18 December 1986, 25.

17. Lovelock, reference 15, 107–108.

18. Schumacher, E F, *Small is Beautiful: Economics as if People Mattered*
(London: Blond and Briggs, 1973), 72, 156.

19. Dobson, Andrew, *Green Political Thought* (London: Unwin Hyman,
1990), 13.

20. Naess, Arne, "The Shallow and the Deep Long-Range Ecology
Movement: A Summary", in *Inquiry* 16, 1973.

21. Spretnak and Capra, reference 4, 3–4.

22. Roszak, Theodore, *Person/Planet* (St Albans: Granada, 1981), 12.

23. Sandbach, Francis, *Environment, Ideology and Policy* (Oxford: Basil
Blackwell, 1980), 22–28.

24. Cotgrove, Stephen, *Catastrophe or Cornucopia: The Environment,
Politics and the Future* (Chichester: John Wiley & Sons, 1982), 25–32.

25. Porritt, reference 14, 5.

26. Milbrath, Lester W, *Environmentalists: Vanguard for a New Society*
(Albany, New York: SUNY Press, 1984), 50.

27. Rothacher, Albert, "The Green Party in German Politics", in *West
European Politics* 7: 3, July 1984, 109–116.

28. Cotgrove, reference 24, 89.

29. Müller-Rommel, Ferdinand, "Ecology Parties in Western Europe",
in *West European Politics* 5: 1, January 1982, 68–74.

30. Barnes, S, Kaase, M et al. (Eds), *Political Action* (London: Sage,
1979).

31. Hulsberg, Werner, *The German Greens: A Social and Political Profile*
(London: Verso, 1988), 10.

32. Müller-Rommel, reference 29.

33. Capra and Spretnak, reference 2, 10.
34. Alber, Jens, "Modernization, Cleavage Structures, and the Rise of Green Parties and Lists in Europe", in Müller-Rommel, Ferdinand (Ed), *New Politics in Western Europe: The Rise and Successes of Green Parties and Alternative Lists* (Boulder, Colorado: Westview Press, 1989), 195–210.
35. Capra and Spretnak, reference 2, 12–13.
36. Porritt, reference 14, 12–13.
37. Inglehart, Ronald, *The Silent Revolution: Changing Values and Political Styles Among Western Publics* (Princeton, New Jersey: Princeton University Press, 1977), 3–13.
38. Ophuls, William, *Ecology and the Politics of Scarcity* (San Francisco: W H Freeman, 1977); Pirages, Dennis C, *The Sustainable Society* (New York: Praeger, 1977); Rifkin, Jeremy, *Entropy: A New Worldview* (New York: Viking Press, 1980); Robertson, J, *The Sane Alternative: A Choice of Futures* (St. Paul, Minnesota: River Basin, 1979).
39. Pirages, Dennis C, *The Sustainable Society* (New York: Praeger, 1977), 26.
40. Yankelovich, Daniel and Bernard Lefkowitz, "The Public Debate on Growth: Preparing for Resolution", in *Technological Forecasting and Social Change* 17: 2, June 1980, 95–140.
41. Dunlap, Riley E and Kent D Van Liere, "The 'New Environmental Paradigm': A Proposed Measuring Instrument and Preliminary Results", in *Journal of Environmental Education* 9, 1978, 10–19; Cotgrove, reference 24; Milbrath, Lester W, *General Report: US Components of a Comparative Study of Environmental Beliefs and Values* (Buffalo, New York: State University of New York Environmental Studies Center, 1981).
42. Milbrath, Lester W, "Environmental Beliefs and Values", in Hermann, Margaret G (Ed), *Political Psychology* (San Francisco: Jossey-Bass, 1986).
43. Simon, Julian L and Herman Kahn (Eds), *The Resourceful Earth* (Oxford: Basil Blackwell, 1984).
44. Inglehart, reference 37, 22.
45. Inglehart, Ronald, "Value Change in Industrial Societies", in *American Political Science Review* 81: 4, December 1987, 1289–1303.
46. Inglehart, reference 37, 3.
47. See reviews in Sandbach, reference 23.
48. Inglehart, reference 45.
49. *Ibid.*
50. Rüdig and Lowe, reference 12.
51. *Ibid.*
52. Eckersley, Robyn, "Green Politics and the New Class: Selfishness or Virtue?", in *Political Studies* 37: 2, June 1989, 221.

Chapter 10

1. Council for Environmental Quality, *Environmental Quality 1971* (Washington DC: US Government Printing Office, 1971), viii.
2. Falk, Richard A, "Environmental Policy as a World Order Problem", in *Natural Resources Journal* 12: 2, April 1972, 161–171.
3. Council on Environmental Quality, *The Global 2000 Report to the President: Entering the Twenty-First Century* (Harmondsworth: Penguin, 1982), Letter of Transmittal.
4. Cleveland, Harlan, "The Extrapolation of Metaphors: A 'Book Review' of the US Government's Global 2000 Study". Address to OECD, 1 April 1981 (unpublished).
5. *Ibid.*
6. Council on Environmental Quality, reference 3, 1.
7. Council on Environmental Quality, *Global Future: Time to Act* (Washington DC: CEQ, 1981).
8. Simon, Julian L, "Global Confusion, 1980: A hard look at the Global 2000 Report", in *The Public Interest* 62, Winter 1981, 3–20.
9. Kahn, Herman and Ernest Schneider, "Globaloney 2000", in *Policy Review* 16, Spring 1981, 129–147.
10. Simon, Julian L and Herman Kahn (Eds), *The Resourceful Earth: A Response to Global 2000* (Oxford: Basil Blackwell, 1984).
11. Kahn and Schneider, reference 9.
12. Council on Environmental Quality, reference 3, 16.
13. United Nations Environment Programme, *Register of International Treaties and Other Agreements in the Field of the Environment* UNEP/GC/INFO/11 (Nairobi: UNEP, May 1984).
14. Burhenne, Wolfgang (Ed), *International Environmental Law: Multilateral Treaties* (Berlin: Erich Schmidt Verlag, 1985).
15. Lyster, Simon, *International Wildlife Law* (Cambridge: Grotius Publications, 1985), 10–11.
16. *Ibid.*
17. Lyster, reference 15, 151.
18. Haigh, Nigel, *Vienna Centre Project ECO I. Collaborative Arrangements for Environmental Protection in Western Europe* (London: IEEP/European Cultural Foundation, 1985), 4.
19. *Ibid.*
20. Haigh, reference 18, 4.
21. *Ibid.*, 5.
22. *World Conservation Strategy* (Gland: IUCN, UNEP, WWF, 1980), 15; Lyster, reference 15, xxiii.
23. Lyster, reference 15, 206.
24. Maltby, Edward, *Waterlogged Wealth* (London: Earthscan, 1986), 94.
25. *Proceedings of the Conference on the Conservation of Wetlands of International Importance Especially as Waterfowl Habitat* Doc. CONF/4, Cagliari, Italy, November 1980.

26. Lyster, reference 15, 191.
27. Maltby, reference 24, 94–95.
28. Lyster, reference 15, 209, 237.
29. Haigh, reference 18, 8.
30. Haigh, Nigel, *EEC Environmental Policy and Britain* (London: Environmental Data Services, 1983), 4.
31. Allen, Robert, "European Con Year", in *The Ecologist* 1: 6, December 1970, 4–7.
32. *Ibid.*
33. Johnson, Brian, "Common Market v Environment", in *The Ecologist* 1: 11, May 1971, 10–14.
34. Haigh, Nigel, "Devolved Responsibility and Centralization: Effects of EEC Environmental Policy", in *Public Administration* 64: 2, Summer 1986, 197–207.
35. Haigh, reference 30, 1.
36. Haigh, reference 34.
37. Ellington, Athleen and Tom Burke, *Europe: Environment* (London: Ecobooks, 1981), 10.
38. Sandbrook, Richard, "The UK's Overseas Environmental Policy", in *The Conservation and Development Programme for the UK: A Response to the World Conservation Strategy* (London: Kogan Page, 1983), 330–331.
39. *Ibid.*, 331.
40. Lowe, Philip and Jane Goyder, *Environmental Groups in Politics* (London: George Allen & Unwin, 1983), pp. 164–165.
41. *Ibid.*, 171.
42. Cowling, Ellis B, "Acid Precipitation in Historical Perspective", in *Environmental Science and Technology* 16: 2, 1982, 110A–123A.
43. Smith, Robert Angus, *Air and Rain: The Beginnings of a Chemical Climatology* (London: Longmans, Green & Co), 1872.
44. Cowling, reference 42.
45. Organisation for Economic Cooperation and Development, *The OECD Programme on Long Range Transport of Air Pollutants* (Summary Report) (Paris: OECD, 1977).
46. McCormick, John, *Acid Earth: The Global Threat of Acid Pollution* (London: Earthscan, 1989), 75–76.
47. Wetstone, Gregory S and Armin Rosencranz, *Acid Rain in Europe and North America* (Washington DC: Environmental Law Institute, 1984), 142.
48. McCormick, reference 46, 76.
49. Wetstone and Rosencranz, reference 47, 142–143.
50. McCormick, reference 46, 79.
51. *Ibid.*, 85.
52. Gribbin, John, *Carbon Dioxide, Climate and Man* (London: Earthscan, 1981), 12.
53. Bolin, Bert, "Changes of Land Biota and Their Importance for the Carbon Cycle", in *Science* 196: 4290, 6 May 1977, 613–615;

Woodwell, George M, "The Carbon Dioxide Question", in *Scientific American* 238: 1, January 1978, 34–43.

54. Molina, Mario J and F S Rowland, "Stratospheric Sink for Chlorofluoromethanes: Chlorine Atom-Catalysed Destruction of Ozone", in *Nature* 249: 5460, 28 June 1974, 810–812.

55. *Stratospheric Ozone Depletion by Halocarbons: Chemistry and Transport Panel on Stratospheric Chemistry and Transport* (Washington DC: National Academy of Sciences, 1979); "Environmental Assessment of Ozone Layer Depletion and its Impact", in *Ozone Bulletin* 6, 1981; National Research Council, *Causes and Effects of Changes in Stratospheric Ozone: Update* (Washington DC: National Research Council, 1984).

56. Organisation for Economic Cooperation and Development, *The State of the Environment 1985* (Paris: OECD, 1985), 36; Chemical Manufacturers Association, quoted in Holdgate, Martin, Mohammed Kassas and Gilbert White, *The World Environment 1972–1982* (Dublin: Tycooly Publishing, 1982), 44.

57. Schneider, Stephen H and Starley L Thompson, "Future Changes in the Atmosphere", in Repetto, Robert (Ed), *The Global Possible: Resources, Development and the New Century* (New Haven, Connecticut: Yale University Press, 1985), 405.

58. Downing, Thomas E and Robert W Kates, "The International Response to the Threat of Chlorofluorocarbons to Atmospheric Ozone", in *American Economic Review* 72: 2, May 1982, 267–272.

59. World Resources Institute/International Institute for Environment and Development, *World Resources 1987* (New York: Basic Books, 1987), 195.

60. Watson, Robert T et al., *Present State of Knowledge of the Upper Atmosphere: An Assessment Report* Publ. 1162 (Washington DC: NASA, 1986), 14–15.

61. *Ibid.*, 15.

62. Ylisela, Jim, "Scientists Probe the Ozone Hole for Clues to its Cause", in *Christian Science Monitor*, 6 October 1987, 18.

63. Aeppel, Timothy, "Ozone Accord Shows Concern Over Global Climate", in *Christian Science Monitor*, 17 September 1987, 8.

64. Holdgate, Martin, Mohammed Kassas and Gilbert White, *The World Environment 1972–1982* (Dublin: Tycooly Publishing, 1982), 30–31.

65. di Castri, Francesco, Malcolm Hadley and Jeanne Damlamian, "MAB: The Man and the Biosphere Program as an Evolving System", in *Ambio* 10: 2–3, 1981, 52–57.

66. UNESCO, *Backgrounder: The MAB Programme* (Paris: UNESCO, 1982), 3.

67. WRI/IIED, reference 59, 158–159.

68. Kerr, Richard A, "Greenhouse Warming Still Coming", in *Science* 232: 4750, 2 May 1986, 573–574.

69. UNEP/WMO/ICSU, *An Assessment of the Role of Carbon Dioxide and*

of Other Greenhouse Gases in Climate Variations and Associated Impacts (Geneva: World Meteorological Organisation, 1985), 12.

70. WRI/IIED, reference 59, 159.
71. *Ibid.*, 78.
72. Eckholm, Erik, *Down to Earth* (New York: W W Norton, 1982), 8.
73. International Board for Plant Genetic Resources: Consultative Group on International Agricultural Research, *Annual Report 1981* (Rome: IBPGR, 1981).
74. Plucknett, D L, N J H Smith, J T Williams and N Murthi Anishetty, "Crop Germplasm Conservation and Developing Countries", in *Science* 220: 4593, 8 April 1983, 163–169.
75. United Nations Environment Programme, *The Environment in 1982: Retrospect and Prospect* Paper prepared for the Session of a Special Character, Doc. UNEP/GC (SSC)/2, Nairobi, 29 January 1982, 34.
76. Holdgate reference 64, 622–623.
77. *Ibid.*, 15.
78. Organisation for Economic Cooperation and Development, *Economic and Ecological Interdependence* (Paris: OECD, 1982), 3.

Chapter 11

1. World Commission on Environment and Development, *Our Common Future* (Oxford: Oxford University Press, 1987).
2. *Ibid.*, 310–312.
3. WCED, reference 1, 313.
4. Redclift, Michael, *Sustainable Development: Exploring the Contradictions* (London: Methuen, 1987), 14.
5. For details on the preparations for UNCED, see Chapter 2 of Grubb, Michael, Matthias Koch, Koy Thomson, Abby Munson and Francis Sullivan, *The Earth Summit Agreements: A Guide and Assessment* (London: Earthscan Publications, 1993).
6. Thompson, Koy, "The Rio Declaration on Environment and Development" in Grubb et al., *ibid.*, 86.
7. McConnell, Grant, "The conservation movement – past and present", *Western Political Quarterly* 7: 3, September 1954, 463–478.
8. Downs, Anthony, "Up and Down With Ecology – The 'Issue-Attention' Cycle", *The Public Interest* 28, Summer 1972, 38–50.
9. Bowman, James S, "The Ecology Movement: A Viewpoint", *International Journal of Environmental Studies* 8: 2, 1975, 91–97.
10. Sandbach, Francis, *Environment, Ideology and Policy* (Oxford: Basil Blackwell, 1980), 1–10. See also Dunlap, Riley E and Kent D Van Liere, "Further Evidence of Declining Public Concern with Environmental Problems: A Research Note", *Western Sociological Review* 8, 1977, 108–112; Honnold, J and L D Nelson, "Age and Environmental Concern: Some Specification of Effects", Paper

presented at annual meeting of the American Sociological Association, Toronto, 1981.

11. Schoenfeld, Clay, "Environmentalism: Fad or Fixture", *American Forests* 78: 3, March 1972, 17–19.

12. See, for example, Milbrath, Lester W, *Environmentalists: Vanguard for a New Society* (Albany, New York: State University of New York Press, 1984); Council on Environmental Quality, *Environmental Quality 1980* (Washington DC: US Government Printing Office, 1980), 401–423.

13. Holdgate, Martin, Mohammed Kassas and Gilbert White, *The World Environment 1972–1982* (Dublin: Tycooly Publishing, 1982), 629.

14. Eckholm, Erik, *Down to Earth* (New York: W W Norton and Co, 1982), 199.

15. Holdgate et al., reference 13, xvi.

16. Tolba, Mostafa, Osama El-Kholy, E El-Hinnawi, Martin Holdgate, D F McMichael and R E Munn (Eds), *The World Environment 1972–1992: Two Decades of Challenge* (London: Chapman and Hall, 1992).

17. Bowman, reference 9.

Chronology of Key Events

1863	passage of Alkali Act and creation of Alkali Inspectorate (Britain)
1864	publication of *Man and Nature* by George Perkins Marsh; Yosemite Valley (California) given protection for public use and recreation
1865	Commons, Open Spaces and Footpaths Preservation Society founded (Britain); creation of the Indian Forest Service
1867	East Riding Association for the Protection of Sea Birds founded (Britain)
1872	Yellowstone National Park created; Robert Angus Smith coins the term "acid rain"
1879	Royal National Park created (Australia)
1881	Society for the Protection of Birds founded (Britain)
1883	Natal Game Preservation Society founded (South Africa)
1892	Sierra Club founded (United States)
1895	National Trust founded (Britain)
1900	Convention for the Preservation of Animals, Birds and Fish in Africa signed in London
1907	Inland Waterways Commission created (United States)
1908	(May) White House Conference of Governors on Conservation, Washington DC
1909	North American Conservation Congress, Washington DC; Wildlife Preservation Society founded (Australia); International Congress for the Protection of Nature, Paris

1913   Consultative Commission for the International Protection of Nature founded (Switzerland)
1914   Swiss National Park created
1922   International Committee for Bird Protection founded (based in London)
1933   International Conference for the Protection of Fauna and Flora, London
1934   International Office for the Protection of Nature founded (based in Belgium)
1934–38   Dust Bowl
1940   Western Hemisphere Convention opened for signature
1945   (October) creation of the Food and Agriculture Organisation of the United Nations (FAO)
1946   creation of the UN Educational, Scientific and Cultural Organisation (UNESCO)
1948   publication of *Our Plundered Planet* by Fairfield Osborn and *Road to Survival* by William Vogt; International Union for the Protection of Nature founded
1949   publication of *Sand County Almanac* by Aldo Leopold; (August–September) UN Scientific Conference on the Conservation and Utilisation of Resources, Lake Success, New York; (August) International Technical Conference on the Protection of Nature, Lake Success, New York
1951   the United States launches its nuclear test programme
1952   Britain launches its nuclear test programme
1953   Third International Conference for the Protection of the Fauna and Flora of Africa, Bukavu, Belgian Congo
1954   the United States holds its hydrogen bomb test BRAVO on Bikini Atoll
1956   Clean Air Act signed (Britain)
1958   publication of *The Affluent Society* by John Kenneth Galbraith
1960   publication of first Red Data Book on endangered species
1961   (September) World Wildlife Fund founded; Arusha Conference on nature conservation in Africa
1961–73   Minamata (Japan)
1962   (July) First World Conference on National Parks, Seattle, Washington; publication of *Silent Spring* by Rachel Carson

1963 Partial Nuclear Test Ban Treaty signed

1964 (July) International Biological Programme created (closed 1974)

1965 Bangkok Conference on nature conservation in Southeast Asia; Adlai Stevenson uses Spaceship Earth metaphor

1966 publication of first photographs of earth taken from space; (October) Aberfan disaster (Britain)

1967 (March) *Torrey Canyon* runs aground (Britain)

1968 San Carlos de Bariloche Conference on nature conservation in Latin America; publication of *The Population Bomb* by Paul Ehrlich; formation of the Club of Rome; (September) Biosphere Conference, Paris

1969 (January) Santa Barbara blowout (United States); creation of Friends of the Earth (United States)

1970 (April 22) Earth Day (United States); European Conservation Year; creation of the Department of the Environment in Britain, and the Environmental Protection Agency in the United States

1971 publication of *The Closing Circle* by Barry Commoner; (November) Man and the Biosphere programme created

1972 publication of *The Limits to Growth* and *A Blueprint for Survival*; (June) United Nations Conference on the Human Environment, Stockholm; Greenpeace founded

1973 UN Environment Programme created (based in Nairobi); publication of *Small is Beautiful* by E.F. Schumacher; emergence of Chipko Andalan movement in India; British green party founded as People

1974 (April) Canberra II meeting, Geneva; (May) UN General Assembly calls for the establishment of a New International Economic Order; (October) Founex II meeting in Cocoyoc, Mexico; (November) death of Karen Silkwood; (December) European Environmental Bureau founded; UNEP Regional Seas Programme launched

1977 UN Conference on Desertification, Nairobi

1978 (March) accident at Three Mile Island nuclear power station, Pennsylvania

1978–79 evacuation of Love Canal, upper New York state

1979 (October) the Swiss elect the first national green legislator in the world; (November) Convention on

Long-Range Transboundary Air Pollution signed in Geneva; launch of World Climate Programme

1980   (January) formation of German green party; (March) launch of the World Conservation Strategy; publication of *Global 2000*

1983   (March) German greens win their first Bundestag seats

1984   (March) creation of the 30 Percent Club; (October) news breaks of Sahelian famine; (October) first meeting of the Brundtland Commission; (December) accident at Union Carbide plant, Bhopal, India

1985   (March) Convention on the Protection of the Ozone Layer signed in Vienna

1986   (April) accident at Chernobyl nuclear power station, Ukraine

1987   publication of the Brundtland Commission report *Our Common Future*

1988   (December) murder of Chico Mendes

1992   (June) UN Conference on Environment and Development, Rio de Janeiro; (November) UN Commission on Sustainable Development created

Index